Österreichische Zeitschrift für öffentliches Recht
Supplementum 1

Agreements

of International Organizations and the Vienna Convention on the Law of Treaties

Edited by K. Zemanek
Assisted by L.-R. Behrmann

Springer-Verlag
Wien · New York 1971

Professor Dr. K. Zemanek and Dr. L.-R. Behrmann
Institute for Public International Law and International Relations
University of Vienna

Library of Congress Catalog Card Number 75-155281
Printed in Austria

With 2 Figures

ISBN 3-211-81010-2 Springer-Verlag Wien - New York
ISBN 0-387-81010-2 Springer-Verlag New York - Wien

Introduction by the Editor

It is, I think, not necessary to argue at great length the significance of the subject treated in the present volume. Since nearly 2000 treaties to which international organizations are parties are published in the UN Treaty Series, it is quite natural to ask why they were excluded from the application of the Vienna Convention on the Law of Treaties of 1969.

The history of the Convention is, rather, confusing in this respect. For twelve years the United Nation's International Law Commission included agreements of international organizations in its preparatory work, only to limit the scope of the final draft to treaties between States. At the UN Conference on the Law of Treaties, which worked from that draft, it was again proposed to extend the application of the Convention to agreements concluded by international organizations, but that proposal was withdrawn because of the widespread feeling that the extension would require the revision of numerous provisions in the Convention, for which task the Conference felt unprepared. It adopted, however, a recommendation to the General Assembly to refer the study of these agreements—back to the ILC, which the General Assembly did at its 24th session (1969).

Thus the ILC will have to test the validity of the argument that the Vienna Convention on the Law of Treaties needed many revisions to be applicable to agreements concluded by international organizations. This task will be facilitated if comparative studies are made from which it can draw.

Seen in this perspective, it was fortunate that the Curatorium of the Hague Academy of International Law had selected the subject "Agreements concluded by international organizations, among themselves or with States" for the 1969 session of its Center for Studies and Research, because it allowed a number of younger scholars of various backgrounds and different formations to prepare such comparative studies and to discuss them in common. I had the privilege of acting as Director of research for the English speaking section.

We used two different approaches for our work: Some participants examined the formal aspects of all agreements concluded by one international organization or of a group of similarily structured agreements (e.g. headquarters agreements), whereas others investigated a particular problem of treaty law in all available agreements. Through this combination of horizontal and vertical analysis it was possible to discuss each problem in three different contexts: that of a particular organization's treaty practice, that of a specific subject matter and that of the general law of treaties, and to study their respective influence. The discussions were extremely fruitful* and it was generally felt that the subsequent reports should be made available in print.

Unfortunately, the common publication of all papers proved impossible. They would have filled a volume of nearly 800 pages and no funds could be found for such an ambitious endeavour. Thus, the more modest project of the present special supplement to the *Österreichische Zeitschrift für öffentliches Recht* was undertaken, which makes it possible to present 6 out of 15 papers**.

Any selection is necessarily subjective and the responsibility for selecting the papers for the present volume is mine. I attempted as fair a representation of the section's work as possible. The first three reports are examples of the horizontal approach, the last three of the vertical. They were written by people of different training and varying concepts. It is hoped that the volume gives the reader an exact impression of the dimensions of the problem under discussion and testifies also to the scholarly merit of collective research into complex legal problems as undertaken in the Hague Center.

Vienna, May 1971

Karl Zemanek

* At least to no small extent for me. My own conclusions are published in the Memorial issue of the University of Toledo Law Review dedicated to Josef L. Kunz (1971).

** It is, however, hoped that other reports may appear individually in legal periodicals. One has, in fact, already been published: T. Modeen, The deposit and registration of treaties of international Organizations. Possible application of the rules of the Vienna Convention on the Law of Treaties. 39 Acta Academiae Abonensis, (1971), Ser. A, Nr. 3.

Contents

Part I

Part II

List of Abbreviations

AFDI	Annuaire Français de Droit International
AJIL	American Journal of International Law
BYIL	British Yearbook of International Law
GAOR	General Assembly Official Records
HLR	Harvard Law Review
LNTS	League of Nations Treaty Series
RCADI	Recueil des Cours de l'Académie de Droit International
RGDIP	Revue Générale de Droit International Public
UNCIO Docs.	Documents of the United Nations Conference on International Organization
UNTS	United Nations Treaty Series
YILC	Yearbook of the International Law Commission
ZaöRV	Zeitschrift für ausländisches öffentliches Recht und Völkerrecht

Österr. Zeitschr. f. öffentl. Recht, Suppl. 1, 1—55 (1971)

Co-operation Agreements and the Law Relating to Agreements Concluded by International Organizations

D. M. McRae
LL.M. (Otago), Assistant Professor of Law, University of Western Ontario, Canada

Introduction

The Convention on the Law of Treaties adopted by the United Nations Conference on the Law of Treaties at Vienna on 22 May 1969[1] was expressly limited to treaties concluded between States[2]. Thus the decision of the International Law Commission, taken at its 14th Session, to exclude from any present codification of the law of treaties agreements concluded by international organizations, was approved[3]. The increasing number of agreements entered into by international organizations makes, however, the task of ascertaining the rules governing them one of primary importance. The purpose of this paper is to examine one class of agreement, that is co-operation agreements, in order to determine whether the rules of the Vienna Convention could be utilized in a codification of the law relating to at least some of the agreements of international organizations. It is not intended to analyse the provisions of the Vienna Convention article by article, but simply to consider those areas in which *prima facie* some difficulty exists in applying the Vienna rules automatically to agreements concluded by international organizations.

The selection of co-operation agreements as the class of agreement to be considered has certain special consequences and an analysis of

[1] A/CONF. 39/27. The treaty was opened for signature on the following day.

[2] Art. 1. Art. 3 provides that the fact that the Convention does not apply to agreements concluded by other subjects of international law does not affect the legal force of such agreements.

[3] (1966) 2 YILC, p. 186. The Vienna Conference, however, adopted a resolution recommending that the General Assembly refer the study of agreements entered into by other subjects of international law to the International Law Commission. A/CONF. 39/C. 1/2.

these agreements can be made only in the light of an understanding of the place of inter-organizational relations generally in international law. Though international law has developed, as its very name indicates, from relations between States, inter-organizational relations involve entities which, it is now accepted, have a legal existence separate from their member States[4]. They must, therefore, be studied at a level removed from inter-state relations and this applies, no less, to co-operation agreements. It is not suggested that rules of international law which have been developed from the relations of States cannot apply to the relations of international organizations, but rather that such rules are not necessarily applicable[5]. The primary actors in inter-organizational relations are the organizations themselves and it is to their practice that attention must first be turned. Further, the study of co-operation agreements, which are bilateral arrangements between international organizations[6], is freed from certain doctrinal difficulties which arise when the relations of organizations with States are in issue. Thus, for example, whether a particular State, or a majority of States, has accorded recognition to an organization would appear to be irrelevant to the question of the capacity of that organization to entertain relations with other organizations[7].

Inter-organizational relations must also be viewed as involving entities which are independent of each other. As an organization is created by the common will of its member States they alone have the right to restrict or expand that organization's independence. Thus unless the founding States of two organizations subject the one to the authority of the other then, initially at least, the organizations must act, with respect to each other, on a basis of equality. A relevant analogy may be drawn with the external relations of States; as the constitution of each sovereign State is derived independently of the will of other States no State can claim legal authority over any other—each

---

[4] It appears that recent Communist writers would accept this proposition, see Paszkowski, "The Sources of the Treaty-Making Capacity of the United Nations," (1962) 17 *Panstwo i Prawo,* p. 796 (in Polish, résumé in English), Valki, "The Juristic Personality and Treaty-Making Power of International Organizations," (1968) *Questions of International Law,* p. 285.

[5] Of course any rules having the status of *jus cogens* would automatically apply.

[6] There is no bar, in theory at least, to the conclusion of multilateral co-operation agreements, in which case the rules of the Vienna Convention concerning multilateral agreements would be relevant, e.g., Arts. 19—23, concerning reservations.

[7] Unless, perhaps, capacity to enter into relations was dependent on the possession of "international personality," which in turn was based on "recognition," see *infra.*

must treat the others as independent entities, indeed the Charter of the United Nations stipulates so.

The approach taken here also requires a distinction to be borne in mind between the internal relations of an international organization, that is the relations between its organs and its member States, and the external relations of the organization with other entities operating in the international field, including both States and other international organizations. It is not suggested that an immutable legal distinction can be made, but many of the problems relating to the law concerning agreements concluded by international organizations will be clarified if these two areas are separated. Primarily the internal relations of an organization are governed by the constitution, which stipulates the rights and duties of the member States and of the various organs of the organization[8]. On the other hand, the external relations of an organization will not necessarily be governed solely by the internal rules of that organization, for the entity with which the organization is dealing may not have been a party to the creation of, nor assented to, those rules. Since an organization will not generally be a party to the constitution of its contracting party[9] then in the absence of contrary evidence it is not subject to the rules stipulated in that constitution[10].

To argue otherwise entails accepting the proposition that a group of States can, by creating an international organization, impose rules upon entities created by other States, or even upon those other States themselves. Such a view is inconsistent with the principles of the independence and equality of States[11]. The absurdity of the argument is also evident when the question is asked, which of two contracting organizations is entitled to have its internal rules govern their relations? Conceivably it would be adequate in some situations to allow each institution to be governed by its own internal rules, but what if they conflict? Moreover, is each organization entitled to rely on the other as having complied with its internal rules? At what stage can each be assured that the other has entered into a binding commitment?

[8] These relations are, of course, governed by general rules of international law but, except in so far as they are in the nature of *jus cogens*, such rules are of less relevance because the member States have stipulated their own special rules to apply.

[9] If on the other hand one organization was a member of another then the two would not always be independent; certain of their relations would be those of organization and member entity.

[10] This point will be elaborated *infra*.

[11] Art. 24 of the Covenant of the League of Nations indicated a recognition of the fact that the independence of international organizations cannot be compromised without their consent, for it provided that the consent of international unions was required before their bureaus could be placed under the direction of the League, see Ray, *Commentaire du Pacte de la Société des Nations* (1930), p. 675.

What is the effect of the agreement if one of the parties fails to comply with its own constitution?

The basic problems, then, are largely those which had to be faced with respect to the treaties of States, that is, what rules ought to determine whether an entity has entered into an engagement under international law and what consequences should international law attach to such an engagement? As will be seen, the solutions must be similar to those adopted for States and will proceed from a distinction between the internal rules of the entity, which govern the activities of the members, and the external rules which govern its relations with other independent entities.

The term 'co-operation agreement' is not a scientific one and some attempt must be made to describe the class of agreements to which it refers[12]. In a general sense all relations between organizations are co-operative, thus 'co-operation agreements' can include everything from the United Nations relationship agreements[13] to a loan agreement concluded between the International Bank for Reconstruction and Development (IBRD) and the International Finance Corporation (IFC)[14]. However, the latter agreement extends the category too far, and in this paper 'co-operation agreements' will be those agreements designed to associate one or both of the parties in the work of the other. The classification, then, is according to content and the types of terms found in co-operation agreements are generally well known, including provisions concerning consultation[15], reciprocal representation[16], and the exchange of information and documents[17]. There are different categories of agreements, some going further than the mere enumeration of forms of co-operation and making practical provision for joint action. This may be done either by a term in a general co-operation agreement[18] or by a separate agreement provid-

---

[12] At this stage a description can only be tentative and whether co-operation agreements constitute a distinct class of agreement will be considered later.

[13] See Arts. 57 and 63 of the UN Charter.

[14] See e.g., 506 UNTS, p. 225.

[15] See agreement between ILO and OAS (70 UNTS, p. 223), Art. I, "The OAS and the ILO will consult regularly on matters of common interest ..."

[16] *Ibid.*, Art. V (1), "The ILO will, subject to effective reciprocity, invite the OAS to attend the meetings of the International Labour Conference ..."

[17] See agreement between ILO and FAO (18 UNTS, p. 335), Art. 4 (1) "Subject to such arrangements as may be necessary for the safeguarding of confidential material, the fullest and promptest exchange of information and documents shall be made ..."

[18] See agreement between FAO and OAS (UN Doc. ST/SG/3, p. 41), Art. III (1) "The OAS and the FAO may through their competent organs, conclude special agreements or arrangements for joint action with a view to attaining objectives of common interest."

ing, perhaps, for technical assistance from one organization to the other[19]. In all cases, however, the basic function of the agreement is to associate organizations in the work of each other.

Capacity to Conclude Agreements

The first question which arises with respect to agreements entered into by international organizations[20] is whether the contracting organizations have a capacity, recognized by international law, to conclude such agreements. Many of the arguments relating to this issue have revolved around the intractable topic of international personality. The adherents to the view that international organizations possess international personality consider either that "treaty-making" capacity implies the possession of personality[21], or that "treaty-making" capacity is a consequence of the possession of international personality[22]. However, a confusion of these two positions is not uncommon so that personality becomes both dependent upon and a criterion for "treaty-making" capacity[23].

Writers have sought to determine the existence of international personality from various sources. At one end of the scale the suggestion has been made that the basis for personality is to be found in the constitution[24] of the organization concerned, either from its express terms[25] or from both the express and implied terms[26]. An extension of this view seeks to derive personality from the constitution in a broader sense, that is, including not only the constituent instrument but also the practice of the organization itself in interpreting its constitutional authority and the manner in which it con

---

[19] See agreement on technical assistance between ILO and UNRWA (182 UNTS, p. 201).

[20] Valuable preparatory work in this field has been done by C. W. Jenks, see "Co-ordination: a new problem of international organization," 77 RCADI (1950-II), p. 151: "Co-ordination in international organization: an introductory survey," 28 BYIL (1951), p. 28.

[21] See Carroz et Probst, *Personnalité Juridique internationale et Capacité de Conclure des Traités de l'ONU et des Institutions Specialisées* (1953), p. 84.

[22] *Ibid.*, p. 85.

[23] This danger is referred to by Bowett, *The Law of International Institutions*, 2nd ed. (1970), p. 303, and the decision of the International Court of Justice in the *Reparations Case, ICJ Reports* (1949), p. 174, is not completely free from this sort of reasoning.

[24] Constitution is meant here in the narrow sense of "constituent instrument."

[25] Kelsen, *Law of the United Nations* (1950), p. 330.

[26] Cf. Hahn, "EURATOM, The Conception of a Legal Personality," 71 H.L.R. (1958) 1001.

siders its proper functions should be carried out[27]. A more recent view is that the personality of an international organization is an objective fact, from which "treaty-making" capacity is a natural consequence[28]. From this it follows that there is no need to establish by other means (either through constitutional provisions or through the organization's interpretation thereof) any basis to personality or capacity to conclude agreements.

For present purposes, however, entry into the controversy over personality would be unprofitable. Since the concern here is a more narrow one, that is, the capacity of international organizations to conclude a particular class of agreement[29], whether or not organizations possess a general international personality is largely irrelevant[30]. In any event more guidance can be obtained from organizational practice than from taking a stand on a rather theoretical issue. The approach, therefore, will be to look to the constitutional authority of organizations and their practice in carrying out the functions prescribed for them.

The provisions of the constitutions of international organizations concerning co-operation and the conclusion of co-operation agreements are varied, but certain classes of provision can be discerned. First, there are those constitutions which authorize both co-operation with other organizations and the conclusion of co-operation agreements. This is done expressly in the constitution of the Food and Agriculture Organization (FAO) which provides for the maintenance of relations and the conclusion of agreements for co-operation with the United Nations[31], and also provides for the conclusion of agree-

[27] This appears to be the position taken by the International Court in the *Reparations Case (supra).*

[28] Seyersted, "Objective International Personality of Intergovernmental Organizations, Do their Capacities Really Depend upon the Conventions establishing them?" 34 *No.T.I.R.* (1964—65), p. 10. For a criticism of Seyersted's view see Seidl-Hohenveldern, "The Legal Personality of International and Supranational Organizations," 21 *Revue Egyptienne de Droit international* (1965), p. 35.

[29] Although, it must be admitted, the majority of agreements concluded between organizations have in fact been co-operation agreements.

[30] This would not be so if Seyersted's view was accepted, for capacity to conclude agreements would then be a consequence of inherent personality. Of course this moves the enquiry to a different level, i.e., what entities can be regarded as 'international organizations'?

[31] Art. XII (1) "The Organization shall maintain relations with the United Nations as a specialized agency within the meaning of Article 57 of the Charter of the United Nations."

(2) "Agreements defining the relations between the Organization and the United Nations shall be subject to the approval of the Conference." The inclusion of a separate provision concerning relations with the UN is general among the constitutions of the Specialized Agencies.

ments with other organizations[32]. In certain cases, however, the power to conclude co-operation agreements, either with a particular organization[33], or with a specific group of organizations[34], or with organizations generally, is implied. The implication arises very clearly in the constitutions of a number of the Specialized Agencies where not only is co-operation authorized but also an organ is designated to conclude any "agreement[35]" or "formal arrangement[36]" which may result from such co-operation. On the other hand the implication of authority to conclude agreements may arise from reading a provision concerning co-operation together with a separate provision bestowing a general "treaty-making" authority[37]. A further implication may arise where the constitutional provision relating to co-operation is expressed in terms so broad that it may be concluded that the discretion left to the competent organ is wide enough to allow it to conclude an agreement should it consider that this is necessary. In such cases the authority to conclude the agreement derives from the co-operation provision itself and is not referable to any separate "treaty-making" authority. Co-operation provisions which confer a

[32] Art. XIII "(1) In order to provide for close co-operation between the Organization and other international organizations with related responsibilities, the Conference may enter into agreements with the competent authorities of such organizations, defining the distribution of responsibilities and methods of co-operation.

(2) The Director-General may, subject to any decision of the Conference, enter into agreements with other intergovernmental organizations for the maintenance of common services, for common arrangements in regard to recruitment, training, conditions of service and other related matters, and for interchanges of staff." See also the constitutions of ICAO (Art. 65), IFC (Art. IV s. 7), IAEA (Art. XVI).

[33] The constitutions of both UPU (Art. 9) and ITU (Art. 29) refer to the conclusion of an agreement with the United Nations but only refer to "co-operation" (ITU Art. 30) and "collaboration" (UPU Art. 10) with other organizations.

[34] The UN-Charter (Art. 63) authorizes the conclusion of agreements with the "specialized agencies" referred to in Art. 57. However, the report of Committee II/8 at the San Francisco Conference shows that it was intended that ECOSOC would be able to conclude agreements with other "intergovernmental agencies" as well as the specialized agencies. See 10 UNCIO (1945) 272, Doc. 861, II/55 (1). See also Art. 134 of the Charter of the OAS as revised by the Buenos Aires Protocol of 27 February 1967 (in force 27 February, 1970).

[35] See WMO Convention, Art. 26 (a), WHO Constitution, Art. 70.

[36] See UNESCO Constitution, Art. XI (1).

[37] Thus the responsibility of the Commission of Euratom for the maintenance of "appropriate relations" with international organizations as provided in Art. 199 of the Euratom Treaty must be read together with Art. 101 of the Treaty which authorizes the incurring of obligations by "concluding agreements or conventions with ... an international organization." See also EEC Treaty, Art. 229 (co-operation) and Art. 228 (conclusion of agreements); IMCO Constitution, Art. 26 (conclusion of agreements) and Arts. 45 (co-operation with the UN), 46 (Specialized Agencies), and 47 (other organizations).

broad competence are characterized by the the use of terms such as "upon such terms and conditions as the ... (organ) may determine[38]," and the conclusion of "suitable" or "appropriate" arrangements[39], and "shall co-operate in such a manner as the ... (organization) may deem appropriate[40]."

The second main class of constitutions are those which make provision for co-operation with other organizations in relatively direct terms, without including any provision from which it may be implied that there is an authority to conclude co-operation agreements. This type of provision generally goes no further than mentioning that the organizations may "co-operate" with other organizations[41]. Thirdly, mention must be made of those organizations whose constitutions provide neither for co-operation with other entities, nor for the conclusion of agreements. Two important constitutions which fall into this category are the Charter of the Organization of African Unity (OAU) and the Pact of the League of Arab States (LAS). In the latter case, however, the Council of the League is given the task of "determining the means whereby the League will collaborate with the international organizations which may be created in the future[42]. Further, one of the purposes of the OAU is to "promote international cooperation[43]." Nevertheless in neither of these cases can it be concluded that the organization possesses a clear constitutional authority to enter into relations or co-operate with existing international organizations[44].

The Council of Europe also appears, at first sight, to fall into this category, for its constituent instrument contains no co-operation or "treaty-making" provisions. Article 15, on the other hand, authorizes the Committee of Ministers to "consider the action required to further the aim of the Council of Europe, including the conclusion of con-

---

[38] OECD Convention, Art. 12. Cf. COMECON Charter, Art. XI which provides that the nature and form of relations with other organizations shall be "determined by the Council in agreement with the international organizations concerned."

[39] See ILO Constitution, Art. 12. The constitution provides only for the conclusion of arrangements for representation in deliberations of the organization.

[40] Agreement establishing the Asian Development Bank, Art. 2. Art. 14 of the Agreement establishing the Inter-American Development Bank authorizes the Bank to "enter into arrangements" with other organizations.

[41] See IMF Articles of Agreement, Art. X, IBRD Articles of Agreement, Art. V, Agreement establishing the African Development Bank, Art. 2 (2).

[42] Art. 3. To regulate such relations, however, would require an amendment of the Pact by a two-thirds majority, see Art. 19.

[43] Art. II (1) (e).

[44] The Charter of the Organization of Central American States (ODECA) also lacks provisions relating to co-operation or the conclusion of agreements.

ventions and agreements." Acting pursuant to this authority the Committee of Ministers at its Eighth Session, in May 1951, adopted a resolution authorizing itself to "... conclude with any inter-governmental organization agreements ... to define the terms on which such an organization shall be brought into relationship with the Council of Europe." This resolution is included in the Council's group of "texts of a statutory character[45]" and may be regarded as part of the Organization's constitution in the broader sense.

This threefold classification of constitutions into those which authorize co-operation and the conclusion of co-operation agreements, those which authorize co-operation *simpliciter* and those which authorize neither[46] is somewhat arbitrary. In the first instance the category of constitutions which include a "treaty-making" power is clearly the largest, resulting in a need for further sub-divisions and explanation, and some of these further divisions overlap. Thus within one constitution there may be found only an implied authority to enter into agreements with one organization while in respect of other organizations an express power exists[47]. Further, some constitutions, though authorizing the conclusion of co-operation agreements, limit such conclusion to a particular class of organization determined on technical grounds[48], or on the ground of related interests[49], or to a particular class of agreement[50]. In spite of this lack of precision the classification adopted is sufficient to indicate the variety of types of provisions that occur and the lack of uniformity in their enunciation. It is important to bear this great variety in mind when considering the extent to which constitutional limitations on the competence of an organization to conclude agreements have been acknowledged and adhered to in practice.

A glance at the United Nations Treaty Series shows the impressive body of agreements concluded by the United Nations and the Spe-

---

[45] Drawn up by the Minister's Deputies at their 40th Meeting (June 1963) and published in the European Treaty Series, No. 1.

[46] Although they do not prohibit either co-operation or the conclusion of agreements.

[47] This is true of the FAO provision concerning relations with the UN (*supra*), where authority is given to "maintain relations" (Art. XIX (1)) and an organ is designated to conclude any "agreements" (Art. XII (2)). Thus an authority to "maintain relations" by concluding agreements arises by a clear implication.

[48] Thus the Asian Development Bank is authorized to co-operate with "... public international organizations ... which are concerned with the investment of development funds in the region..." (Art. 2 (v) of the Agreement establishing the Bank).

[49] IMCO may co-operate with organizations "whose interests and activities are related to the purposes of the Organization" (Art. 47).

[50] The Council of the Caribbean Organization is authorized to conclude "technical assistance agreements" with other organizations (Art. 7 (f) (i)).

cialized Agencies among themselves[51]. First, there are the relationship agreements concluded by the United Nations with the Specialized Agencies in accordance with the provisions of Articles 57 and 63 of the Charter[52]. Secondly, there are the "inter-agency agreements," that is, co-operation agreements concluded between the Specialized Agencies themselves and with the International Atomic Energy Agency (IAEA). Not all, however, of the Specialized Agencies have entered into such agreements, those which have concluded arrangements being ILO, UNESCO, FAO, WHO, WMO, ICAO, IMCO, and IAEA[53]. All of these Agencies have constitutional authority to conclude agreements which is either express, or may be implied. The only Agency on which some doubt may be cast is the ILO, but in view of the content of the agreements which involve, *inter alia*, the sending of representatives to meetings, it would seem that there is authority to conclude such arrangements[54]. Certainly the Agencies which have not entered into formal agreements are ones whose authority to do so is doubtful[55]. Whether this is because they regard themselves as prohibited from doing so, either under their constitutions or as a result of some independent norm of international law, is not clear, but there seems no evidence to suggest that they feel themselves under an obligation, independent of their constitutional limitations, to refrain from concluding agreements. A mere failure to act does not necessarily imply that the failure resulted from the feeling of an obligation to refrain[56]. One explanation for this lack of

---

[51] Mention should, perhaps, be made of the co-operation agreements concluded during the existence of the League of Nations, of which there appear to have been two. First, an agreement between the League and the International Institute of Agriculture (IIA), see *League of Nations Official Journal* (1932-II), 1752, and secondly, an agreement between the ILO and the IIA, see 5 *ILO Official Bulletin* (1922), p. 98.

[52] Relationship agreements have been concluded with all of the Specialized Agencies, which are so designated, by virtue of Art. 57 of the UN Charter, on the conclusion of the agreement. An agreement has also been concluded with the IAEA (281 UNTS, p. 569) although the Agency is not technically a Specialized Agency and enjoys a special status with the UN.

[53] All of the inter-agency agreements, including those with the IAEA have been published in the United Nations Treaty Series.

[54] Art. 12 (2) of the ILO Constitution authorizes the conclusion of agreements relating to representation in meetings of the ILO.

[55] E.g., UPU and ITU. While the ITU has "consistently declined to conclude any formal agreement on this point" it has "informally agreed" to certain procedures of consultation with other Agencies, see Schneider, *Treaty-Making Power of International Organizations* (1959), p. 35.

[56] See the classical formulation of this principle, there relating to customary rules of international law, by the Permanent Court of International Justice in the *Lotus Case*, PCIJ (1927). Ser. A, No. 10.

co-operation arrangements may be that the organizations concerned regard their function as being of such a narrow and technical nature that the conclusion of agreements with other Agencies would serve no practical purpose. This would seem particularly cogent in the case of the financial organizations, whose counterpart to co-operation agreements would be financial arrangements.

Apart from the agreements concluded within the United Nations family, there are a considerable number of agreements which have been concluded between the Specialized Agencies and organizations which are not related to the United Nations. The ILO has been particularly active[57], but agreements have also been entered into by FAO[58], UNESCO[59], WHO[60], IAEA[61], and the United Nations Secretariat has also concluded arrangements[62]. Such a list does not purport to be exhaustive for there are many agreements concluded between the Specialized Agencies and other organizations which are not readily available from official sources. These agreements are often concluded by an exchange of letters without any formal procedure being adopted[63]. In many cases they are not published separately and can only be found in the records of the Agency concerned, or in the minutes of the meetings of its competent organs[64].

---

[57] Agreements have been concluded with OAS, EEC, ECSC, OAU, LAS, the Council of Europe (CE), Asian Productivity Organization (APO), Commission for Technical Co-operation South of the Sahara (CTCA), African and Malagasy Organization for Economic Co-operation (AMOEC) (all published in the United Nations Treaty Series), Euratom *(Journal Officiel des Communautés (J.O.D.C.)* 475/61) and OECD. The agreement with OECD is in substance a continuation of the previous agreement with OEEC, see 37 *ILO Official Bulletin* (1954), p. 392.

[58] Agreements have been concluded with OAS *(op.cit.)*, Council of Europe (CE Doc. A 28254), EEC and OECD (both unpublished exchanges of letters).

[59] Agreements have been concluded with OAS, Council of Europe, International Bureau of Education (IBE), International Commission for Weights and Measures (ICWM) and LAS (all published in the United Nations Treaty Series).

[60] Agreements have been concluded with the International Council for Military Medicine and Pharmacy (ICMMP) and the Pan American Sanitary Organization (PASO) (both published in the United Nations Treaty Series).

[61] Agreements have been concluded with the Inter-American Nuclear Energy Commission (IA-NEC) and OECD (a continuation of the agreement with OEEC) (both published in the United Nations Treaty Series).

[62] Agreement with OAU, on behalf of the Economic Commission for Africa (548 UNTS 514), and agreement with the Secretary-General of the Council of Europe, exchange of letters dated 15 December 1951 (CE Doc. A 7395).

[63] E.g., UN Secretariat agreement with the Secretary-General of the Council of Europe, *supra*. The legal nature of such agreements will be considered *infra*.

[64] This applies equally to certain agreements between the Specialized Agencies and UN organs; thus various agreements between UNESCO and UNRWA are to be found in the decisions of the Executive Board of UNESCO.

Organizations outside the United Nations system have also concluded a number of co-operation agreements among themselves. First, the relationship agreements between the Organization of American States (OAS) and its Specialized Organizations may be mentioned[65]. These agreements are similar in some respects to the United Nations relationship agreements in that they create a regime between the central organization, in the first case the OAS and in the second case the United Nations, and the various organizations with which they are concluded. To a certain extent in both cases the provisions of the agreements go beyond mere co-operation and envisage closer forms of association and even subordination[66]. European organizations have also concluded a number of co-operation agreements. The Council of Europe particularly has established relations with other organizations through the conclusion of agreements, generally in the form of an exchange of letters[67] and similar procedures have been followed by the European Communities and OECD[68]. In most cases the agreements have not been formally reproduced, although some of the agreements of the European Communities have been published in the *Journal Officiel des Communautés*[69].

It seems clear from the practice of international organizations in concluding co-operation agreements that no necessary nexus exists between constitutional authority to conclude agreements and the fact that such agreements have been concluded. In the case of the United

[65] The original OAS Charter provided only for agreements between the Council and the Specialized Organizations relating to the transmission of budgets by the latter to the Council (Art. 99). Nevertheless between 1949 and 1953 more general co-operation agreements were concluded by the Council with the Pan American Institute of Geography and History, Pan American Institute for the Protection of Childhood, Pan American Sanitary Office, Inter-American Statistical Office, Inter-American Indian Institute, Inter-American Commission of Women, and Inter-American Railway Congresses Association (all of these agreements are published in the *Annals of the OAS*). However, the Buenos Aires Protocol of February 1967, amending the OAS Charter, places no restriction on the types of agreement to be concluded between the Council and the Specialized Organizations (Art. 134).

[66] An example of subordination occurs in the UN relationship agreement with UNESCO where a veto is given to ECOSOC and the General Assembly over membership in that organization, Art. II.

[67] E.g., agreements with Euratom (CE Doc. A 58 407) and the European Conference of Ministers of Transport (CE Doc. A 58405).

[68] The agreements concluded by OECD are largely unpublished, but see agreement with the Council of Europe (CE Doc. I 557). For examples of agreements concluded by the European Communities see following note.

[69] E.g., an exchange of letters between Euratom and the International Commission for Weights and Measures (*J.O.D.C.* 614/66) and an exchange of letters between EEC and the Commission Centrale pour la Navigation du Rhin (*J.O.D.C.* 1027/61).

Nations relationship agreements, and to a lesser extent the inter-agency agreements, their conclusion is directly referable to a specific constitutional provision, but the relationship of many other agreements to constitutional authority is less clear and both the OAU and the LAS, neither of which have any constitutional authorization for the conclusion of agreements, have entered into agreements with some of the Specialized Agencies[70]. Thus an attempt to search for the basis for the capacity of international organizations to conclude co-operation agreements in their constituent instruments would be fruitless; the provisions are not uniform, nor are they rigidly adhered to in practice.

One method of avoiding this dilemma is to adopt the approach taken by some writers on the question of personality, that is, to attempt to find the basis, in this case for the capacity of organizations to conclude certain agreements, in the constitution of the organization taken as a whole, including not only the constituent instrument of the organization but also the decisions of organs and the way in which the organization's functions have been developed in practice[71]. This would mean that if by its practice an organization showed that it considered itself competent to conclude co-operation agreements then it must be regarded as having capacity to do so under international law. But such an answer says little more than, if an organization finds a willing contracting partner and concludes an agreement then it must be regarded as having a capacity recognized by international law to do so. In other words capacity under international law is expanded every time an organization concludes a new category of agreement. As a legal basis for that capacity therefore this view is inadequate, for under the guise of providing a rule limiting capacity it simply leaves the matter to the contracting organizations themselves. The purported limitation on the capacity of organizations is thus an illusion.

A recently propounded view is that capacity to conclude agreements, and hence co-operation agreements, is based on a customary rule of international law recognizing that capacity[72]. This view is

---

[70] OAU has concluded an agreement with ILO (550 UNTS, p. 389), while LAS has entered into agreements with both ILO (302 UNTS, p. 344) and UNESCO (see Khalil, *The Arab States and the Arab League* (1962), p. 92).

[71] This is the "implied powers" approach, see Weissberg, *The International Status of the United Nations* (1961), 37, Bowett, *op.cit.*, p. 303. See also Socini, *Rapports et Conflits Entre Organisations Européennes* (1960), p. 75.

[72] Schneider, *op.cit.*, p. 135—142, Chiu, *The Capacity of International Organizations to Conclude Treaties and the Special Legal Aspects of the Treaties so Concluded* (1966), p. 34. Chiu does have some reservations, see *infra*. See also Seyersted, *loc.cit.*

derived from an examination of the practice of international organizations and an enumeration of the types of agreements so far concluded. It is, however, doubted whether the practice that exists can really be said to be adequate for such a conclusion, particularly in view of the lack of uniformity in constitutional authority and in the practice of concluding agreements. Insufficient is known of the organizations which have not concluded agreements in spite of the fact that they have constitutional authority, expressed in relatively general terms, to co-operate with other entities. Furthermore, the somewhat rigorous requirements which are needed to establish the existence of a customary rule of international law, recently reiterated by the International Court of Justice, that practice should be "... both extensive and virtually uniform ... and should moreover have occurred in such a way to show a general recognition that a rule of law or legal obligation is involved[73]" are far from satisfied. Some further and more definitive practice of organizations is required before it can be said that a customary rule of international law has developed, although it cannot be denied that the present practice provides a good basis for the future development of such a rule.

As the existing attempts to determine the basis of the capacity of international organizations to conclude co-operation agreements have been rejected the task is now to formulate a more satisfactory basis. In doing so the writer is led to place primary importance on the practice of international organizations as evidence of a desire to conclude agreements with each other. Any legal basis for capacity must therefore facilitate rather than impede future practice along the same lines. Thus an attempt to declare existing agreements, or in so far as it is possible to conjecture any future agreements, illegal or ineffective under international law would be destructive of the harmonious development of inter-organizational relations. Starting from the organization's practice, then, the fact that they have entered into co-operation agreements suggests that they do not regard themselves as having any incapacity under international law. Nor, it may be added, do there appear to have been any instances of States lodging objections to the conclusion of such agreements on the ground of lack of capacity. It is argued, therefore, that no rule of international law exists which prohibits international organizations from concluding co-operation agreements. Thus, provided that an organization is an entity having an existence recognized by international law then it has the capacity to conclude co-operation agreements[74].

---

[73] *North Sea Continental Shelf Case* (1969), *ICJ Reports*, p. 43.

[74] Capacity here refers only to capacity under international law as far as it concerns the external relations of organizations, and does not purport to affect the

Capacity, then, at present rests not on any positive rule according it but on the fact that it relates to an activity of entities operating on the international level which is not contrary to a specific prohibition imposed by international law and does not infringe some related rule or conflict with some interest protected by international law[75]. As the practice of international organizations develops and the interests of States and organizations become more clearly defined rules may develop, or have to be formulated, to qualify or modify the capacity of organizations to conclude agreements. This does not prevent, however, the more immediate formulation of a rule to cover the present situation.

It has been stated that the existing practice is insufficient to allow the conclusion that a customary rule of international law conferring capacity to conclude co-operation agreements has developed, although the practice may form the basis of a future rule. On the other hand, with a view to codifying[76] rules governing co-operation agreements it would seem that the best approach would be to formulate a positive rule recognizing capacity. In other words the practice presses towards the development of a rule so that its statement in a codification of the law of inter-organizational agreements is a necessary measure for the progressive development of international law. A positive rule would not only acknowledge the present trend in practice but would itself, if accepted, provide a vital link in the development of international law on the subject.

In the light of the above argument the following rule is suggested,

"International organizations possess the capacity under international law to conclude co-operation agreements with each other[77]."

---

organizations internal competence as stipulated by its constitution. This point will be developed later. Moreover, the international character of an organization does not depend on any specific provision of its constitution or on its constitution in the broader sense. Again, this will be considered further *infra*.

[75] It is not sufficient to categorize this view as one which would allow as legal all that is not specifically prohibited. The determination of the legality of an act under any legal system involves an enquiry into the nature of the act and all relevant rules and affected interests. In the present case the conclusion of co-operation agreements by international organizations does not conflict with general rules of international law, nor does it impose on an interest that the law protects.

[76] In this sense codification means the reduction to a written form of rules of international law, whether they are rules *de lege lata* or *de lege ferenda*.

[77] It might be argued that the most which could be stated in a codification of the law relating to inter-organizational agreements is that international law does not prohibit the conclusion of co-operation agreements—thus avoiding the formulation of a rule. However, the mere inclusion of such a statement would, if the codification became law, elevate it to the status of a rule. The consequences would, therefore, be identical.

Some further explanation is required; first, what, in this context, is an 'international organization'? As yet no definition of an international organization has been universally accepted, nor is it likely that one, satisfactory for all purposes, will be found[78]. For the present it will be sufficient to outline the principal characteristics of organizations able to conclude co-operation agreements, without attempting a comprehensive definition. First, it is clear, the organization must be an organization of States: based on agreement[79]. Secondly, the organization must have some institutional element[80] in that the entity should possess an organ (or organs) identifiable separately from the individual wills of the States which comprise it. In practice this separate identity manifests itself when one speaks of action being taken by the "General Assembly," or by the "EEC Commission," rather than by the individual member States. Thirdly, and in determining whether an entity possesses capacity to conclude agreements this criterion seems decisive, the entity must be endowed with a function in the international field which involves it in the conduct of relations with other entities[81].

The second question which arises from the rule formulated above concerns the relationship of the international capacity of an organization to conclude co-operation agreements to its competence as expressed in its constitution, which, was earlier stated to be the source only of the internal rules of the organization. The issue is whether a co-operation agreement concluded without constitutional authorization, or in the face of specific prohibition, can be regarded, as between the contracting organizations (i.e. externally) as valid. According to the rule enunciated here international capacity[82] would not be affected by constitutional limitations[83]. However, some quali-

[78] It may be noted that the Vienna Convention on the Law of Treaties does not attempt to define a 'State.'

[79] Neither the consensual basis to an organization nor the requirement that its members, at least predominantly, are States seems to be seriously doubted in present doctrine.

[80] See Rosenne, "Is the Constitution of an International Organization an International Treaty?" (1966) *Communicazioni e Studi*, 25.

[81] In general the international responsibilities of an organization make it necessary for that entity to enter into relations with other organizations in order to properly carry out its functions, and to avoid duplication of the others' work. A comparison may be made between an organization such as the UN which has wide international responsibilities and an entity established solely for the purpose of acting as a clearing house for information between its member States. In the latter case there would be less reason for the conduct of external relations.

[82] I.e. capacity recognized by international law.

[83] Constitutional limitations, it has been argued earlier, are created by the members of an organization and can therefore be effective only between them.

fication should be introduced. Though the principle of the security of treaty relations, as between States, requires that, in general, lack of express constitutional authority to conclude an agreement should not prejudice the agreement where the other party has acted in good faith, where there is a clear constitutional prohibition with regard to such an agreement a different approach must be taken. Article 46 of the Vienna Convention on the Law of Treaties provides that a violation of the internal law of a State does not invalidate consent given to a treaty "unless that violation was manifest and concerned a rule of ... fundamental importance[84]." Such a provision is also necessary in a codification of the law concerning inter-organizational agreements in order to invalidate consent in the case of a manifest violation of the constitutional provisions of one of the parties[85].

The inclusion of a provision similar to Article 46 of the Vienna Convention would also limit the appeal of the argument in favour of limiting the capacity of organizations to the conclusion only of those agreements whose content is consistent with the organization's functions[86]. This position is based, in part, on the view that to acknowledge the international capacity of an organization to conclude (in theory) any agreement will encourage organizations to extend their competences beyond those originally intended by their member States. This, however, overlooks two factors. First, in practice the States whose interests it is sought to protect are none other than the States making up the organs which, it is believed, will, by exercising

[84] A violation is manifest if it would be "objectively evident to any State conducting itself in the matter in accordance with normal practice and in good faith" Art. 46 (2).

[85] The conclusion, for example, of an agreement between the Council of Europe and the North Atlantic Treaty Organization whereby the former agrees to provide the latter with armed forces would fall within the provision. (Art. 1 (d) of the Statute of the Council of Europe provides, "Matters relating to National Defence do not fall within the scope of the Council of Europe.") In certain cases the interpretation of what constitutes a "manifest violation" may be difficult. Such matters as the previous relations of the parties, the public nature of the organization's activities and the attitude of member States could, however, be taken into account.

[86] Schneider, *op.cit.*, p. 135, "... organizations may conclude agreements ... provided ... they do not exceed the scope and limits of their competences in concluding such agreements. The extent of treaty-making power is thus restricted to the extent of competences." Chiu, *op.cit.*, p. 47, "... in a determination of the limitations on the capacity of an international organization, its functions and purposes are the principal guide." See also Socini, *op.cit.*, p. 75, who considers that organizations are competent to conclude agreements, "pourvu que ces accords rentrent dans l'accomplissement de leurs fonctions et soient nécessaires pour atteindre leurs buts." See further ILC 1962 Draft Articles on the Law of Treaties, 2 YILC (1962), p. 27, Art. 3.

their international capacity, increase their competence and powers. The organs can only act when they are authorized by at least a majority of their member States[87]. International capacity, therefore, remains only theoretical unless it is accompanied by internal authority. Secondly, the members of an organization are primarily the entities competent to interpret their constitution and determine the proper functions of the organization. Thus they may seek to extend their functions beyond those objectively ascertainable by reference to the constitution. To limit the international capacity of an organization to the conclusion of agreements which fall within its functions (which must mean those which objectively can be seen to fall within its functions) may in fact restrict the competence of the member States to subjectively determine the functions of their organization. If the member States of an international organization desire to broaden the functions of their organization then this is a matter for them and not one that a third party should deny them. On the other hand, the inclusion of a provision relating to "manifest violation" guards against flagrantly unconstitutional action by an incompetent organ[88].

Thus the general rule enunciated above should stand and no restrictions should be imposed on the international capacity of organizations to conclude co-operation agreements. This is, of course, subject to the proviso that the consent of an organization is not properly given if the conclusion of the agreement constitutes a "manifest violation" of its constitution. In this way any gross extension of the functions of an organization negates consent, while lesser extensions of the organization's functions do not affect the validity of the agreement. Such a solution is consistent both with the right of the members of an organization to interpret their constitution and with the principle of the security of treaty relations.

The Competence of an Organ to Conclude Agreements on Behalf of an International Organization

Once it has been established that international law recognizes the capacity of international organizations to conclude co-operation agreements among themselves, the question arises as to the organ com-

[87] This may not be so if it is the Secretary-General or an organ of restricted membership which acts, but in general, it will be seen, it is the plenary organ which is constitutionally competent to conclude agreements.

[88] The point made earlier may perhaps be emphasized. Because the members are primarily entitled to interpret their organization's constitution and hence its functions, then limitations based on the organization's constitution (in the broader sense) are no limitations at all.

petent to actually consent to the conclusion of an agreement and so bind the organization. While this is basically a matter of the external law of organizations, in that the issue is whether a contracting organization can rely on a particular organ's competence to bind the other party in the international field, the internal aspect cannot be neglected. Thus with a view to the codification of the law concerning the agreements of international organizations great emphasis must be placed on the organ which internally is recognized as competent to commit the organization to a binding undertaking. Although the practice of States in this field has been susceptible of codification[89], certain complications arise with organizations. First, the practice of issuing "full powers," which in inter-State relations approached the status of a rule of law prior to the conclusion of the Vienna Convention[90], has no counterpart in the relations of international organizations[91]. Secondly, there is no organ in an international organization which is in a position equal to that of a Head of State, or Head of Government, or Minister for Foreign Affairs and who could, therefore, by virtue of office be able to commit the organization to a binding undertaking[92]. Thirdly, the practice of organizations in agreement-making is as yet in a primitive stage, thus any conclusions drawn from it must be tentative and the recognition of a competent organ to some extent arbitrary.

In attempting to determine an organ to be regarded as competent[93] reference must first be made to the constitutional identification of the competent organ by the organizations themselves, to see if there exists among them a consistent practice. The constitutions of many organizations do in fact contain an express stipulation as to the organ possessing the power to consent to the conclusion of certain agreements. This is so with the United Nations[94], and the Specialized

[89] Vienna Convention on the Law of Treaties, Art. 7.

[90] See generally Blix, *Treaty-Making Power* (1960), Ch. V.

[91] In certain organizations, it will be seen, there is a practice of referring, in the opening of negotiations with another organization, to a resolution of the competent organ of the organization authorizing the negotiating organ to act. This cannot, however, be regarded in the same light as "full powers" which involve an official authorizing instrument.

[92] Arguments that the Secretary-General of an international organization is the equivalent of the Minister for Foreign Affairs in a State are unconvincing in view of the different structure of States and organizations and the different functions of the two organs.

[93] I.e. an organ which international law will recognize as capable of giving the consent of an organization to the conclusion of agreements.

[94] Art. 63, UN Charter. Even this, however, is not clear for the Charter provides that ECOSOC "may enter into agreements" but that such agreements shall be "subject to approval by the General Assembly." It seems accepted, nevertheless, that the General Assembly is the competent organ.

Agencies, the constitutions of which often provide specifically for the conclusion of co-operation agreements, and is also true of EEC and Euratom[95]. In other constitutions competence may be implied, for example, where the organ empowered to enter into relations with other organizations is given a wide discretion as to the means by which it shall act[96].

In fact it is difficult to envisage a case where constitutional competence cannot at least be implied; that is, from any constitution it is possible to determine an organ which has the kind of authority which would allow it to conclude co-operation agreements. Where, for example, a constitution simply refers to the competence of an organization to conclude agreements[97], or enter into relations[98], then it can be concluded that in the absence of any contrary authorization the organ with either the primary or the residuary competence will have the necessary authority. This can be taken further and applied to those constitutions where no authority is provided either to enter into relations with other organizations or to conclude co-operation agreements. If these organizations are in fact competent (internally) to conclude such agreements, as the practice of some would indicate, then it may be implied from their constitutions that a particular organ is competent to express the consent of the organization.

The implication may not necessarily be found in the constituent instrument itself, but may be indicated in the constitution in the broader sense. In the case of the OAU ultimate authority generally rests with the Assembly of Heads of State and Government[99] to which the Council of Ministers is responsible[100]. In practice, however, the Council is the organ which authorizes and administers the activities of the Organization, although it is ultimately subject to the Assembly. Thus the OAU's co-operation agreements have been entered into under the authority of the Council[101]. The League of Arab

[95] E.g., FAO Constitution, Art. XII, EEC Treaty, Art. 228, Euratom Treaty, Art. 10.

[96] Examples have been mentioned earlier and include the constitutions of OECD, ECSC and COMECON.

[97] E.g., EEC Treaty, Art. 231, "The Community shall establish close collaboration with OECD of which the methods shall be determined by common accord."

[98] E.g. IMF Articles of Agreement, Art. X, "The Fund shall co-operate ... with any general organization and with public international organizations."

[99] OAU Charter, Art. VIII "The Assembly ... shall be the supreme organ of the Organization."

[100] OAU Charter, Art. XIII.

[101] A similar position pertains in the ILO where the constitution does not stipulate separate functions for the Governing Body and the Conference. In practice the conclusion of agreements falls within the competence of the Governing Body.

States, on the other hand, possesses only one organ which is at all competent to act on behalf of the organization[102], so that it must be concluded that that organ is competent to give the consent of the Organization to the conclusion of agreements[103].

A comparison of the constitutional authority outlined above does not give rise automatically to a presumption in favour of any particular organ as being generally competent to conclude co-operation agreements on behalf of its organization. In most cases it is the plenary organ which is able to act on behalf of the organization, but in some cases the executive organ[104] or the chief executive official[105] has been accorded competence. The Specialized Agencies generally adopt the first alternative, but in the case of the World Meteorological Organization a different technique has been employed whereby co-operation agreements are "subject to approval by two-thirds of the Members which are States, either in Congress or by correspondence[106]." Among the organizations outside the United Nations family the plenary organ also seems predominantly competent[107]. In the case of the EEC, however, the "treaty-making" competence is divided between the Commission and the Council with the latter having the broader competence[108].

However, the practice of international organizations in concluding co-operation agreements does not wholly represent a faithful adherence to constitutional authority. In the main, it is true, the organ endowed with competence by the constitution is the one which consents to the conclusion of agreements. This can be verified either by

---

[102] LAS Pact, Art. 5 (2) "The Council shall be entrusted with the function of realizing the purpose of the League ..."

[103] One must assume with both OAU and LAS that the organizations themselves regard their agreements as being constitutionally authorized.

[104] Thus it is the Executive Board of UNESCO which is competent to approve "formal arrangements" with other organizations (Art. XI), not the General Conference. Cf. ECSC Treaty which authorizes the High Authority to "maintain appropriate relations" with certain organizations (Art. 93).

[105] FAO Constitution, Art. XIII (2).

[106] Art. 26 (a).

[107] In this context the concept of a "plenary" organ is somewhat inadequate, as in a number of organizations there are more than one "plenary," in the sense of being fully representational, organs.

[108] Art. 228. The Commission, it would seem, is competent to conclude co-operation agreements, but this is not without doubt, see Pescatore, "Les Relations Extérieures des Communautés Européennes," 103 RCADI (1961-II), p. 119, and cf. Mégrét, "Conclusion, Formes et Effets des Accords Internationaux Passés par la CEE," 19 *Revue du Marché Commun* (1963), p. 22. See also Raux, *Les Relations Extérieurs de la Communauté Economique Européenne* (1966), 202—206.

reference to provisions of the agreement itself[109], or by referring to the records of the relevant organ when approval of the agreement was given[110]. The United Nations relationship agreements and the inter-agency agreements all provided that they were to come into force on the approval of the competent organs of the respective organizations, but a number of the agreements between the Specialized Agencies and other organizations adopted a different procedure and provided for entry into force on the date on which the agreement was signed by the "authorized representatives" of the two organizations[111]. In such cases the consent of the competent organ would be manifested by authorizing the signature of the agreement. The difference between the two methods, however, appears merely procedural.

While the competent organ can, and sometimes does, delegate its "treaty-making" authority[112], in a number of cases agreements have been concluded by other organs in circumstances from which it is difficult to infer that a prior delegation had been made. For example, the Secretary-General of the United Nations has concluded agreements with certain organizations even though it would seem from the Charter and preparatory work that this is in the province of ECOSOC and the General Assembly[113]. With many of the informally concluded agreements of those organizations outside the United Nations family it is difficult to establish precise authorization by the

---

[109] Agreement between ILO and FAO (18 UNTS, 335), Art. 9, "This agreement shall come into force on its approval by the Governing Body of the ILO and the FAO Conference."

[110] Verification is a relatively simple matter where the records of the organizations are public (subject to delays in publication). On the other hand it is more difficult with an organization which does not publish unrestrictedly its official records.

[111] E.g., Art. 7 (i) of the agreement between ILO and OAS (70 UNTS, p. 225).

[112] The World Health Assembly at its first session authorized the Director-General to enter into agreements, under certain conditions, with the Directors-General of other organizations, to establish or participate in joint committees, WHO Official Records (1948), No. 13, p. 324.

[113] Detter ("The Organs of International Organizations Exercising their Treaty-Making Power," 38 BYIL (1962), p. 421, 436) quotes from a letter from the UN Secretariat to the ILC Special Rapporteur on the Law of Treaties, Sir Humphrey Waldock, as follows,

"Where the Secretary-General concluded an agreement with the Government of a State on behalf of the Organization, ... there is of course no question of credentials or full powers since, as the Chief Administrative Officer of the Oganization unter Article 97 of the Charter, his power of making treaties on behalf of the Organization in the performance of his functions is implied."

It is probable that the same reasoning is applied to the conclusion of agreements with other organizations. Detter, however, concludes that express authorization is more generally used.

competent organ, although in some cases it may well be implied. The Secretary-General of the Council of Europe, for example, has concluded agreements by an exchange of letters with a number of organizations. Though his approach to another organization with a view to establishing relations has been authorized by the Council of Ministers it is not clear that in all cases the expression of consent to the ultimate agreement stemmed from the Council and not from the Secretary-General himself[114]. On the other hand, when the result of the negotiations is an agreement drawn up in the traditional treaty form then explicit reference is made to the approval of the Council of Ministers[115]. Formal approval by the Commission of the EEC seems to be lacking in those agreements concluded simply by the signature of the President of the Group for External Relations of the Commission, although the agreements appear to constitute an undertaking by that body and, therefore, by the Community itself[116].

It can be seen that neither the constitutions nor the organizations' actual practice indicate a single organ as solely competent to conclude agreements on behalf of international organizations. Yet for the codification of the law concerning inter-organizational agreements some organ must be stipulated as one on which organizations can rely as being competent to bind their contracting party. The writers who have considered the matter have variously suggested that competence should repose in the plenary organ[117], the executive body[118], the chief executive official[119], the most powerful organ[120], or a plurality

---

[114] See agreement, by exchange of letters, with the WHO Regional Office for Europe, where the Secretary-General of the Council of Europe stated, in his letter of 9 September 1952, that he had been "authorized to *open negotiations* with the World Health Organization" (emphasis added), CE Doc. A 10046.

[115] The difference is understandable on practical grounds, for where the Secretary-General's opening letter was followed by negotiations then it was logical to embody the terms finally agreed upon in a formal agreement. On the other hand if the reply to his letter simply confirmed the terms there set out then no further stage was needed, the two letters being sufficient to constitute the agreement.

[116] E.g., agreement with ECAFE consisting of a letter of the Commission dated 24 January 1959 and a letter of the Executive-Secretary of ECAFE, dated 27 February 1959. (The agreement is as yet unpublished.) Such agreements give rise to a related issue, which be discussed *infra*, that is, what person or organ can be relied upon as competent to communicate the consent of the duly authorized organ of an organization to the other contracting party.

[117] Brierly, ILC Special Rapporteur on the Law of Treaties, A/CN. 4/23, p. 24.

[118] Detter, *op.cit.*, p. 423.

[119] Chiu, *op.cit.*, p. 90. See also Fitzmaurice, "The Law and Procedure of the International Court of Justice," 29 BYIL (1952), p. 1, 13.

[120] Detter, *op.cit.*, p. 426.

of organs[121], but ultimately a solution must be found which will best accord recognition to existing practice without either impairing the security of treaty relations or providing a mandate for organs to assert a competence which under their constitutions they do not possess. This latter point emphasizes that in reality the issue being considered here is simply a different aspect of the problem discussed earlier, that is, how far can an organization be permitted to deny the international validity of an agreement on the ground that a provision of its constitutional (internal) law has not been complied with, or has been infringed. The conclusion then reached was that in general the fact that an engagement does not comply strictly with internal requirements cannot be allowed to invalidate the consent of an organization unless there is a "manifest violation" of its constitution.

In part at least the same considerations should apply here. An organization should be able to rely on certain organs of another organization as being competent to consent to the conclusion of an agreement, without being affected by incidental violations of the others constitution, provided, of course, that the former organization is acting in good faith. On the other hand, a manifest violation of the constitution ought to invalidate any agreement[122].

From the constitutional provisions and practice referred to above it was concluded that, in general, the competent organ is the plenary organ, although in a number of cases the executive organ or the chief executive official has given assent to the conclusion of an agreement. Thus the rule should be as follows,

"(a) The plenary organ[123] of an international organization can be relied on by other organizations as being competent to express the consent of its organization to the conclusion of agreements.

(b) Where the constitution stipulates otherwise or where the practice of an organization[124] indicates that the chief executive official or some other executive official or organ is, by virtue of his or its officie, authorized to express the consent of the organization then such official or organ may also be relied on."

---

[121] Balladore-Pallieri, "La Formation des traités dans le pratique internationale contemporaine," 74 RCADI (1949-I), p. 490.

[122] The agreement would, in such circumstances, be rendered void.

[123] The argument in favour of the "most powerful" or "supreme" organ is rejected; although it may cover both where the plenary organ is competent and where the executive organ has competence, the interpretation of what constitutes the "most powerful" organ is too subjective. It is not clear whether power should be measured in respect of external competence or in respect of internal authority over member States. In any event the rule suggested does not in any way incapacitate other organs from representing the organization—reliance can be placed on their authority provided there is some degree of evidence of that authority.

[124] Cf. Vienna Convention on the Law of Treaties, Art. 7 (1) (b).

This rule must, of course, be read subject to the "manifest violation" qualification, so that an organization cannot claim that it has relied on an organ in accordance with this rule if the result is such a violation of the other's constitution. In practice the rule would operate through a series of presumptions. If an organization sought to deny that it had given consent to an agreement then the other party would simply have to show that the rule here enunciated had been complied with[125]. If this was done then there would be a presumption in favour of the validity of the agreement. However, if the organization had relied on an organ not covered by the rule then there would be a presumption of invalidity, to be rebutted by showing some further evidence which would indicate that reliance was justified[126].

To a limited extent, it is true, an organization, in concluding an agreement with another organization, must look to the other's constitution to determine whether the organ with which it is dealing is competent to conclude the agreement. Of course an organization cannot be required to undertake a detailed investigation of the other's constitution or become involved in a dispute with that organization over the interpretation of its constitution. As already mentioned each organization is primarily competent to interpret its own constitution and for this reason weight must be attached to an assertion of competence by an organ. On the other hand, if that assertion is apparently in contradiction to the constituent instrument of the organization then a duty must be cast upon the other party to make further enquiries[127].

In substance, then, the position is similar to that proposed under the Vienna Convention of the Law of Treaties, but because of the lack of practice leading to a definite presumption in favour of a particular organ an international organization cannot be wholly protected when it relies on an official or organ other than the plenary organ. It must, before placing reliance on that entity, look to the constitution and practice on the other party. Under the Vienna Convention the "full powers" procedure and the stipulation of certain organs which *ipso facto* can be regarded as representing their State certainly makes for more stability in treaty relations, but the differences in the structure and practice of organizations makes impossible an automatic transposition of the rules developed for States. Under the above rule, however, the principle of the security of treaty relations and the integrity

---

[125] I.e., that consent had been given by the plenary organ or by an organ which the constitution of the organization or its practice indicated was competent.

[126] E.g., reference to a resolution of the competent organ of the organization conferring authority on the organ granting consent.

[127] For example, it is possible that an organization will have adopted a practice which differs from the strict terms of its constituent instrument.

of the internal operations of an organization are both preserved, without either encouraging an incompetent organ to attempt to enter into engagements in violation of its organization's constitution or involving the other contracting party in too detailed an examination of internal competence as set out in the former's constitution.

The Procedure for the Negotiation and Conclusion of Agreements

Though the identification of the organ competent to consent to the conclusion of agreements may in the day to day operations of organizations be a question of academic interest, the procedure for the negotiation and conclusion of such agreements is of great practical importance. The former issue becomes significant only in the event of a dispute, but the latter question affects the whole agreement-making process. It is thus essential in any codification of the law to make provision for procedures by which agreements can be drawn up, and this can best be done by looking to the practice of the organizations themselves. In accordance with the method previously adopted constitutional provisions for the negotiation and conclusion of agreements will first be discussed, followed by a consideration of the actual methods adopted by international organizations in practice.

The first of these matters can be dealt with relatively simply, for in the main the constitutions of organizations include no provisions concerning the procedure for concluding agreements. Apart from stipulating the organ which is competent to conclude agreements the constitution is generally silent. In two cases, however, the constitution of organizations authorize separate organs to negotiate and grant consent to the conclusion of an agreement. Article 65 of the Charter of the United Nations provides that ECOSOC shall "enter into" the relationship agreements, which shall be approved by the General Assembly. In the EEC such a division of powers also exists, Article 228 of the Rome Treaty providing that agreements "shall be negotiated by the Commission," and that, "subject to the competence conferred upon the Commission in this respect, such agreements shall be concluded by the Council . . ."

In practice the procedure of negotiating agreements varies among different organizations, although three main types are discernible. First, there are those agreements which have been negotiated by formal committees established by the contracting organizations for this purpose. Such a procedure was adopted by the United Nations and the Specialized Agencies for their relationship agreements. At its First Session, in 1948, ECOSOC established a Committee on Negotiations with Inter-Governmental Agencies[128], which then met with committees established by the Agencies themselves, and proceeded to the work of preparing draft agreements[129]. The conclusion of this procedure was signified by the initialling of the agreement by the Chairman of the United Nations Negotiating Committee and the leader of the Agency's negotiating committee[130]. The negotiation of the inter-agency agreements also followed this pattern[131]. Outside the United Nations a more simple procedure of negotiation has often been utilized, involving meetings of representatives of the secretariats of two organizations, which have not been designated as official negotiating committees.

Thus the agreement reached between the ILO and the OEEC was the result of consultations between the Director-General of the ILO and the Deputy Secretary-General of OEEC and members of their staffs[132]. Similarly the letter of the President of the EEC Commission to the Director-General of UNESCO which sets out the terms of co-operation between the two organizations[133] refers to "les conversations qui ont eu lieu récemmement entre nos répésentants pour déterminer les modalités de la cooperation à établir entre nos deux institutions . . .[134]" Under this procedure the terms resulting from the consultations of the two groups of representatives were subsequently embodied in the exchange of letters, or more formal agreement, of the two organizations. The negotiations lacked formality, however, in that in general no initialled text resulted from the discussions[135].

---

[128] ECOSOC Official Records, 1st Session, 171 (1946), Res. 1/11. The Committee was composed of members of ECOSOC with the President of the Council as Chairman. See 1 *Repertory of Practice* (1955), p. 688.

[129] The agreement with the International Atomic Energy Agency was negotiated by the Advisory Committee on the Peaceful Uses of Atomic Energy which was authorized to so act by General Assembly Resolution 1115 (XI) at its 11th Session, 1956.

[130] See 3 *Repertory of Practice* (1955), p. 326—342, Chiu, *op.cit.*, p. 129—131.

[131] For an account of the negotiation of two of the inter-agency agreements entered into by WHO see WHO Official Records (1948), No. 6, p. 156—161.

[132] These consultations are referred to in the exchange of letters and text of conclusions which constitute the agreement between ILO and OEEC, see 37 *ILO Official Bulletin* (1954), p. 392.

[133] Letter dated 2 September 1964, signed "Jean Rey, Membre de la Commission." This letter, together with the reply of the Director-General of UNESCO, dated 15 September 1964 constitutes the agreement between the two organizations (UNESCO Official Records, 67 EX/29). In fact negotiations had been in progress since 1962, see UNESCO Official Records, 63 EX/14.

[134] The agreement between the EEC and FAO refers to similar previous discussions.

[135] This may be compared with the negotiation of the UN relationship agreements referred to above.

The third and most simplified procedure is one common among organizations outside the United Nations family and one which does not involve, on the face of it, any negotiation of the agreement at all. In these cases a representative, generally the Secretary-General or an equivalent ranking official, writes to another organization suggesting terms on which the two entities should co-operate. The reply of the other organization constitutes an agreement by an exchange of letters. This is the way in which the Council of Europe has concluded a number of its co-operation arrangements[136], as has the EEC[137]. In such circumstances there is no real negotiating procedure, it has been fused with the procedure of concluding the agreement[138]. It seems that increasingly a simplified conclusion of agreements is being preferred to drawing up an agreement in the traditional treaty form[139].

The actual conclusion of agreements has, to some extent, been discussed already and it may be recalled of those agreements which were formally concluded that the approval of the organ competent to give consent was often made a condition precedent to its entry into force. In some cases the agreement was signed but entry into force was delayed until the approval of the organ stipulated in the agreement was given[140]. In other cases it was to enter into force when signed by the "authorized representatives" of the two organizations[141].

Where the simplified method has been adopted the procedure for conclusion varies. In most cases the agreement enters into force on signature but this does not mean that approval of the competent organ has not been given. The power to approve may have been delegated

---

[136] See the agreements of the Council of Europe with the EEC (CE Doc. A 58406) and with the UN (CE Doc. A 7395).

[137] E.g., agreement with the Council of Europe, *supra*, and agreement with the Economic Commission for Europe (letter of the Executive-Secretary of ECE dated 20 September 1958, reply of the President of the Group for External Relations of the EEC dated 7 October 1958) referred to in Raux, *op.cit.*, p. 212.

[138] In practice the letters may have been preceded by some kind of informal discussions between the representatives of the organizations, perhaps merely by telephone.

[139] It is perhaps significant that after the transformation of OEEC into OECD the new organization simply confirmed, with some minor alterations, the existing arrangements with other organizations by exchanges of letters. Only in the case of the Council of Europe was a new agreement drawn up.

[140] E.g., the UN relationship agreements. A variation is provided by the agreement between FAO and the Council of Europe, where it is stated that the agreement shall enter into force on the approval of the Council of FAO and the Committee of Ministers of the Council of Europe, "but shall remain subject to confirmation by the Conference of FAO" (CE Doc. A 28254).

[141] See the agreement between ILO and OAS, *supra*, Art. 7.

to the negotiating organ prior to the commencement of negotiations[142], or the proposal of relations may have been scrutinized by the competent organ before the reply, which together with the initial letter constitutes the agreement, is sent[143]. Nevertheless in certain cases it would seem that agreements have entered into force without specific approval from the competent organ. This applies particularly to exchanges of letters where the reply of one of the organizations constitutes the necessary element for an agreement concluded in that manner when possibly it was the intention of the other party that its communication should only be exploratory[144].

The above discussion indicates that the procedure for negotiation and conclusion of agreements is significant in its lack of formality. It is difficult, therefore to follow with any degree of precision the various stages, normal in the conclusion of inter-state treaties, of negotiation, authentication[145], approval and exchange of ratifications. The last of these does not really exist at all, although an analogous procedure has been utilized in certain cases. In such agreements it is provided that entry into force shall occur once there has been notification to each organization of the approval of the other's competent

---

[142] E.g. delegation by the First World Health Assembly to the Director-General of WHO of a power to conclude agreements relating to joint committees (mentioned above).

[143] The Director-General of UNESCO in his reply to the letter of the EEC Commission stated, "Je suis heureux de vous informer que j'ai soumis le texte de cette communication au Conseil executif de l'UNESCO qui m'a autorisé à accepter les propositions qui y sont contenues."

[144] For example, with respect to the agreement between the Council of Europe and the WHO Regional Office for Europe (CE Doc. 10046) it is clear from the letter of the Secretary-General of the Council that he had authority to "open negotiations" with the World Health Organization, but the exchange of letters which constitutes the agreement between the two entities makes no reference to approval being given by the Committee of Ministers of the Council of Europe. Dupuy, "Le Droit des Relations entre les Organisations Internationales, 100 RCADI (1960-II), p. 498, refers to the fact that half of the co-operation agreements concluded by the Council of Europe were signed by the Secretary-General "après qu'il eut reçu des instructions du Comité de Ministres." He does not refer to any resolutions and it is probable that he has in mind the more formally concluded agreements, e.g. agreement with ILO, CE Doc. A 7396.

[145] The lack of a developed procedure for authenticating draft agreements may give rise to difficulties where the agreement has been drawn up in "treaty-form," for the organ giving approval may not be sure that the terms to which it is assenting are the terms to which the other party has agreed. On the other hand where the procedure adopted is an exchange of letters then the letter of each is authentic evidence for the other. There is no theoretical difficulty, however, in applying Art. 10 of the Vienna Convention to the more formally concluded agreements.

organ[146]. The practice is not, however, general. Some correlation may be seen between the formality of the negotiating and concluding procedure and the form of the instrument finally agreed upon, for where the procedure is more formal an agreement in traditional inter-State treaty form generally results, whereas when a more simplified method has been adopted the result generally is an exchange of letters. As will be seen later, however, the decisive element for determining the legal nature of an agreement is not the form used but whether rights and duties have been created.

The identification of an organ competent to represent its organization for the purposes of negotiating and communicating the consent of the organization to an agreement is a matter of some importance[147]. When an international organization wishes to conclude an agreement with another organization then obviously it must be concerned to deal with an organ which is competent to negotiate on behalf of the other party, so that at the end of negotiations it will not be confronted with a repudiation of all the work done so far[148]. Similarly, if an organization receives a letter from another suggesting terms for co-operation, a reply to which could constitute an agreement by exchange of letters, then obviously it will be imperative to ensure that the organ which sent the letter is competent to make such an offer on behalf of its organization[149]. Further, when an executive official states that the competent organ has approved an agreement the other party must know if it is entitled to rely on the statement or whether it must seek some further proof. The matter is not made any easier by the fact that few constitutions stipulate a negotiating organ, and is complicated further by the fact, already mentioned, that no practice of issuing "full powers" has been developed by international organizations. The question, then, is whether an organization can rely on statements of an organ of another organization that it is competent to negotiate, or that approval has been given by the competent organ to the conclusion of the agreement.

---

[146] Agreement between ILO and ECSC (*J.O.D.C.* 167/53), Art. 14, "The present Agreement shall enter into force as soon as the Director-General of ILO and the Chairman of the High Authority of ECSC have notified each other of the approval of the agreement of the Governing Body of the ILO and the High Authority of the Community."

[147] See Detter, *op.cit.*, p. 427—437.

[148] The existence of an obligation to refrain from acts detrimental to the object and purpose of the agreement prior to its entry into force will be discussed *infra*.

[149] This is, of course, closely related to the question of who has authority to conclude an agreement, for the processes of negotiation and conclusion in such a case are simultaneous.

In practice, of course, the chances of an organ stating that it is competent when in fact it is not are somewhat slight, but the case of an organ mistakenly believing that it is competent or exceeding the limits of its competence is more real. Generally, too, reliance will be placed on the simple assertion[150] of an organ that it is authorized to fulfil a particular task; it is unlikely, therefore, that an organization would go to the trouble of checking the credentials of a negotiating committee or querying the competence of the Secretary-General of another organization. It would seem, too, that the practice which has been discussed is of little assistance in settling upon a particular organ as being the one on which reliance can be placed, although it does allow certain conclusions to be drawn.

First, as no "full powers" are granted to negotiating committees the ability to point to a resolution of the competent organ of the organization establishing the committee and defining its functions seems sufficient evidence of authority. Secondly, the administrative organ of an organization has, in some cases been accepted as competent to negotiate, and even conclude, co-operation agreements. With some organizations such a power may be considered as a concomitant of that organ's administrative functions[151], and in certain cases as a result of specific authorization to promote relations with other organizations[152]. Certainly there is a practice, particularly in the Council of Europe and OECD, for the Secretary-General, when sending a preliminary communication concerning co-operation, to refer in detail to the contents of the resolution authorizing him either to negotiate or to enter into an agreement. In view of the difficulty of verifying whether the letter accurately states the terms of the resolution, or whether the resolution was passed at all[153], a contracting organization ought to be able to rely on the Secretary-General's letter.

Thirdly, where an administrative organ has stated that the competent organ of its organization, has given its approval to an agreement, then the other party has generally been content to rely on that assertion, and has not felt obliged to obtain any further proof. Excessive enquiries by an organization into the authority of the organs of another organization might be interpreted as an unwarranted interference in the internal affairs of that other organization.

[150] A communication suggesting that an agreement be concluded would generally imply authority in the organ form which it emanates.

[151] E.g., UN Secretary-General under Art. 97 of the Charter, see Detter, *op.cit.*, p. 436.

[152] See OAS Charter, Art. 118, "The General Secretary shall ... (h) establish relations of co-operation, ... with ... international organizations."

[153] Some difficulties may arise through delays in the publication of records, and even through their accessibility.

Admittedly the points outlined above are debatable and could be subject to qualification, but in an area where practice is so imperfectly developed a large measure of progressive development must be introduced into any codification of the law and this it has been attempted to do. Any rules finally decided upon must, as it has already been mentioned, facilitate the negotiation and conclusion of agreements by international organizations. The primary considerations, again no different from those already stated, are the integrity of the constitutions of organizations and the necessity of being able to rely upon the competence of certain organs. This latter point is simply a further aspect of the principle of the security of treaty relations. Again the principle of good faith and the limitation that a "manifest violation" of the constitution of either party invalidates the agreement must apply. In the light of these considerations the following rules are suggested:

"(a) An international organization may rely on a negotiating committee as being authorized to represent another organization, for the purpose of negotiating agreements, provided that the committee is able to invoke an act of the competent organ of its organization authorizing it to negotiate[154].

(b) An international organization may rely on the chief executive official of another organization, or another executive official if by virtue of his office he has apparent authority, as being authorized to represent that organization for the purpose of negotiating agreements.

(c) An international organization may rely on the chief executive official of another organization, or another executive official if by virtue of his office he has apparent authority, as being authorized to communicate the consent of that organization to the conclusion of agreements."

These rules require certain comments. First, more stringent evidence of authority must be required in the case of negotiating committees than for the chief executive official, or even, perhaps, for another official with apparent authority. Of course, where the official is not the Secretary-General of his organization then a greater degree of proof would required.

Secondly, the inclusion of a provision acknowledging the competence of "other executive officials," provided they have "apparent authority," might be questioned. Its addition is justified, however, on the ground that agreements are in fact negotiated and concluded by officials who are not the chief executive official of their organization. Particular examples are the President of the Group for External

[154] Detter *(op.cit.)* states, "In the law of international organizations, the act of authorization concerns rather the internal relationships within the organization" (p. 436). While it is agreed that primarily this is so, authorization must also be accorded some external significance.

Relations of the Commission of the EEC and Directors of Regional Offices of some of the Specialized Agencies[155]. Of course no simple answer can be given to the enquiry as to what constitutes "apparent authority." This will depend on the work of the official concerned, including his general responsibilities, his previous practice and the nature of specific tasks entrusted to him[156]. Naturally reliance could not be placed on his authority if this would amount to a manifest violation of the constitution of his organization. In spite of the difficulties which may arise it seems desirable to recognize the competence of these officials in order to facilitate inter-organizational relations[157].

Reference might also be made to the possibility of distinguishing between the different types of co-operation agreement which can be concluded in order to attribute separate consequences concerning competence to each category. In other words one could, perhaps, acknowledge the competence of certain officials with respect to the negotiation and conclusion of "administrative arrangements," but deny their capacity with respect to more substantial agreements. The feasibility of such a distinction will be discussed later, but it may be pointed out here that a limitation as to the types of agreements that can be negotiated or concluded is inherent in the "apparent authority" qualification, in that the negotiation or conclusion of agreements on matters of substance within the competence of another organ would, in general, be outside the official's apparent authority.

The question of authority to negotiate becomes important when one considers including in a codification of the law relating inter-organizational agreements a provision similar to Article 18 of the Vienna Convention of the Law of Treaties. Under this Article a State is obliged to "refrain from acts which would defeat the object and purpose of a treaty" after signature, but before entry into force, or after the expression of consent but before the treaty enters into force. Clearly if such a provision is to apply to agreements concluded by

---

[155] The agreement between the Council of Europe and the WHO Regional Office for Europe has already been mentioned.

[156] Cf. Detter, *loc.cit.*, who again quotes from the UN Secretariat communication to ILC Special Rapporteur, Sir Humphrey Waldock as follows (p. 434), "Where an Under-Secretary of the United Nations, signs an agreement on behalf of the United Nations, his authorization for doing so is deemed to have derived from the Secretary-General express or implied in the normal courses of administration and no full powers or any other form of specific authorization to sign such agreement have been considered necessary."

[157] The convenience, for example, of a regional organization dealing directly with a regional office of an international organization, rather than with the parent organization, is a relevant consideration.

organizations the necessity of having negotiated with a competent organ is of primary importance. Whether, on the other hand, the existence of such a rule can be implied from the practice of organizations is an issue separate from its desirability, and probably the most that can be said is that the practice of organizations is insufficiently developed to allow the conclusion that a rule has emerged. However, in substance Article 18 is little more than a practical embodiment of the principle of good faith and to that extent would be equally applicable to the agreements of international organizations no less than to inter-State treaties.

So far no attempt has been made to formulate rules concerning the technical procedure of negotiating and concluding agreements, equivalent to those provided in Articles 9 to 17 of the Vienna Convention. The Vienna rules were developed from a wealth of State practice and it is difficult to apply them automatically to the agreements of international organizations where matters such as authentication and signature *ad referendum* are of doubtful relevence. Thus the only practical alternative at present is to leave a broad area of discretion to contracting organizations themselves and provide only for those cases where a *lacuna* would otherwise exist[158]. The following rules are therefore suggested:

"(a) In the negotiation and conclusion of agreements international organizations may adopt whatever procedure they deem adequate.

(b) The consent of an international organization to the conclusion of an agreement may be expressed by signature, approval or by such other means as the parties may agree.

(c) An agreement shall enter into force in such manner as the parties may agree. In the absence of any contrary provision, either express or implied, an agreement shall enter into force on the latest signature or approval[159]."

These provisions endeavour, as far as possible, to facilitate a simplified procedure for the negotiation and conclusion of agreements, which would appear from the practice to be consistent with the wishes of the organs of international organizations. It does not, however, prevent the future development of more detailed rules to deal with specific aspects of procedure. To attempt at present to formulate such rules would be an exercise in mere conjecture.

---

[158] The rules in the Vienna Convention concerning procedure are generally not mandatory but are subject to the parties' contrary agreement.

[159] In a number of agreements concluded by an exchange of letters, particularly among organizations outside the United Nations family, no provision for entry into force is made and it must be assumed that they were intended to come into effect upon signature.

The Form and Legal Nature of Agreements Concluded by International Organizations

The question of what constitutes a legally binding agreement between international organizations must now be considered. "Co-operation agreements" have already been described, in general terms, as including those agreements by which organizations seek to associate themselves in the work of each other, but now a more detailed investigation must be made. The enquiry has three purposes. First, the question must be asked whether co-operation agreements are binding under international law. Secondly, if they are binding should they be regarded as constituting a separate category from other agreements entered into by international organizations? Thirdly, again assuming that co-operation agreements are to be regarded as legally binding should some distinction be made as to types of agreements for co-operation and separate legal consequences attached to the different types? Although these questions overlap the primary investigation is into the legal nature of co-operation agreements; the question of differing legal consequences can only arise in respect of agreements recognized as binding under international law. It is important also to keep in mind the purpose for which any distinction, either between co-operation agreements and other types of agreement or within the class of co-operation agreements itself, is to be made. While one may refer, as a matter of convenience, to "formal" and "informal" agreements, the distinction is legally irrelevant if the same legal consequences are to flow from each type.

Form is the obvious starting point for a discussion of categories of agreements and their legal nature, for there the differences are visible and easy to comprehend. The co-operation agreements already considered can be classified into four different types. There are, first, those which have been concluded in the traditional treaty form, that is with preamble, substantive clauses and final provisions[160]. Secondly, there are those which have been concluded by an exchange of letters. This includes a vast number of agreements in varying degrees of formality. In some cases the agreements form a single unity, the letters being in identical terms and both bearing the same date[161].

---

[160] The UN and OAS relationship agreements and the inter-agency agreements are the most prominent examples.

[161] The agreement of the EEC with the Commission Centrale pour la Navigation du Rhin (CCNR) comprises two sets of letters, containing identical terms, between the Presidents of the CCNR and the EEC Commission and the Secretary-General of CCNR and the Executive Secretary of the EEC Commission, all dated 6 June 1961, *J.O.D.C.* 1027/61.

In other cases the two letters are quite separate and the terms of agreement have to be derived from both of the letters read together[162]. Thirdly, organizations have concluded agreements simply by passing parallel resolutions. Certainly in many instances it is doubtful whether what has resulted is a legally binding agreement[163] but in some cases the resolutions are passed as a result of consultations between the two bodies with a view to defining the terms on which they should co-operate[164].

The fourth category of agreements pose a little more difficulty in that their contractual nature is not always easy to ascertain. These agreements are based on a unilateral declaration by one organization with respect to its relations with another and involve action by both organizations on the basis of that declaration. Though the view that every time an international organization invites another organization to be represented in its meetings an irrevocable offer is created cannot be accepted[165], where the constitution of an organization makes reference to the participation of another organization in its work, and this relationship is carried out in practice, then there seem to be good grounds for concluding that some form of agreement exists. Two important examples are the Protocol to the ECSC Treaty concerning relations with the Council of Europe and the special relationship accorded to the European Communities by Supplementary Protocol No. 1 to the OECD Convention[166]. Both of these protocols, in the light of subsequent relations of the organizations, have definite contractual aspects[167].

The question to be considered, then, is whether these agreements, either taken as a whole or in respect of certain types of them, can be regarded as legally binding agreements under international law. At

---

[162] E.g., Council of Europe agreement with the UN (CE Doc. A 7395). Raux, *loc.cit.*, describes the more formal exchanges of letters as "accords *stricto sensu*" and the less formally concluded ones as "accords *lato sensu*" (p. 196—199).

[163] A doubtful case is where two organizations simply invite observers to their meetings by identical resolutions.

[164] E.g., agreement between the League of Nations and the Institute of Agriculture concluded by resolutions of their respective organs (League Council and Institute's Governing Authority), *League of Nations Official Journal* (1932-II) 1752.

[165] Cf., Raux, *op.cit.*, p. 217, who takes a contrary view.

[166] The Former contains detailed provisions concerning co-operation.

[167] Thus each Protocol gives rise to two different types of obligation; one is owed to the other Organization and derives from the contractual nature of the Protocol and the other is an internal obligation cast upon the organs of the organization, that is, an obligation to carry out the terms of the constitution, including those of the Protocol.

least two writers have doubted such a status. Writing in 1949 Parry suggested that the relationship agreements of the United Nations constitute a "regime[168]" and he said, "Whether the rules applicable to inter-organizational treaties are—or will be—the same as those applicable to inter-state treaties is doubtful[169]." Some four years later Fawcett[170] also cast doubt on the legal nature of co-operation agreements. He considered that whether an agreement could be considered a legal agreement depended on the intentions of the parties to create legal relations, which is not necessarily to be presumed. The decisive tests for such an intention are whether the parties have indicated that the agreement is to be governed by international law and whether they have provided for the settlement of disputes by a compulsory judicial process[171].

The whole question of the binding nature of co-operation agreements involves two separate queries. First, are co-operation agreements a class of agreements recognized by international law as capable of creating binding rights and obligations? Secondly, is a particular co-operation agreement, in the circumstances of the case, legally binding? The second question is dependent on the first, for an arrangement cannot have any legal effect if it falls within a class unrecognized by the legal system. On the other hand, the first question cannot be answered by simply referring to a particular co-operation agreement and showing that the parties intended so create legal rights and obligations, for this is not a matter which they alone can decide. One may enquire whether the parties to co-operation agreements intend to create rights and obligations and whether they intended them to be binding. Further it may be asked whether they have intended that their agreement should be submitted to a system of rules[172] and that

---

[168] "The Treaty-Making Power of the United Nations," 26 BYIL (1949), p. 108, 139. Although Parry considered that it was difficult to classify some of the provisions of the agreements as creative of legal obligations he did not regard them as being entirely devoid of legal consequences for he also said that they were "international statutes establishing a species of international administrative law" *(idem)*.

[169] *Idem.*

[170] "The Legal Character of International Agreements," 30 BYIL (1953), p. 381.

[171] Provision for the settlement of disputes may not necessarily be found in the agreement itself, but may be implied by the parties' acceptance of the compulsory jurisdiction of the ICJ under Art. 36 of the Statute of the Court, Fawcett, *op.cit.*, p. 387. It must be noted that Fawcett's view would exclude most of those arrangements concluded in a form different from the traditional treaty form, and, indeed, many of the latter.

[172] This is, in part, implied in the intention that the agreement should be binding.

the consequences of that system should therefore be applied to their agreement. But whether that system of rules will ascribe such consequences is to be decided not by the parties to an agreement, but by the system itself.

Such a question is hardly a matter of law; rather it is one of policy. A decision will therefore be influenced by individual values and preferred conceptions of a desirable international legal order. It will involve an answer to questions such as, should international law be extended to govern the relations of entities other than States[173]. Ultimately this must be a decision for the established subjects of international law, States, in the light of their policies, their practice and also, it is suggested, the practice of existing international organizations which States have created. However, the issue can be put in a more practical way involving more a matter of necessity. If international law does not ascribe legal consequences to the agreements of international organizations what system of law will? Municipal law clearly is not equipped to deal with many aspects of inter-organizational relations[174], so that if international law rejects them no rules of law at all will apply. The practice of organizations in entering into agreements is indicative of a desire to contract under international law, and it must be assumed, is evidence of the desire of States, members of the organizations, to permit such activity. To fail to acknowledge that international law recognizes the agreements would defeat the intentions of both organizations and States and deny a practice which has with varying effectiveness regulated relations between international organizations since the days of the League of Nations.

Thus it is imperative that co-operation agreements be recognized by international law as agreements subject to that system of rules, and thus capable of creating rights and duties which are legally binding[175]. This is not, however, to assert that every co-operation agreement or arrangement entered into by organizations must automatically be regarded as legally binding. There must first of all be

---

[173] This, in fact, is the question which arguments relating to international personality have sought to resolve and failure to appreciate that the issue is largely a matter of policy has lent an air of unreality to the debate.

[174] Municipal systems, for example, do not generally have law creating or law identifying organs competent to develop or identify rules of international law. This does not prevent, however, organizations from contracting subject to municipal law e.g. a contract for the sale of office furniture.

[175] It is probably too late in the development of international legal doctrine to assert that such agreements are not recognized by international law. Indeed, acceptance that international organizations have capacity to conclude such agreements implies that those agreements have an international legal character.

rights and obligations created under the agreement. On the other hand the fact that such rights and duties may be imprecisely defined does not negative the legal character of the agreement[176]. The fact that a party to an agreement is given a wide measure of discretion in the performance of his obligations does not necessarily deny a basic obligation to perform[177]. Imprecision in the definition of rights and obligations is an issue going to the proof of an agreement's existence but it does not of itself make co-operations agreements either as a class, or individually, inherently incapable of being legally binding agreements.

It has been stated earlier that in determinig whether a particular agreement is a legally binding agreement one must search for some indication that the parties intended their arrangement to be binding and hence subject to a system of rules which will acknowledge that binding nature. It is at this point that Fawcett's view becomes unacceptable, for he appears to determine the existence of an obligation from the presence of a compulsory procedure for the settlement of disputes[178]. This view, apart from its debatable theoratical basis, must be rejected for its total inconsistency with the bulk of inter-organizational agreements concluded in practice. To deny legal character to these agreements would not only be contrary to the intentions of many of the contracting parties but would also frustrate inter-organizational relations[179]. The failure to conclude provisions relating to the settlement of disputes in an agreement should not necessarily be taken to imply the lack of an intention to create legal rights and obligations. It may well be that when the agreement was concluded the parties were not concerned with possible future disputes but rather with laying a framework for practical co-operation. On the other hand if one party fails to carry out the terms of the agreement then the existence of that agreement would certainly be considered as a valid reason for objecting to the failure to perform. In other words,

---

176 It is this point that makes Fawcett doubt the legal character of co-operation agreements, but it may be observed that the provisions of many so-called "law-making conventions" are also imprecisely defined.

177 If a party is able to decide for itself whether or not it will fulfil the obligation under the agreement, then the conclusion must be, not that the obligation is not legal one, but that no obligation exists at all. See Lauterpacht, Report on the Law of Treaties (A/CN. 4/63) (1953), 2 YILC, p. 97.

178 "The process of settlement must be compulsory in the sense that the dispute is justiciable at the instance of any party to the agreement and that the decision given in settlement of the dispute is binding on the parties. This is obvious; for there could otherwise be no relationship of obligation," Fawcett, *op.cit.*, p. 388.

179 The whole purpose of developing legal rules must surely be to facilitate, not frustrate, the settled practices of the entities to which they relate.

co-operation agreements perform an important legal function in providing how certain action should be taken and agreeing that it should be taken.

The test, therefore for determining whether an agreement is legally binding, that is, whether legal rights and obligations have been created, is a composite one. The inclusion of a provision relating to the settlement of disputes is of course one, but only one, of the criteria; whether the language of the agreement is in terms of mutuality or reciprocity[180], whether the agreement has been registered under Article 102 of the Charter of the United Nations, whether a form generally utilized for the conclusion of agreements has been adopted, and the statements of competent organs at the time assent to the conclusion of the agreement was given, are others. None of these criteria is decisive, nor are they exclusive, but all have a certain evidentary value and weight must be given to them before the conclusion can be reached that an agreement entered into by international organizations is not legally binding.

To a certain extent the above argument has answered the second issue raised that is, whether co-operation agreements should be regarded as constituting a legal category separate from other types of agreements concluded by international organizations. Since the test for the existence of an agreement is basically whether rights and obligations, intended to be binding and therefore submitted to a legal order, have been created, and as the position has been taken that international law must ascribe legal consequences to such agreements, then it must be concluded that co-operation agreements are no different from other agreements concluded by international organizations[181]. It was said earlier that the only legally relevant reason for treating co-operation agreements as a separate class is the attribution to them of different legal consequences. However, the only significant difference, as will be seen later, is that such agreements should perhaps be interpreted in a more liberal manner and this is hardly a sufficient justification for affording them a special position in any codification of the law relating to agreements concluded by international organizations, or excluding them from such codification.

There do nevertheless appear to be, at first sight at least, some arguments in favour of dividing the class of co-operation agreements, itself. First, from the simple standpoint of form the earlier discussion has shown that a clear distinction can be made between those agreements which have been formally concluded, including both those in

---

[180] This does not deny the possibility of an agreement existing under which only one of the parties has an obligation, the other having the correlative right.

[181] E.g., headquarters agreements, technical assistance agreements.

the traditional treaty form and some of those concluded by an exchange of letters, and those whose conclusion was informal[182]. Secondly, certain organizations have shown a desire to refrain from concluding more formal agreements; they enter only into less formal "working arrangements[183]." Thirdly, the conclusion of agreements in the traditional treaty form is a cumbersome procedure; the end result certainly produces stability in inter-organizational relations but it prevents agreements "from being as flexible as co-operation should require[184]." Finally, it was mentioned earlier that a division in the types of co-operation agreement which can be concluded might serve as a basis for recognizing the competence of organs to conclude, or negotiate, agreements on behalf of their organizations. The capacity of certain officials to conclude administrative arrangements on behalf of their organization could be recognized without acknowledging any competence to enter into more substantial arrangements involving the organization in far-reaching commitments. In this way the question of the distribution of capacity among various organs could be resolved.

Distinguishing between different types of co-operation agreement becomes particularly significant in the context of a codification of the law, for a decision must at some stage be made whether to include all types of agreement within the scope of the codification, or whether a more restrictive approach is justified[185]. In the light of the preceding discussion it would seem that the arguments in favour of making some distinction are broadly twofold. First, there are those which press for more flexibility in the process of concluding agreements[186], and secondly, there are those which see different consequences attaching to less formally concluded agreements[187]. This latter view results from the apparent assumption that the formality of the conclusion of an agreement determines the strength of the obligation under it. Such an assumption must, however, be rejected for as already stated the test

---

[182] Cf. Raux's distinction between "accords *stricto sensu*" and "accords *lato sensu*" (mentioned earlier). While this is hardly a justification for making a distinction it does show the lines along which one could be made.

[183] Both OECD and EEC appear to have adopted a policy of avoiding, where possible, the conclusion of formal co-operation agreements; in the case of the former only the agreement with IAEA was so concluded.

[184] Schneider, *op.cit.*, p. 141.

[185] The Vienna Convention on the Law of Treaties excludes from its scope oral agreements (Art. 2 (1) (a)) without denying their legal force (Art. 3 (a)).

[186] The view of Schneider and of the organizations which prefer to enter only into informal arrangements.

[187] The view that subsidiary organs can conclude "working arrangements" because they are not as binding as other arrangements, the corollary being that such agreements should not be included in a codification of the law.

for the existence of a binding agreement is the presence of rights and obligations, irrespective of the form used[188]. Once these binding rights and obligations have been established and it has been ascertained that international law attaches legal consequences to that class of arrangement, then a legally binding agreement exists, whether it has been concluded in the traditional treaty form, or by an exchange of notes, or parallel resolutions.

The fallacy in the first argument is in its implied belief that the strength and flexibility of co-operation is to be measured by the type of agreement under which co-operation has been established. Underlying this belief is the idea that where the relations of organizations are regulated by a formal agreement then there will be less scope for their practical development, in that both parties will be limited by the restrictive terms of their agreement. This cannot be accepted for a number of reasons. An analysis of co-operation agreements readily shows that the terms used are broad in scope and capable of leaving a wide measure of discretion to both of the contracting organizations. Also, many agreements[189] make provision for the executive officials of the organizations to enter into supplementary arrangements to facilitate co-operation. Further, in many cases the closest co-operation in fact is found among those organizations which have entered into formal agreements of relationship and co-operation[190]. One might almost conclude that the willingness of an organization to enter into a formal agreement is indicative of its general attitude towards co-operation with other organizations. In short the degree of co-operation which exists between international organizations is not to be measured in terms of the formality of the conclusion of any agreement between them; it is a matter which lies within the respective wills of the organizations themselves. Attitudes to co-operation are influenced by a variety of factors, including the actions of the member States, the spheres of responsibility and common interests of the organizations. Generally if common interest is strong then co-operative relations will be strong, irrespective of the formal aspects of any agreement or arrangement.

Nevertheless a simplified procedure for the conclusion of agreements is desirable from at least one point of view. It might not always be practicable for organizations in their everyday operations to go

---

[188] Form may, of course, be relevant in determing whether the agreement was intended to be subject to international law.

[189] This is so, for example, in all of the UN relationship agreements.

[190] E.g., the relations between the UN and the Specialized Agencies and the Specialized Agencies *inter se*.

through a formal procedure of negotiation, drawing up a text and conclusion of an agreement each time they wish to enter into some arrangement. For this reason the informal exchange of letters has been utilized, thus avoiding unnecessary delay. The growth of this practice has already been mentioned, but the necessity for regarding such agreements as constituting a separate legal category can only be shown by indicating the different rules of law which should be applied to them. Certainly some of the rules which are relevant for other agreements may be irrelevant for informally concluded agreements, for example, such agreements are hardly suitable subjects for registration under Article 102 of the Charter of the United Nations, should such a provision be adopted for the agreements of international organizations. An analogy may perhaps be drawn with the different positions of bilateral and multilateral treaties under the Vienna Convention. Because of the difference in number of the parties to these two types of agreement certain rules which are relevant for the latter have no application with respect to the former[190a]. This is true for example of the rules relating to reservations[191], and those concerning certain aspects of amendment[192]. Formal and informal co-operation agreements could be similarly included in a codification of the law relating to the agreements of international organizations, with separate rules applying to the two types wherever there are differences.

So far the position has been taken that, subject to some minor differences, in substance co-operation agreements which have been formally concluded should be treated in the same way as those concluded in a less formal manner. The major difference is that proof of existence is simpler in the case of more formal agreements. However, the conclusion of agreements by passing parallel resolutions or the implication of an agreement from a unilateral declaration may involve difficult matters of proof. Where resolutions have been passed as a consequence of consultations between the organizations, and where each refers in its resolution to the other, then the matter is a little easier as both instruments, in the case of parallel resolutions, would be related by explicit reference[193].

In proving the existence of an agreement recourse must be had to a variety of sources including the statements of the organs of the organizations, their subsequent practice and, of course, the express

190a However, both types of agreement fall within the scope of the Treaty which simply applies different provisions to them.

191 Arts. 19—23.

192 Art. 40, "Amendment of multilateral treaties."

193 This will be so in the majority of cases.

terms of the resolution or declaration. Ultimately it may well be that the only ground for implying an agreement from two resolutions is that the substance of them is related. Nevertheless this is hardly a sufficient ground for excluding those agreements from the scope of a codification of the law. The question simply becomes one of wording the definition of the word "agreement" broadly enough to catch within it those agreements which are to be implied either from parallel resolutions related only in substance, or from a unilateral declaration. In this respect the terms used in the Vienna Convention seem adequate as they define a "treaty" to include agreements concluded in "two or more related instruments[194]."

It might be argued that some co-operation agreements ought to be excluded from a general codification of the law governing the agreements of international organizations on the ground that they are not agreements between organizations but only arrangements between the individual organs of the organizations. Certainly a number of co-operation agreements have been styled as agreements between organs rather than between the principal organizations[195], and in practice it is a particular organ of an organization which, in fact, carries it out. But this does not make the agreement different from any other inter-organizational agreement. First, though a co-operation agreement may be called an administrative arrangement and primarily concern the secretariats of the organizations involved it does not always follow that the agreement affects only those organs. A common provision in co-operation agreements is one concerning representation in the meetings of each other's organs. This, of course, concerns not only the secretariat but also all those organs whose meetings it is proposed that representatives should attend.

Secondly, a distinction must be made between the process of concluding an agreement and carrying it out, these generally being done by a particular organ or number of organs, and the responsibility of the organization as a whole, which can only arise when the former process has broken down. Certainly specific organs of an organization conclude and carry out agreements, but once the question of responsibility arises it is the organization as a whole which is involved. Thirdly, it is doubted whether an organ of an international organi-

[194] Art. 2 (1) (a). Although the commentary of the ILC does not touch specifically upon the point it was probably intended that the relationship between the two instruments would be by explicit reference. Nevertheless the wording is capable of meaning a relationship by substance and it should bear that meaning with respect to the agreements of international organizations. This could be made clear in any commentary to articles of the law governing these agreements.

[195] E.g., the agreement between the "Secretariat-General of the Council of Europe and the Secretariat of the United Nations," CE Doc. A 7395.

zation can perform any act, effective under international law, which is not the act of its parent, for the former is only recognized as the representative of the latter. Thus, though certain agreements have the appearance of being only inter-secretariat arrangements, they are still agreements between the organizations themselves[196]. There seem, therefore no real grounds for regarding them as a separate legal class.

The conclusion reached then, is that co-operation agreements are, like other agreements concluded by international organizations, agreements which are capable of being binding under international law. The test for determining whether such an agreement has been created is, again like that for other agreements, based on the existence of rights and obligations. The reasons advanced for treating them separately from other agreements of international organizations have not been accepted, nor is it considered that the category of co-operation agreements should be divided. The only substantial difference between types of co-operation agreement is one of form, which is legally irrelevant[197]. A further ground may be adduced. If the rules of law embodied in a codification were not applied to certain categories of co-operation agreement then recourse would have to be made to general rules of international law to determine the law governing those agreements. The result would be that the rules which have already been codified would in substance be the same rules as those which would have to be found by an independent examination of international law[198]. In the result the agreements would all be governed by the same rules.

The above discussion leads to the conclusion that the definition of "treaty" in the Vienna Convention can be utilized satisfactorily to describe agreements concluded by international organizations. The definition would, therefore, be as follows:

> "agreement" means an agreement concluded between international organizations in written form and governed by international law, whether embodied in a single instrument or two or more related instruments and whatever its particular designation.

---

[196] This does not deny the right of secretariats to enter into arrangements between themselves which do not involve any rights and obligations and, therefore, do not involve the responsibility of their organization.

[197] Cf. ILC Draft Articles on the Law of Treaties, 2 YILC (1966), p. 188, "... the juridical differences, in so far as they exist at all, between formal treaties and treaties in simplified form lie almost exclusively in the method of conclusion and entry into force."

[198] Certainly rules *de lege ferenda* have been proposed here, but any search for rules to govern such an excluded class of agreements would be confronted with the same gaps it has been here attempted to fill.

The Interpretation of Agreements

In general there is no reason why the rule of interpretation established by Article 31 of the Vienna Convention on the Law of Treaties[199] should not apply to co-operation agreements concluded by international organizations. Indeed the same can be said of the other rules of interpretation included in the Convention[200]. Of course questions concerning the interpretation of co-operation agreements have infrequently arisen[201], so that it is difficult to ascertain whether any special rules would be applied. Nevertheless it is possible to examine the rules of interpretation to determine the measure in which they are strictly applicable to co-operation agreements, and the extent to which they ought to be modified. These rules can be broadly divided into two categories; first, those which primarily direct attention to the text of the agreement, and, secondly, those which authorize an investigation outside the four corners of the parties agreement. Of course variations of these approaches can be found and both can be utilized for the purpose of ascertaining the "intentions of the parties" or the "objects and purposes" of the agreement. In the result the Vienna Convention has placed principal significance on the text of the agreement, but it has also authorized, as a supplementary means of interpretation, recourse beyond the text to the "preparatory work of the treaty and the circumstances of its conclusion[202]."

Co-operation agreements generally do not define precisely the rights and obligations appertaining to each party, thus there is much scope for differing views as to their interpretation. Hence a mere textual analysis will on its own generally be insufficient to achieve an effective interpretation of the agreement. Thus a more far-reaching approach is apposite, involving not only the actual words used, but also the remaining provisions of the agreement and the purpose of the agreement as a whole. The function of co-operation agreements is something relatively easily stated for their very name indicates that

---

[199] Art. 31 (1) provides "A treaty shall be interpreted in good faith in accordance with the ordinary meaning to be given to the terms of the treaty in the context and in the light of its object and purpose." The remainder of the Article indicates what may be considered to fall within the context and matters which may be read with the context, and also refers to special meanings which may be given to certain words.

[200] Art. 32 (supplementary means of interpretation), Art. 33 (interpretation of treaties authenticated in two or more languages).

[201] The interpretation of certain provisions of the World Bank's relationship agreement with the UN was the subject of an exchange of views between the two organizations in 1967, GAOR, 22nd Session, Annexes, Agenda item 66, Doc. A/6825.

[202] Art. 32.

their purpose is to facilitate co-operation between international organizations. This can be realized in a variety of ways including consultation, reciprocal representation in meetings, exchanging information and documents, and establishing joint committees. Further, from this general principle of co-operation certain more practical rules can be developed, for example, that overlapping in the work of organizations should be avoided and, that organizations with conflicting competences should act in concert and not individually.

These principles are not suggested as obligatory rules binding upon organizations but rather as guides to the interpretation of agreements which establish relations between international organizations. Interpretation is intended to facilitate the relations of organizations and thus the function of their agreement should be the principal guide in achieving that end. To a certain extent the Vienna Convention authorizes such an approach when it allows the "object and purpose" to be considered in the interpretation of a treaty. However, in the context of Article 31 reference to the object and purpose of an agreement is subsidiary to the "ordinary meaning" of the words. The approach to the interpretation of co-operation agreements should therefore be broader.

If, however, it is proposed to look to material beyond the actual terms of the agreement then generally it will be found that co-operation agreements lack preparatory work or other information which would be of assistance[203]. This is particularly so of those agreements concluded in a simplified form. To overcome this, however, recourse could be made to a further source which generally is not available in the case of other agreements, that is, the respective constitutions of the contracting parties.

Since co-operation agreements are concerned with the co-ordination of the activities of the contracting organizations, thereby avoiding duplication in their work, then they involve, to a certain extent, a delimitation of the spheres of competence of each organization. This, of course, is not always express, but may be found, for example, in the recognition by one organization of the other's field of competence[204]. As the delimitation of the competence of an organization is a matter with which its constitution deals, then it may be of assistance for the interpretation of an agreement to have recourse to that constitution. This could, of course, give rise to some difficulty.

[203] Some of the more formally concluded agreements will certainly be preceded by exchanges of correspondence and preliminary reports to each organization.

[204] E.g., UN relationship agreement with IAEA (338 UNTS, p. 407), Art. 1, "The United Nations recognizes the International Atomic Energy Agency ... as the agency, ... responsible for international activities concerned with the peaceful uses of atomic energy ..."

The member States of an organization primarily retain the right to interpret their own constitution; in the event of a dispute between organizations over the interpretation of a co-operation agreement it is possible that an interpretation of the constitution of one would be arrived at which would not be acceptable to the members of that organization. If they themselves had explicitly requested an interpretation of their constitution then the matter would, perhaps, be different, but they may find themselves confronted with an interpretation which they had not requested nor of which they approve. The status of that interpretation *vis à vis* those member States would be a matter of some debate.

To allow reference to the constitution of an organization in order to assist the interpretation of a co-operation agreement may also be regarded as blurring the distinction made earlier between the internal law of an organization, which emanates from its constitution and governs the relations of its member States, and the external law which governs the relations of the organization, as an independent entity, with other entities. If such a distinction was rigidly maintained then it might be argued that recourse to the constitution is an inadmissible attempt to impose the internal law of one organization on the entities with which it enters into relations. To this it must be answered, first, the distinction between the two aspects of the law governing international organizations was not made as an absolute one, for, as already seen, many of the rules regulating the external sphere are derived from the internal law of organizations[205]. Secondly, recourse to the constitution would not be made for the purpose of finally establishing a field of competence, but simply to assist in the elucidation of the terms of a co-operation agreement. In other words the constitutions may be of assistance in showing what, in the light of their constitutional authority, the parties must have intended.

Thus, in spite of the objections which can be made, the constitutions of the organizations party to a co-operation agreement ought to be available, as a supplementary means of interpretation, to aid in the elucidation of that agreement, on the understanding that such a source would only be used to assist in the interpretation of the agreement and would not result in a determination with respect to the constitutions which would in any way be binding on the member States.

---

[205] Thus the question of which organ of another organization is competent to negotiate, or commit its organization to a binding undertaking was in part resolved by referring to constitutional authority, a matter of the internal law of the organization.

The suggestions made here with regard to interpretation could be implemented by the following provisions[206]:

"(1) In the interpretation of co-operation agreements entered into by international organizations primary significance shall be given to their function.

(2) Where a co-operation agreement concluded between international organizations purports to delimit the spheres of competence of the parties to the agreement, recourse may be had, as a supplementary means of interpretation, to the constitutions of those organizations. Any interpretation placed on the constitution of an international organization for the purpose of clarifying the terms of a co-operation agreement shall not bind the member States of that organization[207]."

The Settlement of Disputes

Apart from giving the parties themselves guidance in the way in which they should interpret their agreements, rules of interpretation are really only relevant in the event of a dispute, in which case they can be applied, either by the parties acting in agreement, or by a third party, to settle such differences as exist. Thus they imply a procedure for the settlement of disputes. However, a significant feature of co-operation agreements is their lack of any provision anticipating future disputes and providing for their resolution. It is true that under the relationship agreements with the United Nations a number of the Specialized Agencies have been authorized to request advisory opinions from the International Court of Justice, but "questions concerning the mutual relationships of the Organization and the United Nations or other Specialized Agencies" are excluded[208]. Other co operation agreements are generally silent on the question of settling disputes. In one case[209], however, provision was made that "any difference of opinion as to the interpretation of this Agreement or of any Supplementary Agreements shall be settled by an exchange of views between the parties[210]." If such an exchange of views does not

[206] These provisions would be in addition to the rules of interpretation contained in the Vienna Convention.

[207] This must be distinguished from a determination of competence allocated under the co-operation agreement which may bind the organization, and thus indirectly the member States.

[208] E.g., relationship agreement between the UN and WHO, Art. X (2).

[209] Technical Assistance agreement between ILO and UNRWA (128 UNTS, p. 202). This agreement can only be considered a co-operation agreement in a broader sense. The provision, however, appears unique among technical assistance agreements between organizations.

[210] Art. V (d).

result in settlement of the difference then the matter is to be referred to arbitration[211].

In spite of the almost uniform lack of provision for the settlement of disputes in co-operation agreements the agreements do provide some guidance in the event of a dispute. Again by reference to the general function of co-operation and the manner in which it is intended that co-operation agreements should be carried out, it might be concluded that there is an implied obligation to consult or negotiate in order to settle any differences that may arise. In other words co-operation agreements envisage that they shall be carried out through mutual agreement, which excludes the arbitrary taking of action by one party without recourse to the views of the other. Thus any disagreement should, in the first instance, be the subject of an exchange of views[212]. If these consultations break down then it is for the parties themselves to consider what action should be taken. Of course where there is no provision in the agreement then further action by the parties cannot be regarded as resulting from the agreement itself.

The remaining procedures open to the parties are either conciliation or arbitration. The procedural incapacity provided in Article 34 (1) of the Statute of the International Court of Justice[213], and the non-applicability of the advisory opinion procedure, at the suit of the Specialized Agencies, to the relations of the United Nations with those Agencies, or the relations of the latter *inter se*, makes recourse to the Court of doubtful practical significance[214]. Ultimately, of course, the sanction lies with each organization to refuse to fulfil its obligation under the agreement if the other party remains in breach. While this is hardly the most desirable solution it is a hallmark of "elementary forms of legal relations[215]" which in spite of their deficiencies actually function in practice. Until a hierarchy of authority is established under international law then such a result is the only available solution.

---

[211] Both organizations are to appoint one arbitrator who, in the event of differences between them will appoint a third.

[212] This was done in the disagreement between the UN and IBRD concerning their relationship agreement, referred to *supra*.

[213] Art. 34 (1) provides, "Only states may be parties in cases before the Court."

[214] The UN may, of course, request an opinion, and the Specialized Agencies may request opinions regarding their relations with organizations outside the UN family. The binding nature of such opinions depend on the consent of the organizations concerned, but this applies, no less, to any procedure adopted.

[215] Wengler, "Agreements of States with parties other then States in International Relations," 8 *Revue Hellénique de droit international* (1954—55), p. 113, 130. Wengler would probably regard co-operation agreements as "unilateral promises based on reciprocity."

Thus, at the present, the settlement of disputes arising out of co-operation agreements must largely be left to exchanges of views, or consultation, between organizations and, whenever they agree, to arbitration. Future practice may well develop more adequate techniques, but until this is done it is more desirable to refrain from establishing definite binding rules. The following rule could therefore be made part of a codification:

"Any dispute arising out of an agreement between international organizations shall be settled in accordance with the procedure provided therein. If no such procedure is provided then the parties shall settle their dispute through an exchange of views or, if they so agree, by arbitration."

The Revision of Agreements

Generally those co-operation agreements which have been more formally concluded provide for revision by mutual agreement[216] and denunction by either party on giving the prescribed notice[217]. Thus Article 39 (amendment) and Article 54 (termination and withdrawal) of the Vienna Convention on the Law of Treaties could apply. A problem concerning revision may arise from the power often given to the administrative officers of organizations to make supplementary arrangements in order to implement a co-operation agreement[218]. If in the conclusion of such an arrangement, or where the administrative officers of an organization conclude an agreement independently of any authorization in a prior co-operation agreement, the provisions of the former co-operation agreement are contravened, is the latter agreement invalid or does it overrule the former to the extent of the inconsistency?

If the co-operation agreement itself gives a broad discretion to the officials then their agreement will probably be taken as superseding the former agreement. On the other hand to regard as valid those subsequent agreements for which authority is not provided in the former agreement assumes a norm giving precedence to the latter agreement. It would seem, however, that the better approach is that taken earlier; agreements entered into by subsiduary organs are

[216] E.g, agreement between ILO and the Council of Europe (CE Doc. A 75396), Art. 12 (2) "The Agreement may be modified with the consent of the two parties."

[217] *Ibid*, Art. 12 (3) "Either of the parties may denounce the Agreement by giving six months notice to the other party."

[218] See agreement between the Council of Europe and FAO (CE Doc. A 28254), Art. 6 "The Director-General of FAO and the Secretary-General of the Council will make appropriate administrative arrangements to ensure effective co-operation and liaison between the Secretariats of the two organizations."

agreements engaging the whole organization and not just the organ actually involved in the procedure of concluding the agreement. Thus a subsequent arrangement entered into by the Secretaries-General of two organizations is equally an arrangement of those organizations[219] and must be treated as a later expression of the wills of those organizations, thus overruling, in so far as they are inconsistent, the previous agreement.

The Registration of Agreements

At present those agreements entered into by the United Nations or those of the Specialized Agencies may be deposited with the Secretary-General of the United Nations and published in the United Nations Treaty Series[220]. Whether this procedure should be extended to include the agreements of all international organizations is largely a matter of policy but many co-operation agreements are hardly suitable subjects for inclusion in an official treaty series in view both of their diverse forms[221] and the fact that they concern only the organizations themselves, many of which are not part of the United Nations family. Certainly some form of publication is desirable both from the point of view of legal scholarship and in so far as it serves to discourage the conclusion of secret agreements, but whether this should be centred in the United Nations might be open to question. The practical difficulties involved in collecting these agreements might lead to the conclusion that an alternative procedure is more desirable. Perhaps it would be sufficient simply to require each organization to publish the agreements it enters into.

Conclusions

Once it is accepted that international law imposes no restrictions on the capacity of international organizations to conclude co-operation agreements then there are few areas in which substantial differences from inter-State treaties justify the application of separate rules to these agreements. The chief areas where changes have had to have been suggested are the negotiation and conclusion of agreements, in-

---

[219] This assumes, of course, that the criteria for competence, already discussed, have been fulfilled.

[220] Res. of the General Assembly to give effect to Art. 102 of the UN Charter, Res. 97 (1), 1st Session, A/64/Add. 1 (Art. 10).

[221] This includes the fact that the terms of the agreement may have to be derived from two or more documents, and that the content of the agreement may be of a transitory or administrative nature.

cluding the expression of the consent of an organization to be bound. This is significant for it indicates that modification to the rules of the Vienna Convention on the Law of Treaties is required, in the case of agreements concluded by international organizations, not because of the specific nature of the agreements themselves but because of the constitutional structure of international organizations which differs from that of States. Once international organizations conclude an agreement then in substance that is a binding agreement no different from a treaty concluded between States. However, because of the lack of a clearly identifiable organ which can be presumed to be competent to express the consent of an organization and the practices, dissimilar from those of States, which organizations have developed for the negotiation and conclusion of their agreements, the rules relevant for inter-State treaties are inadequate.

It follows, therefore, that the agreements of international organizations do not differ sufficiently from inter-State treaties to justify the conclusion of a separate convention relating to them which would stand beside the Vienna Convention on the Law of Treaties. The matter could be dealt with simply by the conclusion of a protocol to that Convention modifying the inappropriate Articles and relating the remainder to the agreements of international organizations[222].

It will have been noted that whereas at the outset the class of agreements to be examined was limited to "co-operation agreements," throughout the argument reference has often been made to a wider class of agreements between international organizations and some of the rules have been drafted in broader terms. This has been done where no substantial difference exists between co-operation agreements and other agreements concluded by international organizations and where the experience gathered from the former is relevant in a wider context. On the other hand no attempt has been made to include within the ambit of those rules agreements to which a State is a party, although to a large extent these rules could also be applied to such agreements. It might be argued that the latter class of agreement cannot be assimilated under the same rules, for included in it may be agreements between an organization and one of its member States to which somewhat different considerations would apply. Though a full examination of this contention is beyond the present scope, if the separation of the internal law of an international organization and the law governing its external relations is maintained then no difficulty arises. Under this view a member State of an organization, in the latter's external relations, would in principle be in a

[222] This raises the question whether organizations as well as States should be parties to the protocol and, indeed, to the Convention.

position no different from that of any other entity with which the organization comes into contact[223].

Indeed throughout this discussion one clear indication has emerged. This is that the law concerning the agreements of international organizations can only be placed on a rational basis if the distinction between the internal law of an organization and the external rules governing its relations with other organizations or States, is maintained[224]. No coherent body of rules providing a practical solution to the problems that arise can be developed if the rules which are created by the members of an organization as the internal law of that organization are allowed always to be the standards on which other entities are able to entertain relations with the organization.

Failure to perceive and maintain this distinction leads to manifest inequality in the balancing of interests, with which international law has to be concerned, of the various actors in the international field. To require an organization to assure itself that the constitutional requirements of its contracting party have been faithfully complied with casts upon it too great a burden and may involve it in an analysis and interpretation of the other's constitution amounting to an invasion of that organization's own field of competence. On the other hand reliance cannot simply be placed by an organization upon any organ of another organization which asserts that it is competent to conclude agreements. This goes to the other extreme and gives insufficient recognition to the constitutional integrity of international organizations. The conclusions which have been reached in this study stem from an initial acceptance of the distinction between the two aspects of the law concerning international organizations and from that basis an attempt has been made to give due recognition to the different interests and claims involved.

This approach has certain consequences for the general doctrine of international law, for it continues the existing trend of rejecting a concept of international law which envisages only a single category of rules, rather it requires a conception of international law as a body of rules operating at a variety of different levels[225]. Thus rules of international law which apply in certain fields and to particular entities may not be applicable in other fields and with respect to other entities. This somewhat obvious statement has, in fact, been

[223] Of course the organization will have relations with such a State on the internal level, dealing with it as a member State.

[224] This distinction is not new, see e.g. Broches, "International Legal Aspects of the Operations of the World Bank," 98 RCADI (1959-III), p. 301, 302.

[225] See Friedmann, *The Changing Structure of International Law* (1964), Part III.

denied, when from the simple truism that the constitutions of international organizations are treaties and therefore part of international law certain inadmissible conclusions have been drawn. It has been asserted, for example, that since constitutions of international organizations are treaties the limitations contained in them are "limitations under international law and should therefore be effective also in the sphere of the international relations of the organizations[226]." This, does not follow as a *necessary* conclusion at all. It fails to perceive the essential fact that the members of an organization can only create rules governing their own relations; any limitations under international law upon other entities (either States or international organizations) can only be imposed by international law itself[227].

International law, therefore, is manifested through various rules some of which are of general application while others are of more restricted application, both geographically and in respect of special groups of States. The internal rules of an organization belong in the latter category whereas the external rules are of more universal application in that they apply to all organizations. This does not deny to either the status of rules of law, it merely recognizes respective spheres of application.

Some final remarks may also be made on the desirability of a codification of the rules governing agreements concluded by international organizations. The lack of time for an adequate practice to develop certainly militates against the definition of detailed and precise rules. On the other hand a statement of rules serves the vital function of guiding the conduct of entities to which they relate. In this respect the non-inclusion of a procedure for the settlement of disputes is not fatal, for the rules have the function of guiding organizations in their actions, not telling them what occurs on breach. It is possible, therefore, to develop rules by codifying the uniform practice that exists and providing only for those areas where a present need is felt. The future development of rules relating to the agreements of international organizations will depend on the needs arising out of inter-organizational relations, and their relations with States, and the procedures that are utilized in practice to meet these needs.

---

226 Seidl-Hohenveldern, "The Legal Personality of International and Supra-National Organizations," 35 *Revue Egyptiènne de droit international* (1965), p. 41. It would be a different matter, however, to argue that the limitations contained in the constitution of an organization are binding on other entities because they are so recognized by a rule of international law.

227 If the rules are created by all States then they would be part of general international law, but in such a case the States would be acting in their general capacity of subjects of international law and not as the members of any specific organization.

Österr. Zeitschr. f. öffentl. Recht, Suppl. 1, 57—104 (1971)

The Capacity of International Organizations to Conclude Headquarter Agreements, and Some Features of These Agreements

Liviu Bota
Member of the Romanian Association of International Law and International Relations

I. Introduction

The purpose of the present study is to analyse the Headquarter Agreements concluded by International Organizations in an attempt to test the extent to which the provisions of the Vienna Convention on the Law of Treaties can apply, *mutatis mutandis*, to the treaties concluded by international organizations. Thus, we shall deal with the formal aspects of these Agreements; reference to their material content will be made strictly to the degree it is relevant to the scope of the study.

It is not our purpose to examine all the legal problems involved in the law of treaties of International Organizations, but merely to take up some questions which in our opinion constitute peculiarities of International Organizations in comparison with the law of treaties concluded between States.

Headquarter Agreements are international instruments defining the legal status of an International Organization or of one of its bodies in the State on the territory of which it has its seat[1]. It is not

---

[1] Among other definitions given to Headquarter Agreements we mention:

Cahier, "Accords conclus entre une Organisation Internationale et un Etat dans le but d'établir le statut de cette Organisation dans l'Etat où elle a son siège et de délimiter les privilèges et immunités qui lui seront accordés aussi qu'à ses fonctionnaires," p. 1—Etude des accords de siège conclus entre les Organisations Internationales et les Etats où elles resident (Geneva 1959).

Socini, "Gli accordi diretti a definire lo statuto giuridico di una Organizzazione o di un suo organo decentrato nell'ambito dell'ordinamento interno degli Stati Membri ed eventualmente anche degli stati non membri in cui abbiano sede e cio

the purpose of the Headquarter Agreements to define the international status of the International Organization; nevertheless the international status is expressly or impliedly recognized in Headquarter Agreements: for example art. 1 of the Interim Arrangements on Privileges and Immunities between the Secretary General of the United Nations and the Swiss Federal Council[2] states: "The Swiss Federal Council recognizes the international personality and the legal capacity of the United Nations[3]." The character, the international legal status of an International Organization should be established on the basis of its constitutive act, the provisions of which qualify the respective International Organization for a definit status under international law.

The International Organization appears in such a way in two postures: as international personality and as juridical person in an internal legal order, but the entity as such is a unitarian one[4]. Of course, the legal status of the international organization in international law helds primacy, as it defines the peculiarity of the subject of rights and obligations, while its capacity as juridical person has a complementary role, creating the necessary material conditions for the normal functioning of the organization.

Speaking about International Organizations we have in mind in our study only intergovernmental organizations, created by states for aims compatible with the international legal order, the personality and activity of which are governed by their Constitutive Acts[5]. We

---

tanto in vista di un funzionamento duraturo, quanto in vista di reunioni a carrattere provisorio," p. 83—Gli Accordi Internazionali delle Organizzazioni Intergovernative. Padova: CEDAM, 1962.

[2] 1 UNTS, p. 163.

[3] Cahier has a high regard for the fact that some Headquarter Agreements expressly recognize the international personality of an international organization: "L'accord de siège entre le Canada et l'ICAO du 14 avril 1951 (90) à son art. 2, sect. 2, ne fait que parler de la personnalité juridique interne; il en est de même de l'art. 7 de l'accord de siège entre l'Italie et la F.A.O. du 31 oct. 1950 et de l'art. première de l'accord de siège entre l'UNESCO et la France du 2 juillet 1954. Par contre les Institutions specialisées ayant leur siège en Suisse se sont vu reconnaître la personnalité internationale. Nous avons vu d'ailleurs que ce fut le cas pour la S.D.N. et l'ONU, que c'est dans la tradition, tradition excellente à notre avis, du gouvernement suisse." Op.cit., p. 142.

We do not deny the merit of such recognition, we simply say that this is outside the scope of the Headquarter Agreement. This recognition is important if the Headquarter Agreement was concluded with a State that is not a member of the Organization. For the Member states the problem does not arise.

[4] See Visscher, La protection diplomatique des personnes morales, in RCADI, 1961-I, p. 482.

[5] As for the definitions of International Organization see the first report of Abdullah El-Erian, Special Rapporteur of the International Law Commission on

start from the assumption that these International Organizations are subjects of international law; they are secondary, derived subjects of international law, created by States—the direct and immediate universal and original subjects of international law[6]. In our opinion the term "subject of international law" is synonymous with the term "international personality"; these terms express one quality, that of holder of rights and obligations in international law[7].

The International Organization has a will of its own, distinct from that of the Member States. The existence of this will does not mean that the Organization is independent; it depends always upon the will of States that have created the organization and can dissolve it[8].

Relations between States and Inter-governmental Organizations, in 2 YILC 1963, p. 164.

Because of the fact that El-Erian does not quote authors from socialist countries, for completing the picture, we mention here the definition given by Grigore Geamănu (Romania) in Dreptul Internaţional Contemporan (Bucureşti, 1965, p. 546), "International organizations are forms of coordination of international collaboration in various fields for which states have created a definit legal-institutional framework by adopting a statute, elaborated by mutual agreement, which stipulates the object and the scope of the organization, its organs and their functions required for the attainment of its scope," and the one contained in Course of International Law (in Russian), vol. V, p. 78: "International Organizations are collective organs of the States that have created them; they act on the basis of the Agreement and within the competence given to them by States."

[6] For discussion on International Organizations as subjects of international law see Grigore Geamănu, Dreptul Internaţional Contemporan, Bucureşti 1965, p. 175 as well as N. Ecobescu, k voprosu o mejdunarodnoi pravosubiectnosti OON, in Voprosî teorii i praktiki mejdunarodnovo prava, Moskva 1959, as well as the authors mentioned in these works.

[7] Many authors distinguish the two terms as expressing two different qualities. So, in Oppenheim-Lauterpacht, the term "international personality" is used to denote a body of qualities considering that "international personality may ... be said to be the fact, involved in the very membership of the community of nations, that equality, dignity, independence, territorial and personal supremacy, and the responsibility of every State are recognized by every State" and saying that "full sovereign States are perfect, not full sovereign States are imperfect, International Persons, for not-full sovereign States are only in some respects subjects of International Law."

Siotto-Pintor states that only States are international persons, whereas other entities, the League of Nations for instance, are mere subjects of international law. (See Broches, International Legal Aspects of the Operations of the World Bank, 98 RCADI, 1959-III, p. 317; Siotto-Pintor, Les Sujets du Droit International Autres que les Etats, 41 RCADI, 1932-III, p. 299; Oppenheim-Lauterpacht, 8th ed., note 2, p. 118 and note 2, p. 262.)

[8] Cahier, Op.cit. supra note 1, p. 23.

II. Legal Basis for the Conclusion of Headquarter Agreements

The Practice

To exercise their functions effectively, International Organizations establish headquarters in host States which concede a defined legal status and a number of privileges and immunities to the organizations, their premises and their personnel as well as to delegates of States and of International Organizations to International Organizations. In addition to their Headquarter, these organizations set up a variety of regional centers and offices in Member States, and sometimes even in Non-member States. Permanent representatives are often assigned by them to some of their members. For example the UNTAB has "Resident Representatives" in many countries, the UNHCR and WHO maintain "delegations," "missions of liaison," or "country representatives" in a number of countries, and the ECSC has a permanent mission to the United Kingdom Government, even though that State is not a member of the Community. For these purposes, the International Organization concludes with the host State what we call an Headquarter Agreement.

It is interesting to note that the first agreement ever concluded by an International Organization with a State is an Headquarter Agreement: on October 4th, 1875 the ICWM—International Committee of Weight and Measures—concluded an agreement with France concerning the Committee's headquarters at Pavillion de Breteuil[9]. An other Headquarter Agreement from before the Second World War period, which seems to be also the first Headquarter Agreement ever entered into by Romania with an International Organization refers to the European Commission of the Danube: on August 18th, 1938 an arrangement between the United Kingdom, France, and Romania relative to the exercise of the powers of the European Commission of the Danube was signed[10] which provided in Article 19 that "the privileges and immunities of the employees of the Commission shall be those provided for in the agreement concluded this day between the Commission and the Romanian Government. This agreement may be modified by agreement between the same parties." On the same

---

[9] Reference to it is made by H. Chiu, The Capacity of International Organizations to Conclude Treaties, and the Special Legal Aspects of the Treaties so Concluded, p. 6, note 1, who says that the information was supplied by Mr. Leclerc of the ICWM in his letter of 28 Nov. 1963.

[10] 196 LNTS, p. 113.

day the Commission and Romania entered an agreement regarding privileges and immunities of the Commission's personnel[11].

The number of Headquarter Agreements registered so far with the United Nations Secretariat is close to one hundred. As far as the United Nations family is concerned, all organizations have concluded Headquarter Agreements with the States on the territory of which their seats are located, with the exception of the World Bank and of the International Monetary Fond. The legal régime of these two organizations in the United States of America (they have their headquarter in Washington, D.C.) is governed by the provision of articles VII and respectively IX of their constitutive acts which indicates of privileges and immunities the organizations enjoy on the territory of their member states, as well as by the provisions of the International Organizations Immunities Act of December 25, 1945[12].

Agreements concerning their headquarters were concluded by the United Nations with the USA[13] and Switzerland[14], by ILO[15], WHO[16], WMO[17], ITU[18], UPU[19] with Switzerland, by ICAO[20] with Canada, by UNESCO[21] with France, by FAO[22] with Italy, by IAEA[23] with Austria, by the Council of Europe[24] with France, by OAS[25] with the USA, by the OERN[26] with Switzerland, etc. The United Nations concluded host agreements concerning regional offices with Chile on behalf of the ECLA[27], with Thailand on behalf of the ECAFE[28], with Ethiopia on behalf of the ECA[29], with the

[11] British Command Paper, no. 5946 (1939).

[12] The USA is a member of the Bank and of the Fund and has signed the respective constitutive acts, both of which containing a provision in the sense that a signatory government deposit an instrument with the US government stating that it has taken all the measures to give the respective organization the possibility to carry out its tasks (articles XI, S. 2 (a) and XX, S. 2 (a) respectively). And even more: articles VII, S. 10 and IX, S. 10 respectively states that each of the Bank and the Fund members undertake to take the necessary measures on their territory to make effective from their internal legal order point of view the principles contained in the articles concerning privileges and immunities.

The Presidential Act is applied to all International Organizations located in the USA.

[13] 11 UNTS, p. 11.

[14] 1 UNTS, p. 163.

[15] 15 UNTS, p. 377.

[16] 26 UNTS, p. 331.

[17] 261 UNTS, p. 277.

[18] UN Doc. ST/LEG/SER. B/11, p. 319.

[19] UN Doc. ST/LEG/SER. B/11, p. 321.

[20] 96 UNTS, p. 155.

[21] UN Doc. ST/LEG/SER. B/11, p. 240.

[22] UN Doc. ST/LEG/SER. B/11, p. 187.

[23] 339 UNTS, p. 110—305.

[24] 249 UNTS, p. 207.

[25] 181 UNTS, p. 147.

[26] 249 UNTS, p. 406.

[27] 314 UNTS, p. 49.

[28] 260 UNTS, p. 36.

[29] 317 UNTS, p. 102.

UAR[30], Jordan[31], and Lebanon[32] on behalf of UNRWA. The WHO concluded agreements for its regional offices with Denmark[33], UAR[34], France[35] (with respect to the French Equatorial Africa), India[36], and The Philippines[37]; the ICAO for its regional offices with the UAR[38], France[39], and Peru[40]; the ILO for its offices in Mexico[41], Peru[42], Turkey[43], and Nigeria[44].

It should also be noted that agreements on legal status, privileges, and immunities have also been concluded between an International Organization and a State in which it does not maintain Headquarter or offices, but it conducts operational activities. This kind of agreement is also in the nature of a host agreement. In fact, its contents are quite similar to that of host agreements. For instance, the Bank's Headquarter is at Washington, D.C., and it does not maintain any office in Switzerland (which is not a member of the Bank). But in 1950, it began to make plans to make public issues of its bonds in the Swiss capital market. Since such bonds issues would establish legal relationships in Switzerland between the Bank and private investors, it was deemed highly desirable to clarify the Bank's general legal status in Switzerland and especially its position with respect to judicial process. At the same time, the fact that the Bank was to engage in financial transactions in Switzerland made it desirable to regulate the Bank's position, vis-à-vis the Swiss Government. For these reasons, an agreement governing the Bank's legal status, privileges, and immunities was concluded on June 29th, 1951[45].

Provisions concerning the legal status, privileges and immunities of an International Organization in a State are included in agreements on different matters. This is the case of technical assistance agreements that are concluded between International Organizations and the beneficiary State. As the practice in this field achieved a high degree of uniformity, it was possible to produce model texts of agreements[46].

---

[30] 121 UNTS, p. 107.
[31] 120 UNTS, p. 277.
[32] 202 UNTS, p. 124.
[33] 219 UNTS, p. 168.
[34] 223 UNTS, p. 88.
[35] 209 UNTS, p. 232.
[36] 67 UNTS, p. 44.
[37] WHO Off. Rec. no. 40, p. 111 (1952).
[38] 215 UNTS, p. 371.
[39] 94 UNTS, p. 59.
[40] 95 UNTS, p. 5.
[41] 208 UNTS, p. 225.
[42] UN Doc. ST/LEG/SER. B/11, p. 149.
[43] UN Doc. ST/LEG/SER. B/11, p. 153.
[44] UN Doc. ST/LEG/SER. B/11, p. 154.
[45] 216 UNTS, p. 348. See also Broches, International Legal Aspects of the Operations of the World Bank, in 98 RCAD, 1959-III, p. 374.
[46] See the Models contained in UN Doc. ST/LEG/SER. B/10, p. 361, 369, 374, 377, and 379.

Agreements of the Headquarter Agreements type were concluded also between two or more International Organizations: the United Nations concluded an agreement with WHO concerning the use by the latter of the premises at the Palais des Nations in Geneva[47]; the UN, LN, and UNRRA concluded an agreement for the holding of the Vth session of the UNRRA Council at the Palais des Nations in Geneva[48].

Similar agreements were concluded in connection with the holding of an international conference in a State: the United Nations and Italy signed an Agreement regarding the arrangements for the United Nations Conference on International Travel and Tourism[49].

When the Constitutive Acts of the International Organization contain precise provisions regarding the legal status, privileges and immunities that the organization enjoy on the territory of the member States, it wasn't found necessary to conclude Headquarter Agreements.

So, the Convention concerning navigation on the Danube[50], signed on August 18th, 1948 in Beograd, states that "The Commission shall have the rights of a legal entity in accordance with the laws of the state in which the Commission has its seat" (art. 14) and that "Members of the Commission and officers authorized by it shall enjoy diplomatic immunity. Its official buildings, archives, and documents of all kinds shall be inviolable" (art. 16)[51].

Thus, we see that International Organizations have concluded Headquarter Agreements over a period of almost a century.

The Legal Nature of the Headquarter Agreements

The definition that the Vienna Convention on the Law of Treaties gives to the term "treaty"—for the purpose of that Convention—says that treaty means "an international agreement" concluded between the parties—which in the case of the Vienna Convention are states (as the Convention applies to treaties between states only)[52], "in written form and governed by international law, whether embodied in a single instrument or in two or more related instruments and whatever its particular designation[53]. This means that the treaty is an agreement of will of the parties. So far as the States are con-

[47] 46 UNTS, p. 329.
[48] 1 UNTS, p. 87.
[49] 472 UNTS, no. 6840, p. 173.
[50] 33 UNTS, p. 196.
[51] The seat of the Commission was in Galatzi and later was moved to Budapest.
[52] Art. 1.
[53] Art. 2.

cerned, the question does not pose difficulties, but one may ask whether an International Organization has a will of its own. The doctrine is almost unanimous in considering that an International Organization has a will of its own. Parties to international treaties can be only the subjects of international law[54].

The provision of the Vienna Convention defining its scope as relating to "treaties concluded between States" has to be read in close conjunction with article 2 (1) (a), which states the meaning with which the term "treaty" is used in the Convention, but also with article 3, which contains a general reservation regarding certain other categories of international agreements.

The International Law Commission's commentary to the draft articles that served as the basis for discussion at the Vienna Conference on the Law of Treaties shows precisely that by limitating its scope to treaties between States it was not intended to deny that other subjects of international law, such as International Organization and insurgent communities, may conclude treaties. On the contrary the reservation in art. 3 regarding the legal force of and the legal principles applicable to their treaties was inserted by the Commission expressly for the purpose of refuting any such interpretation of its decision to confine the draft articles to treaties concluded between States[55].

The doctrine is almost unanimous in considering the agreements concluded by International Organizations as "treaties" of international law. There are still some authors, very few, that dispute this. So, C. Parry argues that the General Convention on Privileges and Immunities of the United Nations is not a "treaty" just because it does nothing more but develops the provisions of Articles 104 and 105 of the United Nations Charter, and furthermore he says that "The objection to the treaty-character of the General Convention arising from the relation of that instrument to the obligations of Articles 104 and 105 of the Charter can also be advanced in relation to the two Headquarter Agreements with the United States, a member of the United Nations. There can be no doubt that the United Nations is a "contracting" party to the latter: the only question is whether there is any "contract" given that "throughout its work which resulted in the drafting of the General Convention and of various draft agreements of the Headquarter district, the General Assembly always con-

---

[54] See Geamănu, Dreptul Internaţional Contemporan, p. 479 and the authors there mentioned.

[55] See commentary 5 to article 2 in the Report of the International Law Commission on its eighteenth session, 4 May—19 July 1966, in 2 YILC 1966.

sidered that these two instruments formed an organic whole[56]." The soviet author, V. M. Schourschalov holds a similar view[57].

The arguments brought by C. Parry seem to us unfounded. It is true that the United Nations General Convention on Privileges and Immunities provides in Section 36: "The Secretary-General may conclude with any Member or Members supplementary agreements adjusting the provisions of this convention so far as that Member or those Members are concerned. These supplementary agreements shall in each case be subject to the approval of the General Assembly[58]," but a large number of international agreements were concluded in the development, detailation or execution of some more general instruments and nevertheless, nobody did deny the legal character of these agreements as agreements under international law[59].

Practice shows that both the States and International Organizations consider Headquarter Agreements as treaties under international law.

In Canada, international treaties are published in the Canadian Treaty Series. The Headquarter Agreement between ICAO and Canada was printed in the Treaty Series just like agreements with foreign States[60].

In France, art. 27 of the Constitution of 26 Sept. 1946 provides, *inter alia*, that "treaties relative to International Organization, peace treaties, commercial treaties . . . shall not become final until they have been ratified by an act of the legislature." The Headquarter Agreement between France and UNESCO was approved by the National Assembly Law No. 55-1071[61] and was published in the Journal Officiel[62] as in the case of treaties concluded with foreign States.

The practice of the United States Courts proves that the Headquarter Agreement between the United Nations and the United States

[56] Parry, The Treaty-Making Power of the United Nations in the 26 BYIL, 1949, p. 146.

[57] Schourschalov, Osnovnîie voprosî teorii mejdunarodnovo dogovora. ANSSR, 1959, p. 37 (in Russian).

[58] 1 UNTS, p. 15.

[59] It is enough to mention here that International Space Law tends to develop from general to particular: the Treaty of 27 January 1967 contains the general principles governing the space activities of States. In the further development of these principles, some separate instruments were produced, as for instance the Agreement on the Rescue of Astronauts and the Return of Objects Launched into Outer Space, and some others are in the process of elaboration (e.g. Convention on liability for damage by objects launched into Outer Space).

[60] Canadian Treaty Series no. 7—1951.

[61] Journal Officiel 8106/1955.

[62] Journal Officiel 625/1956.

of America is considered as "treaty" in the meaning given to this word in the Constitution of the United States of America "the supreme law of the land[63]." This view was also held by the Acting United States Attorney-General during the negotiation stage of the Agreement[64].

As far as International Organizations are concerned, we mention as an example of their attitude, that in the course of discussion of the agreement with Egypt relating to the regional office of the WHO in Egypt, the Secretary of the subcommittee of the Fourth World Health Assembly expressed the desire that the courteous treatment granted so far *de facto* to the Organization be accorded *de jure* as well[65].

The Headquarter Agreements concluded by International Organizations are binding for parties. The binding force of these agreements is governed by international law.

The formal legal aspects of the conclusion, registration and application of the Headquarter Agreements reveal their legal nature —instruments under international law, but the argument of substance in favour of this thesis constitutes the material content of these agreements: there is no doubt that the granting of privileges and immunities to a subject of international law belongs to the matter of international law[66]. The conclusion of agreements in simplified form cannot serve as an argument in denying their character in international law.

We don't consider that the establishment of the seat of OECE in virtue of Art. 13 (a) of its Constitution Act which says that the Organization "prendre des décisions que les membres exécuteront" should be included in the field we are dealing with. This opinion is

---

[63] Constitution of the USA, art. VI par. 2. See the cases mentioned in "The practice of the United Nations, the specialized agencies and the International Atomic Energy Agency concerning their status, privileges and immunities: study prepared by the Secretariat" in 2 YILC, 1967, p. 154.

[64] Official Opinions of the Attorney-General of the United States, 40, p. 469 (1946).

[65] WHO, Official Records No. 35, p. 315 (1952).

[66] Fawcett suggests the following tests to determine the legal character of international agreements: "First, have the parties included in the agreement provisions for the settlement by compulsory judicial process of disputes arising out of it? Secondly, have they both accepted the jurisdiction of the International Court of Justice under Article 36 of its Statute in terms which would give the Court jurisdiction over any such dispute? Third, has the agreement been registered under Article 102 of the (UN) Charter or Article 18 of the (LN) Covenant? Fourth, is there an agreement, that the agreement or particular provisions of it are to be governed by public international law, or by a specific system of municipal law, or by the general principles of law recognized by civilized nations?" The Legal Character of International Agreements, in 30 BYIL, 1953, p. 387—388.

shared by other authors too[67]. Freymond calls these decisions as a special category of agreements[68].

The answer to the question whether all agreements concluded by International Organizations are governed by international law is not the same with all the authors. Balladore Pallieri[69] afirms that "agreements" are those instruments which are concluded by International Organizations having international juridical personality; the others, being concluded by International Organizations without this personality are "arrangements" and their legal character is doubtful. We are of the opinion that the name given to a particular instrument is not relevant, and that the agreements concluded by International Organizations as subjects of international law should be distinguished only from the contracts they entered into in their capacity of juridical person in an internal legal order.

It follows that the Headquarter Agreements of International Organizations are "treaties" in the sense given to this term by Art. 2.1 (a) by the Vienna Convention on the Law of Treaties, with, of course, the mention that one of the parties is an International Organization.

The Constitutive Acts

The Constitutive Acts of International Organizations contain very rarely express provisions concerning the Headquarter Agreements. Such provisions can be found in the Constitutive Acts of some regional organizations:

—Council of Europe—art. 40 (b) . . . a special agreement shall be concluded with the Government of the French Republic defining the privileges and immunities which the Council shall enjoy at its seat.

—EFTA—art. 35 (2)—The Council, acting on behalf of the Association, may conclude with the Government of the State in whose territory the headquarters will be situated an agreement relating to the legal capacity and the privileges and immunities to be recognized and granted in connection with the Association.

—OAS—art. 141—The juridical status of the Specialized Organizations and the privileges and immunities, that should be granted to them and to their personnel, as well as to the officials of the General Secretariat, shall be determined in a multilateral agreement. The for-

67 See Socini, Op.cit. supra note 1, p. 37.

68 See Freymond, 11 Annuaire suisse de droit international, 1954, p. 65.

69 Balladore Palieri, La formation des traités dans la pratique internationale contemporaine, 74 RCADI, 1949-I, p. 488.

going shall not preclude, when it is considered necessary, the concluding of bilateral agreements.

Similar provisions are contained in the Constitution of IRO (art. 11, par. 3). This Organization ceased its existence in 1952.

Some Constitutive Acts contain provisions regarding their seat:

—ITU—art. 3, "The seat of the Union shall be at Geneva,"

—UPU—art. 2, "The seat of the Union and of its permanent organs shall be at Berne,"

—WHO—art. 43, "The location of the headquarters of the Organization shall be determined by the Health Assembly after consultations with the United Nations,"

—WMO—art. 7 (functions of the Congress), lit. k, "to determine the location of the Secretariat of the Organization,"

—FAO—art. 9, "The Seat of the Organization shall be determined by the Conference,"

but don't expressly authorize the conclusion of Headquarter Agreements.

The majority of the Constitutive Acts indicate, borrowing the provisions of Art. 104 and 105 of the United Nations Charter, the privileges and immunities that the organization should enjoy on the territory of the member States:

"Art. 104. The Organization shall enjoy on the territory of each of its Members such legal capacity as may be necessary for the exercise of its functions and the fulfilment of its purposes."

"Art. 105. 1. The Organization shall enjoy on the territory of each of its Members such privileges and immunities as are necessary for the fulfilment of its purposes.

2. Representatives of the Members of the United Nations and officials of the Organization shall similarly enjoy such privileges and immunities as are necessary for the independent exercise of their functions in connexion with the Organization.

3. The General Assembly may make recommendations with a view to determining the details of the application of paragraphs 1 and 2 of this Article or may propose conventions to the Members of the United Nations for this purpose."

ILO—art. 40; FAO—art. XV; UNESCO—art. XII; WHO—art. 66—68; WMO—art. 27; ICAO—art. 60; IMCO—art. 50; IAEA—art. XV, etc. Provisions to the same effect can be found in the Constitutional Acts of some regional organizations: Charter of the Council for Mutual Economic Assistance, art. XIII, EFTA—art. 35, OSA—art. 138—142, etc.

On the basis of the provisions contained in Constitutive Acts, within the framework of the United Nations family of organizations, two instruments were elaborated spelling out *la portée et l'étendue* of these provisions: the General Convention on Privileges and Immunities of the United Nations[70] and the Convention on the Privileges and Immunities of the Specialized Agencies[71]. Section 36 of the General Convention on Privileges and Immunities of the United Nations provides for the possibility of concluding supplementary agreements by the Secretary-General with states in order to adapt its provisions to the peculiar conditions of each country.

The United Nations Secretariat maintains that Art. 105 of the United Nations Charter is self-executing. It says[72] that the legislative requirement of Article 105 is directly binding upon Member Governments and their political subdivisions, from the date on which the Charter became effective, and that the essential immunities which it provides are in no way dependent upon accession by a Member State to the Convention on the privileges and immunities of the United Nations. The Report of the Committee which drafted Art. 105 of the Charter, as adopted by Commission IV on judicial organization and subsequently by the Plenary of the United Nations Conference on International Organization at San Francisco in 1945 stated that the first paragraph of Art. 105, as already quoted "sets forth a rule obligatory for all members as soon as the Charter becomes operative" (Docs. 13, UNCIO, Doc. 933 (English). IV/2/42 (2), June 12, 1945). The Preparatory Commission on the United Nations reported in 1945 that the Art. 105 is "applicable even before the General Assembly has made the recommendations referred to in paragraph (3) of the Article or the Conventions therein mentioned have been concluded" (Report by the Executive Committee to the Preparatory Commission of the United Nations (PC/EX/113/Rev. 1, 12 Nov. 1945) chap. V, sect. 5, par. 2).

The United Nations Secretariat asserts[73] also that "the treaty-making capacity possessed by the Organization may only be exercised ... upon the basis of authorization contained, expressly or impliedly, in the provision of the Charter[74]; or in resolutions adopted by one of the principal organs on which Member States are represented."

The Doctrine

The doctrine is almost unanimous in considering that International Organizations have the capacity to conclude treaties.

---

[70] 1 UNTS, p. 115.
[71] 33 UNTS, p. 261.
[72] 2 YILC, p. 246.
[73] 2 YILC, 1967, p. 221.
[74] Among others, art. 105 of the Charter.

Some writers consider that this capacity is stipulated in the Constitutive Acts of the International Organizations. In the Course of International Law published in 1968 in Moscow we read with reference to the privileges and immunities of the United Nations (art. 105 of the Charter) that "The United Nations Charter provides the right of the United Nations to enter into juridical relations with States and with International Organizations and to conclude agreements with them on some problems[75]."

Other consider that the treaty-making power of international organizations is an attribute of their being subjects of international law. "Only by virtue of their capacity of subjects of international law, the organizations can undertake and exercise their rights and obligations different from the rights and obligations of Member States ... by concluding international agreements not only with Member States but with other states and International Organizations as well[76]."

A school of thought esteems that the treaty-making capacity of International Organizations is "implied by the necessity of ensuring the Organization with the ability to perform the functions it was created for[77].

Another group of writers are of the opinion that the treaty-making power of International Organizations should not be derived strictly from the Constitutive Acts, but reference should be made also to the practice followed by International Organizations and consolidated in this field[78].

Finally, H. Chiu, in concluding his study on the capacity of International Organizations to conclude treaties says, "We think that the treaty-making capacity has now been conferred upon International Organizations by a rule of customary international law[79]."

The shortcomings of one or another of these approaches, brought about changes in the position of some authors. So, R. Socini who had maintained that the capacity of International Organizations to conclude treaties should expressly be provided for in Constitutive Acts and not simply "derived" from them[80], changed his opinion after a careful study of the practice[81].

---

[75] 5 Kurs mejdunarodnovo pravo, p. 81.

[76] Lukaşuk, Storonî v mejdunarodnîh dogovorah, p. 126.

[77] See on this school, Rosenne, United Nations treaty practice, in RCADI—1954-II, p. 296.

[78] See Socini, Op.cit. supra note 1, pp. 136—137, and the authors quoted there.

[79] Chiu, Op.cit. supra note 9, p. 211.

[80] Socini, Gli Organizzazioni internazionali a carattere europeo considerate nei loro rapporti reciproci, in 39 "Studi Cagliari," 1957, p. 55.

[81] Socini, Rapports et conflits entre Organisations européens, p. 75.

It seems to us relevant for the matter we are discussing, that some authors consider that as far as the privileges and immunities of international organizations are concerned, there is, or at least it is in the process of formation, a customary rule of international law[82].

---

[82] Abdullah El-Erian summarizes in the following way the doctrine and the practice regarding the place of custom in the law of international immunities:

Some writers state that international immunities, in contrast to immunities of inter-State diplomatic agents, are almost exclusively created by treaty law, and that international custom has not yet made any appreciable contribution to this branch of law.

Several writers acknowledge, however, that "a customary law appears to be in the process of formation, by virtue of which certain organizations endowed with international personality may claim diplomatic standing for their agents as of right," and speak of "l'existence d'une véritable coutume internationale ... ou en tout cas d'un commencement de coutume." One writer has summed up the position, as it has developed since the creation of the League of Nations, as follows:

En voie de création est une règle coutumière qui assure aux organisations internationales et à leurs fonctionnaires supérieurs les mêmes privilèges et immunités diplomatiques qu'au personnel diplomatique. Les étapes de ce développement sont constituées par les arrangements conclus entre la Suisse et la Société des Nations en 1921 et en 1926, ainsi que par ceux qui sont intervenus entre la Suisse, d'une part, les Nations Unies et l'Organisation Internationale du Travail d'autre part, en 1946.

Le fait que certaines conventions internationales ont des contenus identiques, ce qui est particulièrement caractéristique pour les traités d'établissement, de consulat de d'extradition, n'entraîne pas en soi la formation d'une règle coutumière.

A parallel development of concepts can be found in practice. In a diplomatic note by the United States Government dated 16 October 1933 it was stated that:

... under customary international law, diplomatic privileges and immunities are only conferred upon a well-defined class of persons, namely, those who are sent by one state to another on diplomatic missions. Officials of the League of Nations are not as such considered by this Government to be entitled while in the United States to such privileges and immunities under generally accepted principles of international law, but only under special provisions of the Covenant of the League which have no force in countries not members of the League.

When, however, at the end of 1944 the British Diplomatic Privileges (Extension) Act, which provided for immunities, privileges and capacities of the International Organizations, their staff, and the representatives of Member Governments, was introduced in Parliament, the Minister of State explained that where a number of Governments joined together to create an International Organization to fulfil some public purpose, the Organization should have the same status, immunities and privileges as the foreign Governments members thereof enjoyed under the ordinary law. He elaborated that in principle they were entitled to it as a matter of international law which the English courts would regard as being part of the common law. However, legislation was regarded as desirable in order to put the legal position beyond dispute and to define with precision the extent of the prerogatives.

The Swiss Federal Council stated in a message dated 28 July 1955 to the Federal Assembly:

Estimate of Legal Foundation for the Conclusion of Headquarter Agreements

The Constitutive Acts of the International Organizations which have concluded Headquarter Agreements contain provisions regarding the privileges and immunities the Organization should enjoy on the territory of Member States. The Headquarter Agreements spell out the details of these provisions for their application in the specific environment of each country. The source of the Headquarter Agreements goes in such a way back to the Constitutive instrument as it concerns the International Organization.

The Constitutive Act, the fundamental instrument expressing the will of States hat have created the International Organization, is not the only document expressing the will of States regarding the activities of the International Organization. The Convention on Privileges and Immunities supplements the relevant provisions of the Constitutive Acts; the conclusion of General Convention on privileges and immunities of the United Nations was contemplated by the founders of the Organization and the Charter provided for it in Art. 105 (3). Similarly, Art. XV of the IAEA Statut specifies that the legal capacity, privileges, and immunities of the Agency "shall be defined in a separate agreement or agreements between the Agency ... and the members." We have already shown that Section 36 of the United Nations General Convention on Privileges and Immunities provides the possibility of concluding Headquarter Agreements.

Thus, we can affirm that the possibility of concluding Headquarter Agreements is expressly or impliedly provided for by the fundamental documents of International Organizations.

One can wonder whether in fact the express provisions in the Constitutive Acts regarding the conclusion of some Agreements could

---

... une organisation internationale fondée sur un traité entre Etats jouit d'après le droit international d'un certain nombre de privilèges dans l'Etat où elle a fixé son siège ...

... nous étions donc en présence d'un droit coutumier auquel notre pays ne pouvait pas se soustraire ...

The Supreme Court of Mexico in its decision of 28 April 1954 declared that the United Nations Economic Commission for Latin America could enjoy immunities recognized by international law.

Reference may also be made in this respect to article III, section 3 of the Agreement between Egypt and the World Health Organization, which provides:

The Organization and its principal or subsidiary organs shall have in Egypt the independence and freedom of action belonging to an International Organization according to international practice.

See Second Report on Relations between States and Intergovernmental Organizations, in 2 YILC, 1967, pp. 140—141.

be considered as meaning that the organization has the capacity to conclude treaties or whether this capacity belongs to the Member States, and the organization simply implements the will of States as for instance the United Nations Secretariat implements a United Nations General Assembly resolution. The process of concluding Headquarter Agreements—negotiation, signature, approval, registration, demonstrates that these are agreements of the Organization; otherwise, these agreements should be submitted for approval to the body that has elaborated the Constitutive Act, i.e. to the conference of plenipotentiaries of Member States.

The well-known soviet jurist, Kojevnikov, while stating that "international organs" may conclude treaties, considers that the treaties so concluded reflect the delegated treaty-making power of the Member States, as principal subjects of international law[83].

When creating an International Organization, the Member States delegate to it some prerogatives. This situation, however, should not be interpreted as meaning that the treaty-making power "is delegated" by States to the organization for each individual act. That is why an International Organization can be a party only to such agreements the possibility of conclusion of which is expressly or impliedly provided for by its Constitutive Act, or is based upon special authorization of member States. The International Organization can not conclude agreements that contradict the purposes and the principles set forth by Member States, sovereign subjects of international law.

The concept of delegation of powers for each individual case can, if admitted, explain neither the position of the agreements concluded by International Organization, vis-à-vis States that become members of the organization after the conclusion of these agreements, nor the position of States that in the process of the conclusion of the agreements were against these agreements and were in minority.

The normal functioning of an International Organization implies the holding of meetings on the territory of some States, within the premises of an other International Organization, or the establishment of its own seat in a country. Provisions of this nature contained in Constitutive Acts, expression of the will of Member States, allow the conclusion of Headquarter of host agreements by international organizations[84].

---

[83] Kojevnikov, Mejdunarodnoe Pravo, 1964, p. 319.

[84] There are instances when Headquarter Agreements were concluded on behalf of the Member States and not of the organization. This is the case of the NATO. Cahier, in examining the legal status of the NATO says: "... ce qui sert la démonstration de notre conception de l'OTAN, organe commun, est que si l'Organisation avait été considérée comme un sujet distinct, les conventions sur

The large number of Headquarter Agreements concluded over a period of more than a century, the validity of which was never challenged on the ground of unconstitutionality or for having been concluded in violation of limitations on the organizations' capacity, constitutes an additional argument in favour of the right of International Organizations to conclude Headquarter Agreements.

In concluding, one can state that International Organizations may conclude agreements with all those entities which international law recognize to be capable of being parties to agreements provided organizations do not exceed the scope and limits of their competence in concluding such agreements. In this rests one of the peculiarities of agreements concluded by International Organizations: a State cannot commit an excès de pouvoir, as it possesses full-treaty-making power; an International Organization, however, essentially rests upon a multilateral convention of a contractual character, and hence every transgression on its part is, in principle, a breach of a positive international rule.

J. W. Schneider[85] is of the opinion that "the rules which an organization may transgress are either conventional rules, as embodied in the agreements which organizations have concluded themselves, or constitutional provisions, which form another category of conventional rules, or the resolutions which it adopted. In these constitutional provisions a rule may be inserted restricting the treaty-making power of the organization. An agreement concluded by contravening the above rules must probably be declared void, except if resolutions are

---

le statut des forces, du personnel et des quartiers généraux auraient été signées par l'OTAN en son nom au lieu de l'être seulement par les Etats Membres. En effet, certains articles des différentes conventions montrent la volonté des parties de ne pas considérer l'Organisation comme un tout. L'art. 9 du protocole sur le statut de quartiers généraux militaires internationaux de 1952 déclare que les fonds en possession des quartiers généraux, lorsque ceux-ci cessent d'en avoir besoin, seront liquidés, et que le produit de cette liquidation sera réparti entre les parties au traité de l'Atlantique Nord au prorata de leurs contributions. Il apparaît ainsi que les Etats Membres n'ont pas cessé d'être propriétaires de ces fonds. Cette règle est comme nous l'avons vu au deuxième chapitre en parlant des organes communs, une des grandes caractéristiques de ces organes qui ne possedent pas une personnalité propre. Enfin, si on analyse les différents articles de la Convention entre les Etats Membres de l'OTAN sur le statut de leurs forces de 1951, articles ayant pour objet la responsabilité en cas de dégâts causés par les forces armées sur le territoire d'un Etat Membre, cette responsabilité n'est pas collective comme elle devait l'être si l'OTAN avait une personnalité juridique propre (38), mais elle appartient exclusivement à l'Etat dont dépendent les forces armées qui ont causé le dommage" (cf. essentiellement l'art. 8 de ladite convention). Op.cit. supra note 1, pp. 180—181.

[85] Schneider, Treaty-Making Power of International Organizations, 1959, pp. 62—63.

contravened. In this case the agreement should be declared voidable only ... The possible restrictions of the treaty-making power are not of great weight."

III. Organs Competent to Conclude Headquarter Agreements

The capacity to conclude treaties belongs in international law to the International Organization. This capacity, however, is exercised by one of its organs which concludes the Agreement in the name of the organization which it commits. A treaty concluded by any organ is thus to be looked upon as a "treaty of the organization."

The Provisions of Constitutive Acts

The Constitutive Acts of International Organizations do not contain but as a matter of exception provisions enabling expressly a definit organ to conclude Headquarter Agreements. The Convention of EFTA, for instance, stipulates in Art. 35 (2) that "The Council, acting on behalf of the Association, may conclude with the Government of the State ..." It is to be noted that under Art. 32 (2) of EFTA Convention, the Council is the plenary organ: "Each Member State shall be represented in the Council and shall have one vote." In the case of the Council of Europe, the Statute of the Council (art. 40-b) authorizes the Committee of Ministers to conclude Headquarter Agreements. The Committee of Ministers is again the plenary organ (art. 14).

Some Constitutive Acts confer to the plenary organ the capacity of determining the seat of the organization's headquarters. The Constitution of WHO provides in art. 43 that "The location of the Headquarter of the Organization shall be determined by the Health Assembly after consultation with the United Nations." Similarly, the Constitution of WMO provides in art. 7 among other functions of the Congress (the plenary organ), "to determine the location of the Organization"; FAO Constitution provides in art. IX that "The seat of the Organization shall be determined by the Conference" (which is the plenary organ)[86].

One should note that in the case of the United Nations, the Security Council is abilitated under Art. 43 to take measures which

---

[86] See also art. X and XV of the FAO Constitution.

could lead to the conclusion of Headquarter or host Agreements with some Member States. The Security Council may, under art. 28 of the Charter, hold meetings at such places other than the seat of the Organization as in its judgment will best facilitate its work. This can bring about the need of concluding a Headquarter-type Agreement.

The Practice

The Analysis of the Headquarter Agreement of International Organizations shows that they were concluded by authorization of the plenary organ. There are no instances of agreements concluded by the United Nations Security Council in virtue of its special tasks just mentioned, under the Charter.

The practice of International Organizations in concluding Headquarter Agreements lacks uniformity[87]. This is true even if one takes the case of just one organization: the United Nations, for instance, has concluded agreements for the granting of a proper treatment to one of its subsidiary bodies that was not invested with the capacity to conclude treaties. This was the case of the exchange of letters constituting an agreement on the statute of the United Nations group of observers in Lebanon[88], or of the Agreement with Jordan concerning the status of some auxiliary organs of the United Nations in that country[89].

Among instances of different type, we note the fact that the International Court of Justice, UNEF or UNRWA have concluded agreements concerning their legal status in the internal order of the states where their headquarters are located. They did it, having been duly authorized for it. The example of the International Court of Justice Headquarters Agreement with the Netherlands is significant from this point of view: Although the Court is a principal organ of the Organization, and the Statute is an integral part of the Charter, the Immunities Convention does not, apparently, extend to the Court because Article 19 of the Statute contains special provisions on the subject, and lex specialis derogat generali. The Preparatory Commission had accordingly been of opinion that Article 105 of the Charter would be inapplicable, and that the General Assembly should postpone consideration of the subject until the Court could be consulted[90]—advice which was acted upon in Resolution 22 C (I). After its inauguration in April 1946, the Court authorized its President to enter into nego-

[87] See Socini, Op.cit., supra note 1, p. 89.
[88] 303 UNTS, p. 271.
[89] 315 UNTS, p. 125.
[90] PC/20, p. 60.

tiations with the Netherlands Foreign Minister and the result of these negotiations is recorded in an Exchange of Notes of 26 July 1946[91] which was duly reported to the Secretary-General of the United Nations and submitted by him to the General Assembly[92]. After some discussion[93], in which representatives of the Court and of the Secretariat participated, the General Assembly, in its Resolution 90 (I) of 11 December 1946, formally approved the Exchange of Notes. However, at the same time it made a number of additional recommendations, which partake of the nature of "understandings" as to the purport of the agreement. Although this may have been something of a unilateral act on the part of the General Assembly, no problem seems to have arisen vis-à-vis the Netherlands Government, whose representative, indeed, was Rapporteur of the Sixth Committee's Subcommittee which dealt with this topic[94].

As a rule, the task of concluding Headquarter Agreements is given to the Executive Head of the Organization, but one should bear in mind that the Executive Head does not act on its own initiative[95] but at the request of the organ with which the capacity to conclude Headquarter Agreements rests, normally the plenary organ. The United Nations-United States Headquarter Agreement of 26 June 1947[96] is edifying:

"The United Nations and the United States of America,

Desiring to conclude an agreement for the purpose of carrying out the Resolution adopted by the General Assembly on 14 December 1946 to establish the seat of the United Nations in the City of New York and to regulate questions arising as a result thereof:

have appointed as their representatives for this purpose:

The United Nations: Trygve Lie, Secretary-General, and

The United States of America: George C. Marshall, Secretary of State."

The United Nations Secretariat maintains[97] that the treaty-making capacity of the Organization is normaly exercised by the

---

[91] International Court of Justice, Yearbook, 1946—47, p. 88.

[92] G.A.O.R. (I, part 2) 6th, p. 246 (A/105).

[93] Ibid., pp. 104—107, 108—111.

[94] This appears as the first instance in which the General Assembly asserted its right to effect changes in an agreement brought to its notice, and actually concluded by another principal organ in exercise of its implied treaty-making power. For the promulgation of the agreement in Holland, see Decree of 5 April 1947 in Staatsblad van het Koninkrijk der Nederlanden, No. H. 79.

[95] The Executive Head would act on its own initiative only in strictly administrative matters, and even then he would try to seek some kind of authorization from the plenary organ.

[96] 11 UNTS, p. 11.

[97] See 2 YILC, 1967, p. 221.

Secretary-General and that in the case of subsidiary organs, such as UNICEF and UNRWA, agreements may be concluded by the body concerned on the basis of resolutions of the parent organ or by the Secretary-General or his representative, acting on his behalf.

The Doctrine

The doctrine is not unanimous in evaluating which is the competent organ to conclude agreements on behalf of the organization.

In the absence of express provisions in the Constitutive Acts regarding the competent organ, the following are the main tendencies manifested in the doctrine.

1. The Competence of the Plenary Organ

Brierly considers in his Report on the Law of Treaties—suggested article 4 (3)—that "In the absence of provisions to the contrary, the capacity of an International Organization to make treaties is deemed to reside in its plenary organ[98]."

Dupuy maintains that even when organs other than the plenary ones conclude treaties they merely exercise the "delegated" power of the plenary organ which should be considered the only one abilitated always with this capacity[99].

Rosenne[100] esteems that "which is the competent body depends, in the case of each Organization, upon the terms of its own Constitution, but is usually that organ in which all the members are represented. Experience has shown that the conclusion of these agreements, and their operation, are not confined to purely technical and legal matters, but occasionally may intrude into the political sphere. While the Secretariat thus represents the Organization considered as a collective entity, it also has to take into account the actual and even potential individual attitudes of its members. Formally the implementation of these agreements is not the direct concern of the General Assembly of the UN. In cases of serious difficulties, however, the General Assembly can be seized of the matter by virtue of its general competence and also by virtue of its concern with the Immunities Conventions (of which, to some extent, the Headquarters and Host Agreements are particularizations)."

---

[98] UN Doc. A/CN. 4/23, p. 26.

[99] Dupuy, "Le droit de relations entre les organisations internationales," 100 RCADI (1960-II), p. 511 and 502—3.

[100] Rosenne, "United Nations Treaty Practice," 86 RCADI (1954-II), p. 406 to 407.

Similarly, Socini[101] affirms that the treaty-making power is exercised by the organ in which all members are represented, because when creating the organization, the states preserve the capacity to promote their objectives.

2. *The Competence of the Most Powerful Organ*

I. Detter[102] reaches the conclusion that "It may ... safely be assumed that the treaty-making power is in principle vested in the supreme organ of the organization." This supreme organ is, as a rule, the plenary organ.

Capotorti[103] is of the opinion that the plenary organ is the most powerful one, but it can delegate its capacity "... all organo esecutivo collegiale." If this "delegation" continues over a long period of time, Capotorti thinks that it may change the structure of the Organization, and then the most powerful organ is another than the plenary organ.

3. *The Competence of Several Organs*

This theory maintains that each organ has treaty-making power in accordance with the distribution of powers in the organization. All organs needless to say, are acting on behalf of the Organization which is in fact engaged by the treaty.

Zemanek[104] shows that no organ has the monopoly over the treaty-making capacity and that the question arises only in the absence of express provisions in the Constitutive Acts. The capacity belongs to the organ that bears the responsibility for the material implementation of the Agreement. With the plenary organ rests, normally, the residual competence for the activity of the organization.

Kasme[105] creates a hierarchy of possibilities; Jenks[106] considers that the representative plenary organ has the general capacity which it exercises for concluding major agreements, while the executive organ (individual or collectiv) is competent to conclude agreements in the implementation of the agreements concluded by the plenary organ.

---

[101] Socini, Op.cit., supra note 1, p. 173.

[102] Detter, "The Organs of International Organizations exercising their treaty-making power," 38 BYIL, 1962.

[103] Capotorti, "Sulla competenza a stipulare degli organi di unioni," in 7 "Communicazioni e studi" (1955), p. 187.

[104] Zemanek, Das Vertragsrecht der Internationalen Organisation. Wien, Springer-Verlag, 1957, p. 68.

[105] Kasme, La capacité de l'ONU de Conclure des Traités, 1960, p. 179.

[106] Jenks, Some Constitutional problems ..., in 22 BYIL, 1945, p. 53.

4. *The Competence of the Executive Organ*

The opinion of Jenks just mentioned, as well as the comments on the practice of International Organizations are not firm accepting the existence of a treaty-making power of the executive organ[107].

Art. 33 of the WHO Constitution provides:

"The Director-General or his representative may establish a procedure by agreement with Members, permitting him, for the purpose of discharging his duties, to have direct access to their various departments, especially to their health administrations and to national health organizations, governmental or non-governmental. He may also establish direct relations with International Organizations whose activities come within the competence of the Organization . . ."

This being so, an agreement made in 1956 between the World Health Organization and Denmark concerning tuberculosis immunization research was concluded by the Director-General, Mr. Candau, whose signature sufficed to bind the Organization. In point of fact, this type of WHO agreement is even more frequently concluded by the (Deputy) Regional Director, who acts on behalf of the Director-General. The agreement on technical assistance with Nepal was, for example, signed by the Deputy Regional Director of the Organization for South-East Asia, acting as 'representative of the Director-General.' In the case of WHO the agreements actually enter into force upon signature, and the Director-General is regarded as competent to bind the Organization by his decision.

I. Detter admits the possibility that the competence of the Secretary-General or Director-General will develop in the field of concluding treaties in the same manner as without any express provisions in the Constitutive Acts, the general sphere of their competence has been extended through practice[108].

In the light of the provisions of the Constitutive Acts, of the practice of concluding Headquarter Agreements and of doctrine, one can draw the following conclusion regarding the organ competent to conclude treaties:

1. There are no general rules of international law regarding the organ competent to conclude treaties on behalf of the International Organization.

[107] We have excluded from our study the European Communities, which in the opinion of some writers give instances of competence of the executive organs. See Pilidis, La Capacité de conclure de traités internationaux des organisations internationales (Paris 1952), p. 152.

[108] Detter, The Organs of International Organizations, in 38 BYIL, 1962, p. 425.

2. There exists no single organ or individual which is the representative and the personification of the organization as a whole, in the sense recognized for states in art. 7 (2) of the Vienna Convention on the Law of Treaties. We don't think that in the absence of specific provisions in the Constitutive Acts it is desirable to establish rules for the designation of an organ or individual as "representative" of the organization in the sense of art. 7 (2) of the Vienna Convention, because the mechanism of each individual organization, having specific features and engaging different responsibilities in each case, could suffer modifications of substance by conventionally establishing such an organ.

3. The fact that the Headquarter Agreements were concluded so far by authorization of the plenary organ does not constitute a sufficiently solid basis for concluding that this type of agreements may be concluded by plenary organs exclusively, because there are provisions in the Constitutive Acts of some organizations that permit the conclusion of such agreements by other organs as well (as it is the case of the United Nations Security Council).

4. In order to determine the competent organ, in the absence of express provisions in the Constitutive Acts, one should resort to examining the whole concept of the Constitutive Act of the respective International Organization, to the practice followed by each individual International Organization.

The practice of the Headquarter Agreements offer neither instances where the material validity of an Headquarter Agreement was challenged on the ground that it was concluded by an incompetent organ in the sense of art. 46 applying to States of the Vienna Convention, nor instances of the sort mentioned in connection with States by art. 48 (error), 49 (fraude), and 52 (coercion by the threat or use of force). Nevertheless, we consider that these articles can apply, mutatis mutandis, to agreements concluded by International Organizations.

IV. The Process of Conclusion of the Headquarter Agreements

In spite of the large variety of procedures employed for concluding Headquarter Agreements, one can distinguish two main patterns: agreements concluded through a complex procedure of negotiations, signature, approval and registration and agreements in simplified form, where one or several stages of the complex procedure are missing.

The process of concluding the Headquarter Agreement between the United Nations and the USA constitute an eloquent example of complex procedure. This agreement served as a model for other similar agreements[109].

On 11 December 1945, the House of Representatives (the Senate concurring) invited the Organization to locate its Headquarter within the USA. The Preparatory Commission made various proposals for the internationalization of the seat of the Organization, and prepared what it termed a "draft" treaty to be concluded by the United Nations with the USA for the location of the Headquarter of the United Nations. At the first part of the first session a new draft, based upon that prepared by the Preparatory Commission, was proposed as a basis for discussion in negotiations between the Secretary-General and the Government of the US. After a brief debate in the Sixth Committee, the General Assembly adopted Resolution 22 (I) B of 13 Febr. 1946. By this resolution the General Assembly authorized the Secretary-General, with the assistance of a Negotiating Committee, to negotiate with the competent authorities of the United States of America the arrangements required as a result of the establishment of the seat of the United Nations in the United States of America. This resolution provided that any agreement with the competent authorities of the United States resulting from these negotiations should be subject to approval by the General Assembly before being signed on behalf of the United Nations. Annexed to the resolution was a draft Convention between the United Nations and the Government of the United States of America intended for use by the Secretary-General as a basis for discussion during the negotiations. This draft Convention had been drawn up by the Sixth Committee[110] on the basis of a "draft treaty" prepared for the purpose by the Preparatory Commission of the United Nations[111].

The Secretary-General and the Negotiating Committee submitted to the General Assembly at its first session a joint report[112] on the negotiations carried out with the authorities of the United States of America. This report contained an annexed draft agreement which had been reached in the course of the negotiations.

---

[109] The legal adviser of UNESCO explained to the Executive Board of that Organization that the Headquarter Agreement between France and UNESCO was based upon similar agreements of the United Nations (UNESCO Doc. EX/SR. 10, p. 44). In fact this is a source for the uniformity of Agreements concluded by International Organization which can be apt to build up a customary practice.

[110] Report of the Sixth Committee to the General Assembly, Doc. A/43/Rev. 1.

[111] Report of the Preparatory Commission of the United Nations, Document PC/20, p. 75.

[112] Document A/67/Add. 1.

The General Assembly referred the report to the Sixth Committee. On that Committee's recommendation[113], the General Assembly, on 14 December 1946, adopted Resolution 99 (I) whereby it recognized that, having decided that the permanent headquarters of the United Nations should be located in the City of New York, the draft agreement resulting from the negotiations between the Secretary-General and Negotiating Committee and the competent authorities of the United States of America would need to be adapted to the circumstances of that site. In this resolution, the General Assembly also adopted the following decisions:

The General Assembly,

. . .

Resolves, therefore:

1. That the Secretary-General be authorized to negotiate and conclude with the appropriate authorities of the United States of America an agreement concerning the arrangements required as a result of the establishment of the permanent headquarters of the United Nations in the City of New York;

2. That in negotiating this agreement the Secretary-General shall be guided by the provisions of the draft agreement set forth in document A/67;

3. That the agreement referred to in paragraph 1 shall not come into force until approved by the General Assembly;

4. That, pending the coming into force of the agreement referred to in paragraph 1, the Secretary-General be authorized to negotiate and conclude arrangements with the appropriate authorities of the United States of America to determine on a provisional basis the privileges, immunities, and facilities needed in connexion with the permanent headquarters of the United Nations. In negotiating these arrangements, the Secretary-General shall be guided by the provisions of the draft agreement set forth in document A/67;

5. That the Government of the United States of America be requested to take the necessary steps as soon as possible to put into effect the Convention on the Privileges and Immunities of the United Nations, and to give effect to such arrangements as may be reached in accordance with paragraph 4 of this resolution.

In the report[114] submitted by the Secretary-General to the General Assembly at its second session, it was stated that in "pursuance of the resolution of 14 December, the Secretary-General resumed his negotiations with the competent United States authorities

[113] Report of the Sixth Committee to the General Assembly, Document A/271.

[114] Document A/371.

and on 26 June 1947 signed, with the Secretary of State of the United States of America, the 'Agreement between the United Nations and the United States of America regarding the headquarters of the United Nations'." An annex to this report contained the text of the agreement, section 28 of which, in conformity with paragraph 3 of the above-mentioned General Assembly resolution, stipulated that it:

. . . shall be brought into effect by an exchange of notes between the Secretary-General, duly authorized pursuant to a resolution of the General Assembly of the United Nations, and the appropriate executive officer of the United States, duly authorized pursuant to appropriate action of the Congress.

Section 20 of the Agreement also stipulated that:

The Secretary-General and the appropriate American authorities shall settle by agreement the channels through which they will communicate regarding the application of the provisions of this agreement and other questions affecting the headquarters district, and may enter into such supplemental agreements as may be necessary to fulfil the purposes of this agreement. In making supplemental agreements with the Secretary-General, the United States shall consult with the appropriate state and local authorities. If the Secretary-General so requests, the Secretary of State of the United States shall appoint a special representative for the purpose of liaison with the Secretary-General.

The text of the agreement was referred to the Sixth Committee, which requested its Sub-Committee on Privileges and Immunities to study it. The Sub-Committee, in its report to the Sixth Committee[115], expressed the following views with regard to sections 20 and 28 of the agreement:

(f) Section 20 provides for the conclusion between the Secretary-General and appropriate United States authorities of any supplemental agreements that may be necessary to fulfil the purposes of the Headquarters Agreement. The Sub-Committee was of the opinion that the Secretary-General should have authority to conclude such supplemental agreements and that the General Assembly should in all cases be informed of their contents. However, wherever, in the judgment of the Secretary-General, the proposed supplemental agreement involved any question of importance for which he had not already received authority, the Secretary-General should obtain the approval of the General Assembly before the supplemental agreement could become operative;

---

[115] Report of the Sixth Committee to the General Assembly, Official Records of the General Assembly, Second Session, Annex 9 b, document A/427.

(f) With regard to section 28, the Sub-Committee was of the opinion that the notes exchanged for the purpose of bringing the Headquarters Agreement into force should be limited to effecting this purpose.

At its 101st plenary meeting held on 31 October 1947, the General Assembly adopted resolution 169 (II), reading as follows:

A

The General Assembly,

Whereas the Secretary-General pursuant to resolution 99 (I) of 14 December 1946 signed with the Secretary of State of the United States of America on 26 June 1947 an Agreement between the United Nations and the United States of America regarding the Headquarters of the United Nations, and

Whereas the Secretary-General in accordance with the said resolution has submitted the said Agreement to the General Assembly;

Having studied the report prepared on this matter by the Sixth Committee,

Endorses the opinions expressed therein;

Approves the Agreement signed on 26 June 1947, and

Authorizes the Secretary-General to bring that Agreement into force in the manner provided in section 28 thereof, and to perform on behalf of the United Nations such acts or functions as may be required by that Agreement[116].

Negotiation

The stage of negotiation as far as International Organizations are concerned is in some cases, stipulated and guided by specific provisions of the Constitutive Acts[117].

---

[116] For the text of this Agreement which came into force on 21 November 1947 by an exchange of notes, in accordance with section 28, see 11 UNTS, p. 11.

[117] For example: Art. 4 of the Charter of the African and Malgasy Union for Economic Cooperation states the capacity of the Union to negotiate on behalf of each of the Member States with organizations and third States.

Art. 43 (3) of the United Nations Charter: The Agreement or Agreements shall be negotiated.

Art. 101 of Euratom Treaty: Such agreements or conventions shall be negotiated by the Commission in accordance with the Council's directives;

UN Doc. E/ICEF/321 of 15 Nov. 1956, p. 6: "Regional offices are responsible, jointly with the Headquarter for inter-alia, the negociation of Agreements with Governments," p. 21: "Area and Country Offices: Responsibilities: To represent UNICEF in its relations with appropriate governmental officials of assisted countries and with other International Agencies engaged in similar work in the country area." A Government dealing with these organs should be satisfied that they are qualified to conduct negotiations etc. Quoted by Schneider, The Treaty-Making Power of International Organizations, footnote 4, p. 63.

Negotiation for the conclusion of Headquarter Agreements on behalf of International Organizations were conducted by:

—an individual organ, as a rule the Secretary-General or the Director-General of contracting International Organization, duly authorized for it by the organ invested with the exercise of the treaty-making power. (This is the case for the majority of the Headquarter Agreements);

—mixt organs: sometimes the individual organ was assisted by a collective organ having consultative functions (for instance, the Headquarter Agreement between the United Nations and the United States)[118];

—collective organs, as it was the case for the General Convention on Privileges and Immunities of the United Nations.

The majority of the Headquarter Agreements do not contain reference to the organs that have carried out the negotiations. Sometimes the representatives of the contracting parties are mentioned in the Preamble[119]. They are not called "plenipotentiaries," but who are the "representatives" of the contracting parties "duly authorized" to negotiate and eventually to conclude treaties if not "plenipotentiaries[120]."

There are no "full powers" in the traditional sense which are to be presented to the other contracting party (as is normally the case with state agents), by an Organization. When a Headquarter Agreement is to be concluded on behalf of an International Organization there is an internal act of authorization in favour of a particular agent, e.g. a Secretary-General. This, of course, would be something equivalent of full powers[121].

The authorization may be given to negotiate one particular agreement or several agreements:

The Second World Health Assembly authorized the Director-General or his representative to sign an agreement concerning Privi-

[118] 11 UNTS, p. 11.

[119] Examples: Headquarter agreements between the Council of Europe and France, the United Nations and the United States; the UNESCO and France, the ILO and Mexico of 5. I. 1955.

[120] E.g. The decision of the Executive Board of UNESCO at its 43rd session (Doc. UNESCO 42, Ex. 44): "Autorise le Directeur Général conformément à l'art. XI par. 1 de l'Acte Constitutif, à entreprendre des negociations avec le Secrétaire Général du Bureau d'éducation Ibéro-Americaine en vue de la préparation d'un projet d'accord réglant les relations entre le dit Bureau et l'UNESCO."

[121] The ICAO-France agreement (94 UNTS, p. 59) was originally brought into force between the PICAO and France by an exchange of notes. In his letter the representative of PICAO wrote: "I am authorized by the Council of PICAO to sign the agreement forthwith."

leges and Immunities of the Regional Organization of the WHO in South-East Asia, which was to be concluded with India[122]. Similarly, in the case of the host agreement with Egypt the Director-General was authorized by the Assembly to sign, having been previously charged with the negotiation of the Agreement[123].

Authorization for negotiating a series of Agreements (eventually their signature, too) may be given in very broad and vague terms: By resolution 1237 (ES. III), the General Assembly welcomed the assurance of the Arab States that each member of the Arab League would respect the government established in other member countries, and requested the Secretary General to

'... make forthwith in consultation with the Governments concerned and in accordance with the Charter ... such practical arrangements as would adequately help in upholding the purposes and principles of the Charter in relation to Lebanon and Jordan in the present circumstances, and thereby facilitate the early withdrawal of the foreign troops from the two countries.'

Three months later, in pursuance of this Resolution, the Secretary-General concluded an Agreement with the Government of Jordan on which he made the following report to the Assembly:

'In respect of the subsidiary organ of the United Nations in charge of the Special Representative of the Secretary General stationed in Jordan in furtherance of General Assembly Resolution 1237 (ES-III) of 21 August 1958, an exchange of letters between the Secretary-General and the Jordanian Government in November 1958 provided for privileges, immunities and facilities for the subsidiary organ as well as for the Special Representative and officials of the United Nations assigned to his staff[124].'

An authorization may be given to an executive officer in previous international agreements as it is the case of section 36 of the General Convention on Privileges and Immunities of the United Nations[125].

I. Detter[126] shows that it must be conceded that the authorization is often given in a quite informal way. Thus, it may be difficult to find any record of an act of authorization for a particular agreement: the minutes of the plenary organ may be silent as to whether or not authorization has been given, and the agreement itself may not recite any grant of authority. Even so, this does not neces-

[122] WHO, Official Records, 1949, no. 21, p. 49. It is interesting to note that in this instance the Director-General had been invited to negotiate this Agreement by the Executive Board of the Organization (ibid., 1948, no. 14, p. 26).

[123] WHO, Official Record, 1948, no. 14, p. 26.

[124] A/4132, p. 95. See 315 UNTS, p. 125.

[125] 1 UNTS, p. 15.

[126] Detter, The organs of International Organizations exercising their treaty-making power, in BYIL, 1962, p. 436.

sarily mean that there was no authorization. Only in exceptional cases would an executive officer fail to obtain an authorization or conclude that he could safely act without any kind of authorization. In practice, it will usually be found that there is at least, some form of authorization, however broad may be its terms. The Secretary-General, for example, has been empowered to "take relevant measures" in a certain situation and this may constitute an authorization to conclude such agreements as he would judge to be necessary; i.e. such "necessary" agreements would be considered "relevant measures." By thus authorizing an executive officer to conclude agreements, the competent organ of the organization exercises its treaty-making power; in the example given, the Secretary-General exercises a "delegated" treaty-making power—assuming that he is permitted to conclude the agreements without any further reference back to the organ that has delegated its powers[127].

As for the need of "full powers," the doctrine is not unanimous in evaluating the practice accumulated so far. So, Rosenne writes:

"There is no room for full powers in the traditional sense on the part of the Organization: none are required and none are proffered —and there is no individual capable of issuing them. On the other hand the negotiators on behalf of the Organization may be required to furnish evidence of their authority to act, and this authority may circumscribe with some particularity the extend of their discretion. It would be a function of the Secretary-General to issue such authorization. The Headquarter Agreement provides a good example of this[128]."

Socini considers that in virtue of the general principles of international law the organ competent to conclude the agreement will be the organ competent to issue full powers and in absence of any specific indication, the full powers should be received by the head of the permanent executive body[129].

The question of authorization is of a different nature for the agents of States and for those of the International Organization: in International Organization the act of authorization is not primarily intended as proof to the other party that the agent is competent to conclude the agreement. It is not the equivalent of full powers of diplomats. In the law of International Organization, the act of

[127] Resolution 369 (IV) of 3 Dec. 1949 on convening the UN Conference on Declaration of Death of Missing Persons, reads:

"2. Instructs the Secretary-General: b) to take all other measures necessary for the convening of the conference."

This will include measures for granting privileges and immunities.

[128] Rosenne, in RCADI, 1954-II, p. 412.

[129] Socini, Op.cit. supra note 1, p. 184.

authorization concerns rather the internal relationship within the organization: e.g. between the competent organ and the Secretary General.

As regards procedural aspects of United Nations treaty practice, the following extract from a letter dated 22 November 1961, sent by the Office of Legal Affairs in response to an inquiry by the Special Rapporteur of the International Law Commission on the Law of Treaties as to whether the United Nations issues anything that corresponds to credentials or full-powers, provides a general survey of the arrangements which have been adopted.

... The procedures heretofore followed in the United Nations in this regard have been rather informal. Where the Secretary-General concluded an agreement with the Government of a State on behalf of the Organization, in the implementation of a decision of one of its organs or in the performance of his regular duties, there is of course no question of credentials or full-powers since, as Chief Administrative Officer of the Organization under Article 97 of the Charter, his power of making treaties on behalf of the Organization in the performance of his functions is implied.

On occasion, the Secretary-General has been authorized by an organ of the United Nations to conclude with the Government of a State an agreement for a specific purpose. Thus, in view of the decision to establish the seat of the United Nations in the United States, the General Assembly first adopted a resolution by which it "authorizes" persons appointed by certain Governments, to negotiate with the competent authorities of the United States the arrangements required (resolution 22 B (I), 13 February 1946). Upon receipt of a report by the Secretary-General and the negotiating committee on the negotiations carried out in pursuance of the above-mentioned resolution, the General Assembly further authorized the Secretary-General "to negotiate and conclude with the appropriate authorities of the United States of America an agreement concerning the arrangements required as a result of the establishment of the permanent headquarters of the United Nations in the City of New York, such agreement to come into force only upon approval by the General Assembly" (resolution 99 (I), 14 December 1946). On the basis of this resolution, the Secretary-General signed with the Secretary of State of the United States an agreement between the United Nations and the United States on 26 June 1947 regarding the headquarters of the United Nations and submitted it to the General Assembly for approval. By a third resolution, the General Assembly approved the agreement as signed and authorized the Secretary-General to bring it into force (resolution 169 A (II), 31 October 1947).

Where an Under-Secretary of the United Nations signs an agreement on behalf of the United Nations, his authority for doing so is deemed to have derived from the Secretary-General, express or implied, in the normal courses of administration and no full-powers or any other form of specific authorization to sign such agreement have been considered necessary.

In cases of agreements negotiated and concluded overseas by a Representative of a subsidiary organ of the United Nations, such as the United Nations Special Fund, with the Government of a State the executive head of the subsidiary organ usually issues a letter stating simply that the Representative has been authorized to sign such agreement on his behalf. This letter may be addressed to the Representative or to the Government concerned, depending on the preference of the Government. There have been occasions where a telegram was sent instead of a letter when time was on the essence. In the case of Standard Agreements on Technical Assistance negotiated by a Resident Representative of the United Nations Technical Assistance Board, such Representative receives authorization, again in a similarly informal manner, from the Executive Chairman of the said Board and signs such agreements on behalf of all the participating agencies on the Board, namely the United Nations, the International Atomic Energy Agency and seven specialized agencies . . .[130]

We would rather consider that what the UN Secretariat esteems to be the rule (authorization given "on occasion") is in fact the exeption, and the rule is that such authorization for negotiation or conclusion exists almost always.

The claim that the Secretary-General has an implied treaty-making power under article 97 was challenged. So, I. Detter says that this article, which provides that the Secretary-General of the United Nations is the "Chief administrative officer" of the organization, merely concerns the *jus representationis* of the Secretary-General. Having been designated the chief executive official of the United Nations, he is necessarily competent to act for the Organization in treaty matters; in other words, he is automatically competent to represent the Organization in the negotiation and conclusion of treaties and, as in the case of a Foreign Minister, has no need of credentials or full-powers. It does not, however, follow that authorization has been dispensed with, or that the Secretary-General is free to conclude agreements without any kind of authorization from another organ of the UN. On the contrary, an act of authorization is, as a general rule, required[131].

We are of the opinion that upon the request of the other party, the negotiator on behalf of an international organization should produce evidence of his authority. We don't think advisable to disciplinate in an uniform conventional manner the way in which the evidence should be produced. This should be left to every International Organization to develop its own means, because of the

---

[130] 2 YILC, 1967, p. 222.

[131] Detter, The Organs of International Organizations exercising their Treaty-Making Power, in BYIL, 1962, p. 436.

peculiarities of the profile of each organization. At the same time, the executive head of the Organization as well as the heads of the main—nonsubordinated organs of the International Organization should be deemed to be empowered with the task of negotiating agreements.

There is no negotiation stage in some cases where, let us say, for the purpose of holding an international conference one state offers to the Organization an agreement showing the privileges and immunities it is offering to the participants to the Conference, which is accepted by the organization.

Signature

One should distinguish between the institution of signature indicating the completion of the drafting stage and the institution of signature as a means by which the definitive consent to be bound by a treaty is expressed.

Signature indicating the completion of the drafting stage may be entierly dispensed with in agreements the validity of which depends expressly, owing to a term in the treaty itself, or in the Constitutive Act of the International Organization, upon a subsequent approbatory act. For example, the Headquarter Agreement between Switzerland and the International Labour Organization and the accompanying arrangements, were in fact never signed. These texts were annexed to a procès-verbal which was itself "adopted and signed" by the negotiators. The agreement and the arrangements came into force on 27 May 1946, the Swiss Federal Council having approved it on 17 April, and the Governing Body of the International Labour Organization on 27 May 1946. This was recorded in a formal Exchange of Notes[132]. This institution of signature should be considered to fall within the provisions of art. 10 of the Vienna Convention, as it serves mainly the purpose of authentification.

Signature, as consent to be bound by a treaty, is often disciplinated by precise norms of international organizations contained in acts of regulatory nature or in acts referring specifically to the particular agreement that is to be signed.

As a rule, the Headquarter Agreements were signed by the persons that had negotiated the agreements, and the authorizations were given in general, for both negotiating and signing the agreements. But in some instances the authorization for signing was given separately. This was the case of the host agreement between WHO and Egypt, when the Director-General of the WHO was authorized by the

[132] 15 UNTS, p. 377.

Assembly to sign, having been previously entrusted with the negotiation of the Agreement[133]. Moreover, it was expressly provided that the Director-General should not sign before Egypt had complied with its constitutional requirements for approval of agreements[134]. The Agreement concerned certain Privileges and Immunities to be granted to the Regional Organization of the WHO in the eastern Mediterranean area, and under the authorization given to him the Director-General concluded the Agreement in the form of exchange of letters[135].

Practice shows that as far as Headquarter Agreements are concerned, signature alone cannot be used to create international obligations for the Organization. The signature is always accompanied by an approval of the policy which the agreement is designed to implement, in the form of a resolution by a competent body[136].

Signature is sometime reserved exclusively for the head of the executive organ. In ICAO for instance, only the President of the Council may sign agreements.

However, the Secretary-General has received the authorization to conclude two Headquarter Agreements, the Headquarter Agreement with Canada[137] and the Agreement for Lease of International Civil Air Building[138].

There are instances where Headquarter Agreements were signed in different places and on a different date, the signed text or texts (if done in duplicate) presumably being transmitted by post or by courier from the first signatory to the second. This is the case of the Agreement of 10 Dec. 1951 between UNICEF and Irak concerning the activities of UNICEF in that country, registered with the UN Secretariat under no. 1682. According to the monthly statement of the Secretariat[139] this Agreement was signed at Baghdad and at Paris

---

[133] WHO, Official Records, 1948, no. 14, p. 26.

[134] Ibid., 1950, no. 28, p. 52, Resolution WHO, 383.

[135] Ibid.

[136] If the competent organ is a subsidiary organ which does not normally meet in public, it ought, in its annual report, to give full indications of the policy decisions which were adopted requiring the employment of the treaty-making power. E.g.: The Government of Mexico undertook by the letter of March 3, 1959 that privileges and immunities of the UN General Convention on Privileges and Immunities (to which Mexico has not yet acceded), to participants to ECOSOC session in Mexico City, April 1959. The UN Secretary-General states in his report for 1959 that "in his reply dated 7 April 1959 the Secretary General accepted with gratitude the offer of the Government of Mexico." This reply, it seems, was presumed to bind the Organization. For the shortcomings of this technique see Kasme, La Capacité de l'ONU de Conclure des Traités, 1960, Paris, p. 188.

[137] 96 UNTS, p. 155.

[138] ICAO, Doc. 7310-C. 846, p. 43.

[139] Doc. ST/LEG/SER. A/A/61, p. 26.

on 10 December 1951. The distance between the two cities is over 5,000 km.

When international agreements are recorded in Exchanges of Notes, it is not necessary for the two Notes to bear the same date, and frequently they do not. Unless otherwise stipulated, in such cases the agreement will enter into force as from the date of the reply[140]. The informality goes so far, that some agreements do not bear any date[141].

Approval

"Approval" by an International Organization serves the same function as ratification or approval by States. The Act of approval constitutes the conclusion of the Agreement; this means that the organ which has the right of approval itself exercises the treaty-making power.

Nevertheless, some Headquarter Agreements contain the term "ratification" referring to International Organization, but one should admit it is used with a different connotation then for States. The agreement on a regional office between the FAO and Costa Rica[142] is to be ratified, under art. 139 26 (a) by the legislative Assembly of Costa Rica and the Council of FAO. Similarly, in the preamble of the Headquarter Agreement between the FAO and Italy it is specified that the FAO Conference authorizes "the Director-General to negociate such Headquarter Agreements and to refer them to the Council of FAO for ratification[143]."

There is no uniform practice as to the approval-ratification of Headquarter Agreements:

1. Each of the parties adopts a similar procedure: The Headquarter Agreement between UNESCO and France provides in art. 32 that it enters into effect upon ratification by France and notification of approval by the UNESCO Conference[144].

2. Each of the parties adopts another procedure: The Agreement on Privileges and Immunities between WHO and France was to be signed by France and adopted by WHO[145] under the provisions of art. 13 (S. 34).

3. No provision on the organ that should approve the Headquarter Agreement on behalf of the International Organization: the Headquarter Agreement between ILO and Switzerland was said to

---

[140] See Weinstein, "Exchanges of Notes," in 29 BYIL, 1952, p. 209.

[141] E.g. Agreement between FAO and Brasil, mentioned by Socini in Op.cit. supra note 1, p. 90, footnote 65.

[142] FAO Council Report 15, p. 38; CL 15/13.

[143] UN Doc. ST/LEG/SER. B/11, p. 187.

[144] 357 UNTS, p. 26.

[145] 209 UNTS, p. 231.

enter into force upon approval by the Swiss Federal Council and the "competent authority" of the WHO[146].

4. No provision for approval by International Organization: the Headquarter Agreement between Chile and ECLA[147] stipulated at Art. XII, Section 22 (a): "This Agreement shall enter into force immediately after its ratification by the Government of Chile . . ."

In the practice of concluding Headquarter Agreements by International Organizations it is quite frequent to simplify the process by allowing the agreement to be brought into force upon signature[148].

Entry into Force

The Headquarter Agreements contain as a rule provisions regarding their entry into force. E.q.:

—"This Agreement shall be signed and shall enter into force on the date of ratification by the Government . . ."—Headquarter Agreement between the UN and Ethiopia of 18 June 1958, art. X, Section 24[149].

—"This agreement shall be brought into effect by an exchange of notes between the . . ." Headquarter Agreement between the UN and the USA of 26 June 1948, art. IX, Section 28[150].

—"This Agreement shall become effective from the date of signature"—Headquarter Agreement between the UN and Japan of 25 July 1952[151].

—"Le présent accord, de même que tout accord modificatif éventuel, entreront en vigueur à la suite de l'échange des instruments de ratification par le gouvernement de la République française et de la notification d'approbation par l'Organisation"—Agreement between France and UNESCO of 2 July 1954, art. 32.

—"This supplemental Agreement enters into force with effect from the date of entry into force of the Headquarter Agreement"—Exchange of letters of 17 July 1954 constituting a supplemental agreement between AIEA and Austria, par. 4[152].

---

[146] 26 UNTS, p. 347. In fact this Agreement was approved by the World Health Assembly. There is, at least, one case on record where an agreement received the approval of two organs, the plenary and the restricted: the Agreement on Privileges and Immunities between the WHO and Philippines signed on 22 July 1951.

[147] 314 UNTS, p. 49.

[148] This is often the case of agreements concluded in the form of exchange of notes.

[149] Doc. ONU: ST/LEG/SER. B/10, p. 232.

[150] 11 UNTS, p. 11. [151] 135 UNTS, p. 305.

[152] Doc. ONU: ST/LEG/SER. B/11, p. 240.

In some instances, the date of entry into effect is set up retroactively.

Thus an exchange of notes between the Director-General of the WHO and the Swiss Government[153] provided that the Headquarter Agreement would enter into effect, retroactively, on 17 July 1948. Mr. Zutter, on behalf of the Swiss Government, suggested in a letter that the main agreement would be "... considered as of 21st August 1948, that is to say the date of final approval of the texts by the Federal Council. It remains understood that the date of entry into force has been settled retroactively as from 17 July 1948." Dr. Chisholm, Director-General of the WHO, agreed in his reply to these provisions.

Registration[154]

The Headquarter Agreements were registered in conformity with the Regulations to give effect to art. 102 of the UN Charter adopted by the General Assembly in resolution 97 (I) with modifications contained in resolution 364 B (IV) and 482 (V) of the General Assembly[155].

The problem of sanction provided in Art. 102 paragraph 2 of the UN Charter "no party to any such treaty ... which has not been registered ... may invoke that treaty or agreement before any organ of the U.N." does not arise for International Organization since paragraph 1 of that article stipulated that the obligation to register refers to States only.

V. Some Problems of Application of the Headquarter Agreements: Application in Space and Time

Because of the fact that International Organizations have no territory, the problem of territorial application appears only in relation to one of the contracting parties, the State. The existence of what

---

[153] 26 UNTS, p. 359. This latter date was the date of approval of the two texts by the World Health Assembly (ibid., p. 361). The Agreement would thus be considered to be concluded on one date, 21 August 1948, with retroactive operation from an early date, 17 July 1948.

[154] For a discussion of the question of registration by International Organizations see Broches and Boskey, Theory and Practice of Treaty Registration with Particular Reference to the Agreements of the International Bank, 4 Netherlands International Law Review, 1957.

[155] Socini, Op.cit. supra note 1, p. 90, footnote 65, given two examples of agreements that were not registered with the UN Secretariat: the agreements concluded by FAO with Egypt in 1952 and with Thailand in 1965.

is usually called "the Headquarter district[156]" has no significance in this context since it is part of the territory of the host State[157].

The privileges and immunities granted through Headquarter Agreements are of a functional nature. The following statement by the UN Secretariat seems to clarify the question of space and time application of the material provisions of the Headquarter Agreements:

Section 11 of the General Convention and section 9 of the 1946 Agreement with Switzerland provide that representatives shall enjoy the privileges and immunities listed in those provisions "while exercising their functions and during their journey to and from the place of meeting." In 1961 the Legal Counsel replied to an inquiry made by one of the specialized agencies as to the interpretation to be given to the first part of this phrase, which is also to be found in section 13 of the Convention on the Privileges and Immunities of the Specialized Agencies.

You inquire whether the words "while exercising their functions" should be given a narrow or broad interpretation. By the former, the words could mean only "the period of time during which the representative concerned is actually doing something as a part of his functions as representative," e.g., is present in the room or building where the meeting ... is being held." By the latter, it could denote "the whole of the period during which he is present in the city where the ... meeting ... is being held."

We have not been confronted with such a question here in the United Nations, and the preparatory work on neither of the two privileges and immunities conventions throws any specific light on the point you raise. Nevertheless, I have no hesitation in believing that it was the "broad" interpretation that was intended by the authors of the Convention. This must follow from the fact that the expression "while exercising their functions" is contained in the opening paragraph and qualified each and all of the privileges and immunities provided in the sub-paragraphs, (a) through (g), that follow.

A glance at those sub-paragraphs will clearly show that the privileges and immunities provided by any of them would become meaningless if it is applicable only when the representative is "actually doing something as a part of his functions," "e.g., is present in the room or building where the meeting ... is being held." Such an interpretation would lead to the absurd conclusion that, a representative, immediately after having performed an official function, or after having left the meeting room may, under paragraph (a) for example, be arrested, or detained, or have his personal baggage seized. By the same narrow interpretation, he may, the moment he left the meeting room, have his papers confiscated, or his right to use codes

[156] See for example Art. II Section 2 of the UN-US Agreement, 11 UNTS, p. 11.

[157] An International Organization may, of course, have some territories under its administration. But this aspect is outside the scope of our discussion here.

suspended, or his courier seized, or be conscripted into national service, etc. Should such a narrow interpretation prevail, the basic purpose of the Convention, which is to assure the representatives the independent exercise of their functions, would clearly be totally defeated.

The broader interpretation is also borne out by the fact that the phrase "while exercising their functions" is immediately accompanied and complemented by the phrase "and during their journey to and from the place of meeting." In other words, "while exercising" means during the entire period of presence in the State (not city) for reasons of the conference in question. This is logical because the "journey" necessarily is that to and from the State, not the conference hall. Only this interpretation avoids absurdity and only this is consistent with the immediately following reference in sub-section (a) to "personal baggage." Therefore, in accordance with the general principle that a treaty must be interpreted to effectuate its purpose and not to lead to absurdity, it seems to me, without reference to other criteria of interpretation, that only the "broad interpretation" should have been intended by the phrase in question[158].

Third Parties

The Headquarter Agreements regulate the position of International Organizations as a whole, comprising not only the Organizations' staff but representatives of State to organizations as well, in the territory of the host State.

The representative of a State to an International Organization is not accredited to the host State in whose territory the seat of the organization is situated. Neither the staff of the organization nor the representatives of the Member States enter into direct relationship or transactions with the host State as in bilateral diplomacy. Notwithstanding this fact, the territory of the host State is the field of application of the legal status of representatives of Member States to the International Organization. The Headquarter Agreements, are, from this point of view, arrangements between international organizations and their host state, and they are not pactum in favorem tertii, because it gives rights to organization's member States. These rights are organically different from rights provided for third states by interstate treaties, as in our case, the organization exists as consisting of states, and presuming liaison with non-member states that can, in a way or other, be associated with the work of the organization.

Section 15 of the Headquarter Agreement between the United Nations and the United States provides that privileges and immunities granted to permanent representatives to the United Nations are the

[158] 2 YILC, 1967, p. 176.

same "and subject to corresponding conditions and obligations," as the host State accords to diplomatic envoys accredited to the host State. In practice, the host States trend to interpret this provision as meaning that the regime of Mission to the International Organization should be subject to particular conditions imposed, on the basis of reciprocity, upon the diplomatic missions of a particular State. This interpretation seems to us inappropriate and it is not accepted by the United Nations Secretariat too, which says that its interpretation is supported by an early official interpretation of the position by the Legal Adviser of the United States Department of State, which held it to be

clear that the Charter of the United Nations does not permit the imposition of conditions of reciprocity on the granting of privileges and immunities under article 105. Indeed the purpose of the Charter in respect of article 105 is to provide for the granting unconditionally by Member States of certain privileges and immunities to the United Nations so that it may function effectively as a world organization untrammelled in its operation by national requirements of reciprocity or national measures of retaliation among States.

The State Department Legal Adviser's opinion also notes that the Convention on the Privileges and Immunities of the United Nations "does not admit of reciprocity requirement." He continues:

The background in the negotiation of section 15 of the Headquarter Agreement indicates that the phrase "subject to corresponding conditions and obligations" was inserted by way of compromise to meet a desire on the part of the United States that persons covered by section 15 were not to receive privileges and immunities broader than those accorded to diplomatic envoys accredited to the President of the United States, and that, like diplomatic envoys, such persons might be found personae non gratae and made subject to recall. The negotiating background does not indicate that the quoted phrase was inserted for the purpose of permitting the United States to make the privileges and immunities provided for in Section 15 dependent upon reciprocity. In the case of representatives of members, and resident members of their staffs, the United States may be authorized under the headquarter agreement to bring about expulsion of personal in cases where such action appears to be required. Except for this drastic weapon which the United States may under some circumstances use, the headquarter agreement does not provide for the cancelling of privileges and immunities.

He therefore concluded that even the International Organizations Immunities Act, which has an express authority on reciprocity in its section 9, is not to be interpreted as requiring the United States Secretary of State to enforce any conditions of reciprocity in conflict with the Charter and the Headquarter Agreement, but only as not precluding him from enforcing reciprocity, where otherwise authorized to do so, merely because a foreign national happens to be connected with an International Organization. In addition, he acknowledged that the Headquarter Agreement established its own procedure for requiring a representative to leave the United States in case of abuse of his privileges of residence in activities outside his official capacity, beyond which there exists no grant of authority to withdraw privileges on any grounds determined by the host State[159].

In practice, Permanent Missions to the United Nations try to settle their problems concerning Privileges and Immunities directly with the authorities of the host State, on a bilateral basis and only after failing, they resort to the specific provisions of the Headquarter Agreements[160].

The representatives of Non-member States of an International Organization who attend meetings as observers are not beneficiary of the regime granted to the representatives of Member States under the Headquarter Agreement concluded between the International Organization and the host country or under other statutory provisions of the host State. They cannot be considered "third parties" vis-à-vis the Headquarter Agreement. When the representatives of Non-member States are specially invited to attend meetings or conferences, the representatives concerned must be granted at least functional immunities and a right of entry into the host State, even if they only attend as observers. In the case of the United Nations, they will fall under the provisions of section 11 (5) of the Headquarter Agreement with the USA as "persons invited to the Headquarter District by the United Nations . . . on official business."

---

159 2 YILC, 1967, p. 178.

160 It may be noted that in 1960 when the Chairman of the Council of Ministers of the Union of Soviet Socialist Republics attended the fifteenth session of the General Assembly, the United States declared that he should reside "in the closest proximity to the Headquarters of the United Nations" and that his movements, other than his arrival and departure, should be confined to Manhattan Island. The Union of Soviet Socialist Republics denied the authority of the United States to impose these restrictions and asked the Secretary-General to take up the matter. The Secretary-General requested the United States to reconsider its position, drawing attention to the terms of Section 11 of the Headquarter Agreement and to the interest of the United Nations as a whole that heads of governments should participate in its deliberations. The Chairman of the Council of Ministers was eventually permitted to travel to the premises maintained on Long Island by the Mission of the USSR.

Interpretation

The majority of the Headquarter Agreements contain provisions concerning their interpretation.

Firstly, the Headquarter Agreements are considered as supplementary to the General Conventions on Privileges and Immunities of the United Nations and of specialized agencies. E.g.: Section 26 of the Headquarter Agreement between the United Nations and the United States:

> The provisions of this agreement shall be complementary to the provisions of the General Convention. In so far as any provision of this agreement and any provisions of the General Convention relate to the same subject matter, the two provisions shall, wherever possible, be treated as complementary so that both provisions shall be applicable and neither shall narrow the effect of the other; but in any case of absolute conflict, the provisions of this agreement shall prevail[161].

It should be noted that the United States did not become party to the General Convention of Privileges and Immunities of the United Nations, and other States that are hosts for some specialized agencies are not parties to the Convention on Privileges and Immunities of the specialized agencies.

Secondly, the Headquarter Agreements emphasize the need to create proper conditions of work for the Organizations. So, Section 22 (c) of the Headquarter Agreement between the IAEA and Austria[162] states:

"This Agreement shall be construed in the light of its primary purpose of enabling the IAEA at its headquarters in the Republic of Austria fully and efficiently to discharge its responsibilities and fulfill its purposes."

It may be generally noted that the legal status of the United Nations in the United States is not only governed by the provisions of the Headquarter Agreement, but that also US Public Law 291 specifies certain privileges and immunities which attach to the Organization. It will therefore be necessary to refer to the provisions of this Law, as well as to those of the Headquarter Agreement in dealing with the United Nations. With regard to the specialized agencies which have concluded Headquarter Agreements, the privileges and immunities which they are granted by their host States are exclusively set out in the respective Agreements. In this connection it is necessary to recall that the basic principle of all the privileges and immunities

---

[161] UN Doc. ST/LEG/SER. B/10, p. 211.

[162] UN Doc. ST/LEG/SER. B/11, p. 327.

are set out in the relevant clause dealing with such matters, to be found in the constituent instrument of each organization. Most of these clauses stipulate that the privileges and immunities to be enjoyed by the organization shall be those which are necessary for the fulfilment of its purposes. It is proposed generally to refer only to those clauses which set out specific immunities.

Settlement of Disputes

The disputes that can arise out ouf interpretation or application of the Headquarter Agreements could refer to one of the two capacities of an International Organization: as subject of international law and as juridical person in municipal law of the host country.

As a rule, the Headquarter Agreements contain provisions to the effect that disputes between contracting parties concerning the interpretation or application of the Agreement or of any supplementary agreement which are not settled by negotiations or other agreed mode of settlement, shall be referred for final decision to a tribunal of three arbitrators. The possibility to ask for advisory opinion from the International Court of Justice is also provided for, e.g. Section 21 b of the Headquarter Agreement between the United Nations and the United States:

> The Secretary-General or the United States may ask the General Assembly to request of the International Court of Justice an advisory opinion on any legal question arising in the course of such proceedings. Pending the receipt of the opinion of the Court, an interim decision of the arbitral tribunal shall be observed by both parties. Thereafter, the arbitral tribunal shall render a final decision, having regard to the opinion of the Court[163].

The way in which the tribunal with arbitrators can be formed is not uniform. E.g.: the agreement between France and OACI provides in art. 20 that the disputes will be submitted to a unic arbitrator; The Agreement between France and FISE of 19 January 1949 stipulates in art. 10 that the disputes between the parties will be settled by the Programme Committee of the governing body of FISE.

The International Organizations cannot employ all those means at the disposal of sovereign States to act upon the partner that does not observe its treaty obligations. The difference in the international legal status between States and International Organizations is reflected in the Status of the International Court of Justice, which provides that only States have quality to apeare before the Court[164].

[163] UN Doc. ST/LEG/SER. B, p. 210.

[164] Art. 34 (1).

In such a way, International Organizations cannot stand in contentious cases before the International Court. This does not mean that the International Organizations cannot bring claims against States or that they cannot defend their rights. The International Court of Justice, as well as the United Nations General Assembly were unanimous in confirming this right of the United Nations to present international claims[165] against Member as well as Non-member States[166]. The International Organization can resort for the settlement of disputes to the majority of means provided for the settlement of disputes between States, and it has some means of its own, that individual States have no: collective measures undertaken by Member States.

Some countries among which Romania, and other socialist countries have entered with reservation the General Convention on Privileges and Immunities of the United Nations because of their well-known position toward the means stipulated by the Convention regarding the settlement of disputes.

The study prepared by the Secretariat on the practice of the United Nations, the specialized agencies and the IAEA concerning their status, privileges and immunities[167] gives numerous examples of the way in which the disputes were settled and examines the legal ground for each of the cases.

Writing on this issue, H. Chiu[168] affirms that "the lack of capacity of International Organizations in contentious cases before the International Court of Justice has compelled them to resort to methods, such as arbitration or the advisory opinion, for juridical settlement of disputes ... Such a rule, it is submitted, can no longer reflect the requirements of international life in which International Organizations are playing an increasing role. If International Organizations were granted *locus standi* as parties in contentious cases before the Court and assuming they would accept the Court's compulsory jurisdiction, the international legal character of the agreements concluded by International Organizations would perhaps be put on a much firmer and solid basis."

---

[165] See I.C.J. Reports, Advisory Opinion of April 11, 1949, p. 17, and the debates in the Sixth Committee of the IVth Session of the UN General Assembly on "United Nations."

[166] This question raises the very disputed problem of liability of states and International Organizations which didn't find as yet a general solution. For particular fields, see art. XIII of the Treaty on principles governing the activities of States in outer space of 1967.

[167] 2 YILC, p. 154.

[168] Chiu, The capacity of International Organizations to conclude treaties ..., p. 212.

We don't think that the international legal character of the agreements concluded by International Organizations depends upon the organization's capacity to stand or not in contentious cases before the Court, and we don't think that international life requires at present any modification of the now prevailing rules. The means and ways for the settlement of disputes provided for by relevant clauses of the Headquarter Agreements are sufficient to ensure an efficient application of these agreements. Practice does not offer any instances to the contrary.

Duration of the Agreement

The majority of the Headquarter Agreements contain provisions for the revision, duration of force or denounciation. One should note that, as a rule, the possibility for a State to denounce Headquarter Agreements is limited.

The Headquarter Agreements concluded by Switzerland with ILO, WHO, and OERN, as well as the agreements concluded by WHO for its regional offices, provide that if one of the parties requests, negotiations concerning the revision of the agreements should be engaged. In case these negotiations fail to bring the parties to an acceptable solution over a reasonable period of time (one year) each of the parties will have the right to denounce the Agreement (giving one or two years notice of its intention).

The Headquarter Agreements concluded by the United States with the United Nations (Sections 23 and 24) and with the OAS (Section 36) stipulate that these agreements could be terminated if the respective organization decides to change the seat of its headquarters. The Headquarter Agreement between France and UNESCO does not contain any provision concerning its denounciation by one of the parties, but in the course of elaboration of this agreement, it was stated that the UNESCO reserves its right to change the seat of its headquarters.

VI. Some Concluding Remarks

It is now generally accepted that International Organizations have the capacity to conclude treaties with all those entities which international law recognizes to be capable of being parties to agreements, provided organizations do not exceed the scope and limits of their competence in concluding such instruments and that this treaties are governed by international law.

The Vienna UN Conference on the Law of Treaties, recognizing the importance of the question of treaties concluded between States and International Organizations or between two or more International Organizations, cognizant of the varied practices of International Organizations in this respect and desirous of ensuring that the extensive experience of International Organizations in this field be utilized to the best advantage, adopted a resolution[169] recommending to the General Assembly of the United Nations that it refer to the International Law Commission the study, in consultation with the principal International Organizations, of the question of treaties concluded between States and International Organizations or between two ore more International Organizations.

We share the opinion that a Convention on the Law of Treaties of International Organizations should be elaborated as soon as possible at an international Conference.

The Conference should be opened for participation to all States, without any discrimination. As for the participation of International Organizations, the problems should be settled with priority.

The Vienna Convention on the Law of Treaties is the result of extensive studies made inside, as well as outside the United Nations and of long negotiations among States. It is, in fact, a compromise intended to satisfy the views of all nations. Because of this, the applicable provisions of the Vienna Convention on the Law of Treaties, if this is the will of states, could be incorporated in the future Convention of the Law of Treaties of International Organizations.

---

[169] UN Doc./Conf. 39/26, p. 6.

Österr. Zeitschr. f. öffentl. Recht, Suppl. 1, 105—126 (1971)

Formal Aspects of the Technical Assistance Agreements Concluded by the UN Family of Organizations

Joke M. van Wouw
Assistant Lecturer in International Law at the University of Amsterdam

It is the purpose of this study to describe the formal aspects of technical assistance agreements; its scope has been deliberately limited to the technical assistance agreements concluded by the United Nations family of organizations, that is to say the agreements concluded on their behalf by the Technical Assistance Board (TAB), which has been replaced in 1965 by the Inter-Agency Consultative Board (IACB)[1, 2].

After some general information as to the legal basis of the UN technical assistance activities it contains an analysis of the different sorts of technical assistance agreements and their contents. We will also discuss the negotiating organ on the part of the international organizations (TAB or IACB), the notion "multilateral," since this seems of particular interest with regard to the technical assistance agreements, and the legal character of the agreements, especially the question whether they are to be considered as international agreements governed by international law.

Finally, an attempt will be made to answer the question to what extent the Convention on the Law of Treaties (Vienna 1969) would apply to the technical assistance agreements.

---

[1] This excludes technical assistance agreements concluded by other international organizations, technical assistance agreements concluded by the UN and the specialized agencies under their regular budget, as well as agreements concerning the financing of economic development concluded by the UN family of organizations, for example the Special Fund agreements and the agreements concluded by the World Bank (IBRD).

[2] For a description of the United Nations technical and financial aid programmes, see Kirdar, The Structure of United Nations Economic Aid to Underdeveloped Countries, 1966.

General Background

The technical assistance operations of the UN family are based on the Charter of the UN, the constitutions of the specialized agencies and the resolutions on the matter as adopted by the respective organs of the organizations.

Only some constitutions contain specific references to technical assistance: for instance Article 2, paragraph d, of the WHO constitution of 22 July 1946 defines that one of the functions of the organization "shall be ... to furnish appropriate technical assistance ... upon the request or acceptance of Governments[3]."

Similar provisions can be found in the constitutions of FAO and UPU[4]; but others are silent: neither the Charter of the UN nor the constitutions of the other specialized agencies include particular references to the rendering of technical assistance. An implied authorization to undertake this kind of activity may, however, be found in general articles, such as Article 55 of the UN Charter, describing the functions to be performed by the organization.

For it is submitted that the competence of an international organization to initiate a certain activity is not limited by the absence of specific authorizations in the constituent instrument, but that this competence is determined by the function of an organization as originally outlined in its constitution and subsequently interpreted by the competent organs of the organization. Any resolution, therefore, which provides the legal basis for a new activity has to be regarded as a constitutional one as long as the undertaking comes within the function of an organization as outlined above and is not prohibited by its constitutional provisions[5, 6].

---

[3] The resolutions adopted on the matter by the World Health Assembly and the Executive Board of WHO can be found in the Handbook of Resolutions and Decisions of the World Health Assembly and the Executive Board, Tenth Edition, covering the period June 1948—February 1969, Geneva, May 1969.

[4] Article I, paragraph 3 (a) in the FAO constitution, and Article 1, paragraph 3 in the UPU constitution.

[5] Compare Chiu, The Capacity of International Organizations to Conclude Treaties and the Special Legal Aspects of the Treaties so Concluded, 1966, p. 169. He submits that "the constitutional basis of technical assistance agreements should not be rested on any implied authority from one or more particular provisions of a constitution," because such an "interpretation does not appear applicable to at least some constitutions of the specialized agencies since the latter usually contain no similar provisions"; although the words "no similar provisions" seem to refer

Since the founders of the UN and the specialized agencies could in no way foresee and regulate in advance what would be the evolution of international contacts, what new activities would have to be undertaken and what legal provisions would have to be devised for them, it follows that for most substantive activities the body of resolutions elaborating and interpreting the basic instrument constitutes virtually the only source of information on the legal system underlying a particular activity[7].

The legal principles which evolve from the resolutions on technical assistance[8] show that international organizations cannot provide a country with assistance by unilateral decision[9]. The guiding principles of the Expanded Programme of Technical Assistance (EPTA) (since 1965 United Nations Development Programme (UNDP)), as annexed to the Economic and Social Council (ECOSOC) Resolution 222 A (IX), state explicitly that:

> "Technical assistance for economic development of underdeveloped countries shall be rendered by the participating organizations only in agreement with the Governments concerned and on the basis of requests received from them" (para. 2 (a))[10].

---

back to Article 55 of the Charter (general article on international economic and social co-operation), it appears that, after reading the footnote, reference is really made to specific constitutional provisions which authorize the rendering of technical assistance. Consequently the rejection of the "implied authority" argument seems to be less convincing, the more so as he continues to say that the conclusion of the technical assistance agreements has to be "within the broad purposes" of an organization. Since "the broad purposes" can only be found in the constitution (and subsequent practice), Chiu's reasoning leads back to the argument which he has rejected before.

[6] See "Certain Expenses of the United Nations, ICJ, Advisory Opinion, p. 168: "But when the Organization takes action which warrants the assertion that it was appropriate for the fulfilment of one of the stated purposes of the United Nations, the presumption is that such action is not ultra vires the Organization."

[7] Feuer, Les Aspects Juridiques de l'Assistance Technique, 1957, pp. 19—20.

[8] The resolutions which make up the legal framework for the United Nations Development Programme (UNDP) can be found in International Organisation and Integration, A Collection of the Texts of Documents relating to the United Nations, its Related Agencies and Regional International Organisations, Kluwer, Sijthoff, 1968.

[9] I. Detter, Law Making by International Organizations, Stockholm 1965, p. 171 ff.

[10] Moreover, para. 2 (i) provides that the technical assistance furnished shall not be a means of foreign economic and political interference in the internal affairs of the country and not be accompanied by any consideration of a political nature. ECOSOC resolution 1020 (XXXVII) which launches the United Nations Development Programme (UNDP) does not encroach upon these principles (paras. 1 and 2). This resolution has been approved by GA Res. 2029 (XX) of 22 November 1965, the "merger" Resolution.

This principle which lies at the root of international law[11] implies that the rules set up by the resolutions governing the Programme only become obligations of requesting governments by virtue of express consent, and therefore the conclusion of some sort of agreement is needed.

Different Sorts of Technical Assistance Agreements

There exist two different sorts of technical assistance agreements: the standard agreements and the mutually agreed programmes of operations (plans of operations).

The standard agreements embody the administrative framework in which assistance shall be carried out. Their provisions can be traced back to the first report of TAB to TAC[12]; annex I to this document contains suggested standard clauses for inclusion in agreements on technical assistance between the participating organizations and the recipient countries.

In drawing up the standard clauses the Board sought to ensure that: (a) all subjects mention of which was likely to facilitate the effective provision and utilization of technical services were dealt with, and (b) the agreements to be negotiated were uniform in so far as circumstances would permit. Articles on the furnishing of technical assistance, the co-operation of the government with respect to the provision of technical assistance, the administrative and financial obligations of the parties, facilities, privileges and immunities, and general provisions regarding entry into force, modification, termination, etc. were considered as essential to the smooth operation of the Programme.

---

[11] See, for instance, Art. 2, par. 7 of the Charter, and the "Lotus-case" (PCIJ A 9, p. 18) where it is stated that "International law governs relations between independent States. The rules of law binding upon States therefore emanate from their own free will as expressed in conventions or by usages generally accepted as expressing principles of law and established in order to regulate the regulations between these co-existing independent communities or with a view to the achievement of common aims. Restrictions upon the independence of States cannot therefore be presumed."

[12] Document E/1742. TAC stands for the Technical Assistance Committee. Under EPTA procedures it was composed of States members of the UN or members of the specialized agencies. The Committee, *inter alia,* examined and approved the programme presented to it by TAB, made critical examinations for ECOSOC of activities undertaken and results achieved under the Programme and received reports from TAB on the implementation of and disbursements of funds under the Programme. TAB will be discussed below (p. 114).

The first agreement concluded along these lines was the one entered into between the UN, FAO, ICAO, ILO, UNESCO, and WHO on the one side and the United Kingdom as Administrating Power of the Territories of Cyrenaica and Tripolitania on the other[13].

Since the "Basic Agreements for the provision of technical assistance" only embodied the frame in which technical assistance had to be furnished they envisaged in their first Article, the conclusion of "Supplementary Agreements." These agreements were meant to govern the specific terms of each technical assistance operation[14]. To eliminate the need for formal negotiations for each operation TAB decided to change this practice and drew up the text of a "Revised Standard Agreement concerning technical assistance" in March 1954 which would govern the provision of technical assistance by all organizations participating in the Programme on an uniform basis[15].

Since that time no more Supplementary Agreements were negotiated; assistance is given under "mutually agreed annual programmes of operations" (plans of operations) concluded through correspondence between the agency (agencies) concerned and the requesting government.

The first Revised Standard Agreement (standard agreement) was concluded with the government of Burma[16]. Once such an agreement is concluded with a recipient government it supersedes and replaces the previous basic agreement if there is one[17].

As stated above TAB envisaged the technical assistance agreements to be as uniform as cicumstances would permit. The term "standard" indicates that uniformity is still a characteristic of the agreements. It seems legitimate to conclude that the conditions for the furnishing of technical assistance are primarily set unilaterally by the organizations and that consequently the requesting government has, apart from minor points, no bargaining power, that is to say no power to negotiate the fundamental rules underlying the Programme; States who apply for technical assistance find themselves in a "take it or leave it" position.

---

[13] 76 UNTS (1950), p. 120.

[14] References to Supplementary Agreements can be found in Cumulative Index No. 1 to the United Nations Treaty Series.

[15] E/2842 (8th report of TAB to TAC), p. 71; E/2965 (annual report of TAB for 1956), p. 65; E/3080 (annual report of TAB for 1957), p. 62.

[16] 376 UNTS, p. 122.

[17] See, for instance, Art. VI, para. 4, of the agreements contained in 264 UNTS, p. 94; 248, p. 37 and 259, p. 426; further Art. VI, para. 2, of the agreement contained in 227 UNTS, p. 153.

Contents of the Agreements

The contents of the standard agreements (or "umbrella agreement" as they are called by Sharp[18]) can be summarized as follows[19]:

(a) a preamble in which the parties state that in a spirit of friendly co-operation they have entered into the agreement to give effect to the resolutions and decisions relating to technical assistance of the organizations, which are intended to promote the economic and social progress and development of peoples;

(b) there follow Articles dealing with:

(i) the furnishing of technical assistance; under this head the organizations, acting jointly or separately, and the government undertake to co-operate in arranging, on the basis of the requests received from the government and approved by the organizations concerned, mutually agreeable programmes of operations for the carrying out of technical assistance activities. Such technical assistance shall be furnished and received in accordance with the relevant resolutions and decisions of the assemblies, conferences and other organs of the organizations and may consist of making available the services of experts, organizing and conducting seminars etc., awarding scholarships etc., preparing and executing pilot projects etc., and any other form of technical assistance which may be agreed upon;

(ii) the co-operation of the government concerning technical assistance;

(iii) the administrative and financial obligations of the participating organizations;

(iv) the administrative and financial obligations of the recipient government;

(v) privileges and immunities. All the agreements contain a provision to the effect that the requesting government shall apply to the organizations and their agents the Convention on the Privileges and Immunities of the United Nations where it concerns the UN, the Convention on the Privileges and Immunities of the Specialized Agencies in respect of the agencies, and the Agreement on the Privileges and Immunities of the IAEA where IAEA is concerned[20];

(c) a number of general clauses which comprise entry into force, modification, termination, settlement of disputes, and related questions.

Most standard agreements enter into force upon signature. However, some agreements provide that they will enter into force on the

---

[18] Sharp, Field Administration, 1961.

[19] See the Technical Assistance Board and Special Fund Field Manual, ed. II, 1 August 1965, Section IX-C, Organization and Legislative Framework.

[20] 374 UNTS, p. 147.

date on which the Chairman of TAB (casu quo the Administrator of UNDP) receives from the government a notification of the approval of the agreement by the competent constitutional organ or organs; they shall be provisionally applied as from the date of signature[21]. In some instances ratification on the part of the government is provided for[22].

Duly appointed representatives of the organizations and the government sign the agreement. On the part of the participating organizations the Executive Chairman of TAB (casu quo the Administrator of UNDP) signs or authorizes signature on behalf of the organizations[23]. Authorization is frequently given to the Resident Representatives or regional representatives of TAB (IACB)[24, 25].

The agreements may be modified by agreement between the organizations and the government. No special procedure to this end has been anticipated[26]. Termination is possible by "all or any of the

---

[21] 253 UNTS, p. 12; 321, p. 134; Tractatenblad van het Koninkrijk der Nederlanden 1967, no. 57.

[22] 537 UNTS, p. 214.

[23] ECOSOC Resolution 433 A (XIV) approves of the Executive Chairman's terms of reference as contained in Resolution no. 3 of TAC (E/2238, Annex II). ECOSOC Resolution 1020 (XXXVII) regarding the consolidation of the Special Fund and the Expanded Programme does not seem to impair the original assignment.

See also International Organization and Integration, op.cit., p. 307.

[24] 231 UNTS, p. 267.

[25] The terms of reference of the Resident Representative can be found in UN Doc. TAB/R. 275 and Corr. 1. See also International Organisation and Integration, op.cit., p. 307. For a detailed study of his role and functions see Stoll, Le Statut Juridique du Représentant Résident du Bureau de l'Assistance Technique des N.U. dans l'Etat òu il est Accrédité, AFDI, 1964; Schaaf, The Role of Resident Representatives of the UN Technical Assistance Board, Int. Org., Vol. 14, p. 548; and UN Doc. DP/CM/FIELD/44 and E/AC. 49/3.

[26] Sometimes it is stated that the agreement may be modified "by agreement between the Organizations *concerned* and the government" (537 UNTS, p. 226); other agreements refer to the participating organizations as "Organization(s)" (540 UNTS, p. 122). Both instances do not seem to conform to the standard form of the agreements. Modification would affect *all* the organizations which are party to the agreement. Examples of modification can be found in 529 UNTS, p. 329; 550, p. 424; 511, p. 270, and 519, p. 396. Most of these concern the adding of IAEA and UPU as parties to the agreement and result from an exchange of letters constituting an agreement amending the standard agreement. This also seems the best legal way to make the United Nations Industrial Development Organization (UNIDO) a party to already existing standard agreements. UNIDO has become a participating and executing agency of UNDP pursuant to GA Resolution 2151 (XXI) of 17 November 1966. An exchange of letters between the Administrator and the requesting State would meet the modification requirements and would at the same time imply UNIDO's consent since the Administrator acts on behalf of all the participating organizations.

Organizations as far as they are respectively concerned," or by the government upon written notice to the other parties and shall take effect 60 days after receipt of such notice. Termination has the effect of inactivating any supplementary agreement or plan or operation[27].

All agreements contain a provision regarding the settlement of disputes relating to interpretation or application of the agreements stating that "Any relevant matter for which no provision is made in the Agreement shall be settled by the Government and by the Organizations concerned in keeping with the relevant resolutions and decisions of the assemblies, conferences, councils and other organs of the Organizations," and that "Each party ... shall give full and sympathetic consideration to any proposal for such settlement advanced by the other party." Only very rarely is mention made of a procedure for the settlement of disputes which may arise with respect to matters which are dealt with *in* the agreements. The agreement concluded by the Netherlands, for example, on behalf of Surinam and the Netherlands Antilles, refers such disputes to arbitration[28].

At first this appears to be a rather meagre result; one could say that if a party to a dispute has to rely on the "full and sympathetic" feelings of the other party or parties, an arrangement satisfactory to both parties is not very likely to produce itself. Moreover, matters which are dealt with *in* the agreements are not covered by this phrase, although one may rely on the preamble where it is stated that the parties have entered into the agreement in a "spirit of friendly co-operation." Practice, however, does not seem to be much troubled by the absence of exhaustive legal provisions. First of all the modification clause provides an opportunity to change the contents of the agreements by simple exchange of letters; proposals originating from TAB to that effect have been accepted by the governments without any difficulty[29]. Secondly, it is in the interest of both parties to safeguard the smooth operation of the agreement, since the recipient government is dependent on the services of the organizations, whereas raising the question in some plenary organ or in the Economic and Social Council would do no good to an organization's reputation. Lastly, there is always the possibility to terminate the agreement on both sides.

---

[27] An example of termination can be found in 535 UNTS, p. 412; in a letter, dated 10 March 1965, the Department of Foreign Affairs of the Republic of Indonesia communicated its decision to terminate the standard agreement.

[28] See Tractatenblad van het Koninkrijk der Nederlanden, 1967, no. 57.

[29] For instance 503 UNTS, p. 238; the amendment concerns the adding of IAEA and UPU as Participating Organizations, slight changes in the local cost provisions and the exclusion of technical assistance rendered under the regular programmes of the organizations from the scope of the standard agreement.

As stated above the plans of operations complement the standard agreements in the sense that they contain specific project descriptions. Since assistance under EPTA (UNDP/Technical Assistance (TA) Sector) consists of experts, fellowships and/or equipment, the actual project will give details on the number of experts, which agency will provide the experts, which agency will provide fellowships and equipment, and on the counterpart support to be made available by the requesting State[30]. If, for instance, a project on economic planning is launched, a manpower expert may be provided by the ILO, while a macroeconomist will be provided by the UN. It will depend on the nature of the project which expert will act as teamleader and co-ordinator of the different tasks; the agency which has the major share in the project will have to assume the co-ordinating function. However, this does in no way encroach upon the responsibilities of each expert towards his own agency under his own job description[31].

The Regulation for registration and publication as adopted by the General Assembly at its first session[32] stipulates in Article 4 that every treaty or international agreement to which the UN is a party, has to be registered ex officio by the Secretariat. Since, so far, the UN has been a party to every basic- or standard agreement, all of them have been registered. Neither the supplementary agreements nor the plans of operations have, as a rule, been registered. The Repertory of Practice[33] on Article 104 of the Charter provides some clarification on this point by stating that agreements concerning technical assistance are "essentially administrative arrangements." Whereas this could certainly not apply to the basic- or standard agreements, it

---

[30] WHO uses the text of a model plan of operation either for plans of operation in connexion with a revised standard agreement for projects financed from the Technical Assistance component of UNDP or a WHO basic agreement or for tripartite plans of operation involving UNICEF.

WHO Manual, 1 August 1968.

[31] A change in policy can be noted with regard to the division of responsibilities. In the general execution of the project and day-to-day operations the experts, both belonging to the teamleader's organization and to the other organization(s) participating in the project, may become responsible to the co-ordinator/teamleader. In such a case the teamleader will act as the sole spokesman for the project vis-à-vis the government. Experts of the other organizations may also become financially dependent on the organization to which the teamleader belongs. With regard to Special Fund projects, this practice is already common and has been followed for a long time. It is referred to as "sub-contracting." In such a case the organization which retains the overall responsibility for the execution of the project and provides the money, is called the "Executing Agency" whereas the "service-rendering" organization is referred to as the "Participating Agency."

[32] GA Resolution 97 (I).

[33] Repertory of Practice of UN Organs, N.Y. 1955, Vol. 5, p. 330.

seems to explain why the plans of operations have been excluded from the range of instruments to be registered.

Reasons of a purely practical nature must have caused this labeling[34], for, as submitted below[35] as to substance both types of agreements are governed by international law.

Negotiating Organs

How does the treaty-making process evolve on the part of the international organizations participating in EPTA (UNDP)?

Within TAB[36] (IACB)[37] the respective functions of the organizations seem to be conclusive; the scope of their functions is to be deduced from the relevant constitutional provisions and the interpretation subsequently made by the competent organs. A further delimination of functions is contained in the co-operation agreements concluded between the UN and the specialized agencies[38] and the specialized agencies *inter se*[39].

Whenever its function corresponds to a need within the requesting State, an organization participating in EPTA (UNDP) will be a

---

[34] This view also finds expression in the Report to the President ... by the Chairman of the United States Delegation, the Secretary of State: "Experience had indicated that the registration of every international agreement is unnecessary because many of them are of minor importance and of temporary effect." Department of State Publication 2349 (Conference Series 71), p. 154.

[35] See p. 120 f.

[36] The Technical Assistance Board was set up under ECOSOC Resolution 222 (IX) of 15 August 1949, consisting of representatives of the UN and the specialized agencies which participate in EPTA. The functions of the Board were to co-ordinate and supervise operations under EPTA and to consolidate the requests of each country into an overall programme. The Board made periodic reports to TAC. See Kirdar, op.cit., pp. 32, 33.

[37] The Inter-Agency Consultative Board is the successor of TAB under the UN Development Programme (ECOSOC Resolution 1020 (XXXVII)). The Board advises the Management on the programmes and projects submitted by governments through the Resident Representatives, prior to the submission of these programmes to the Governing Council for approval. The Governing Council is the successor of TAC.

[38] For instance Art. 1 of the agreement between the UN and the ILO—which served as a model for all subsequent UN-agency agreements—provides that: "The United Nations recognizes the International Labour Organization as a specialized agency responsible for taking such action as may be appropriate under its basic instrument for the accomplishment of the purposes set forth therein."

[39] See Articles 2 and 3 of the agreement between IAEA and IMCO, IMCO Basis Documents II.

party to the standard agreement. As a consequence, the decision to conclude a particular agreement will always be based on unanimity between the organizations ultimately taking part in the agreement[40].

The same will apply to the plans of operations, the only difference being that since the scope of their object is limited to specific assistance projects, few organizations will consider it to be within their function to participate in the undertaking[41].

This brings us to another question: do we have to characterize the technical assistance agreements as bilateral, multilateral or do neither of these notions cover the juridical nature of the agreements?

That the standard technical assistance agreements do not constitute bilateral agreements can best be illustrated by their termination provision which states that the agreement may be terminated by all or any of the organizations so far as they are respectively concerned[42]. If, for instance, one organization would for some reason or another cease to take part in the agreement, it should be possible that it continues to function between the others and the requesting State.

What are the criteria for calling an agreement multilateral? First, it seems that more than two subjects of international law have to take part in the agreement and, secondly, every party should be entitled, respectively be subject to rights and obligations towards any other party. As far as the contents are concerned, these rights and obligations do not necessarily have to be the same; the UNCTAD agreement, for instance, embodies rights and obligations which differ as to their substance, dependent on whether a State party to the agreement belongs to the group of developed or to the group of developing countries. The *existence* of legal relations between all the parties can be considered, however, a distinctive feature of multilateral agreements[43]. This structure characterizes the traditional type of multilateral agreement: the so-called law-making treaty, which is "con-

---

[40] This would also seem to have its implications with regard to the question whether TAB (IACB) has some sort of independent juridical personality. We agree with Kirdar, op.cit., pp. 31, 32, that it has not, the more since the Chairman (c.q. the Administrator) signs the agreement *on behalf* of the participating organizations. See also p. 116.

[41] Sometimes, however, a whole range of experts and fellowships is applied for, especially when the requesting State has recently become independent.

[42] In some agreements the world 'organizations' is even written as follows: "Organization(s)." See, for instance, 540 UNTS, p. 110.

[43] See Strupp-Schlochauer, Wörterbuch des Völkerrechts, 1960, p. 252. Bindschedler defines a multilateral treaty (Kollektivvertrag) as follows: "Unter Kollektiv- oder multilateralen Verträgen versteht man Verträge, die mindestens drei, in der Regel eine größere Zahl von Staaten umfassen, wobei jeder Mitgliedstaat als Träger von Rechten und Pflichten gegenüber jedem anderen auftritt."

cluded for the purpose of laying down general rules of conduct among a considerable number of States[44]."

As regards the standard technical assistance agreements the first requirement is certainly fulfilled: the participating organizations and the government are mentioned separately and by name in the preamble and together with the signature, while they are later on referred to as "the Organizations" and "the government." The second criterion, however, does not seem to be fulfilled, because what has been established constitutes in fact only a series of parallel bilateral relations between each of the organizations on the one side and the State on the other. The relationship between the organizations among themselves does not form part of the agreements[45]. The tying together of a number of bilateral relations in one single instrument—the agreement—is certainly due to reasons of pure administrative efficiency.

The same can be said of the signature which is usually performed by the Executive Chairman (c.q. Administrator) on behalf of the participating organizations. That it concerns here an act of representation which has resulted from practical reasoning can be illustrated by a letter from the Resident Representative of the UN TAB in Pakistan to the government of Pakistan[46], where the Chairman refers to himself as "representing the United Nations and the signatory Specialized Agencies[47].

Because of the above the question arises how to qualify the standard technical assistance agreements. Two alternatives present themselves: we could follow Bindschedler: after having defined multilateral treaties as treaties which comprise at least three States while every party should be entitled, resp. be subject to rights and obligations towards any other party[48], he introduces a further distinction by pointing at treaties which create rights and obligations between some of the parties only. He denotes such treaties as "unechte oder Halb-Kollektivverträge (traités mi-collectifs)." By way of example he mentions the peace treaties concluded by the Allied Powers with Bulgaria, Finland, Italy, Roumania and Hungary from 1947 and concludes that "es fraglich erscheint, ob der Vertrag zwischen den Partnern der gleichen Gruppe ebenfalls Rechte und Pflichten schafft."

The standard agreements would certainly fall within this category of "semi-multilateral" or "Halb-Kollektivverträge," because they are

[44] Oppenheim-Lauterpacht, International Law, Vol. I, p. 878.

[45] This relationship is dealt with in agreements and working arrangements between the organizations. See, for instance, as far as the ILO is concerned: The ILO and Technical Co-operation, International Labour Conference, Fifty-first session, Geneva 1967, Appendix II (Co-ordination of Technical Co-operation).

[46] 540 UNTS, p. 124.

[47] See note 40 on p. 115.

[48] See p. 115.

concluded by more than two parties and establish legal relations only between some of them.

The second possibility would be to call them simply multilateral agreements and to interpret the word "multilateral" in a general way so as to include also instruments which establish legal relations between some of the parties only. For one could argue that, since international life confronts us at all times with phenomena which are the outcome of practice, it would be ploughing the sands to devise new classifications the minute a new type of legal activity presents itself. This interpretation would depart little from the traditional definition of multilateral treaties as reflected by Bindschedler[48a].

The choice between these two possibilities does not seem to be a very crucial one. The difference relates exclusively to the question whether legal relations have been established between all the parties to the treaty or only between some of them, and does not purport to the substance of the treaty obligations. Since this looks a bit like introducing distinctions where no basic difference in substance exists, there seems to be no reason, so far, to abandon the traditional conception of multilaterality as outlined above[49].

That the nature of the obligations assumed constitutes the most important element will be illustrated below[50, 51].

[48a] See p. 115. [49] See p. 115 f.

[50] See p. 124 under point 6.

[51] Rosenne, United Nations Treaty Practice, in RdC, Vol. 86, p. 302, states that, referring to the first basic agreement concluded between the UN organizations on the one hand and the United Kingdom as Administering Power on the other (76 UNTS, p. 120), "although this Agreement is bipartite in form, in the sense that all the Organizations join together as parties of the first part, in fact it is multipartite, for it envisages supplementary agreements to be made between the Administering Power and one or more of the Organizations, so that in due course the individual Organizations may well come to have uneven obligations *inter se.*"

This does not seem to clarify much: first of all it is not quite clear what Rosenne means by the phrase "bipartite in form, in the sense that all the Organizations join together as parties of the first part"; if one takes into consideration the characteristics of the standard agreements as outlined above (p. 116), such a denotation does not stand its ground, because first of all, more than two parties are involved, and secondly separate treaty relations have been established between them, or rather between some of them. It appears, however, that Rosenne does not refer to these criteria, but the contents of the obligations, since in proving his contention that the basic agreements are "in fact ... multipartite": he continues by pointing at the uneven obligations which would result from the supplementary agreements.

Apart from the fact that it is difficult to understand how the legal nature of an agreement can be deduced from subsequent agreements, which are legally speaking separate instruments (see below, p. 120 f.), it is submittet that the distinction 'bipartite—multipartite' does in no way relate to the contents of an agreement; this has been illustrated above by the UNCTAD example.

As far as the plans of operations are concerned legal reasoning will, generally speaking, follow the same line. As mentioned before, projects result from an exchange of letters between UNDP (the organization(s) concerned) and the government. They contain separate job descriptions of the experts to be appointed, and details concerning fellowships and equipment.

Parallel legal relations are established, therefore, between the organizations on the one hand and the State on the other hand; for it is not well feasible that in case one organization would cease to take part in the project, the whole project would fall to the ground. If, for instance, an ILO manpower expert would have to withdraw from a project, the macro-economist could as a rule continue his job, the more so as most experts will have acquired such an allround field knowledge that they will be able to continue the project in the event that one or several experts from another organization would have to withdraw.

So far, there seems to exist no basic legal difference between the standard agreements and the plans of operations. In fact both contain a series of bilateral relations, which for reasons of administrative efficiency, run through UNDP and are, for the same reason, laid down in one and the same instrument: either the standard agreement, or the plan of operation.

It may occur, however, that due to the nature of the project the obligations of the different organizations get so interlinked, that it becomes hard to distinguish separate bilateral treaty relations: a project on occupational health and safety, for instance, constitutes such an organic whole that an industrial hygienist, provided by WHO, in the carrying out of his job, will have to rely on ILO experts in the fields of occupational health and worksmen's compensation and occupational safety. This has probably been the reason why the organizations consider to introduce the Special Fund practice of subcontracting[52] also in the Technical Assistance Sector of UNDP.

In the event this practice will be introduced on a more permanent basis where it concerns such "interlinked" projects, we need not worry anymore about the meaning of the notion multilateral, because in such a case the plan of operation will constitute a bilateral agreement between the "Executing Agency" and the State[53].

---

[52] See note 31 on p. 113.

[53] Only in case this would not become common practice on may wonder whether it would not be appropriate to introduce McNair's terminology (McNair, The Law of Treaties, Oxford 1961, pp. 29, 30).

He distinguishes between bipartite and multipartite treaties on the one hand and bilateral and multilateral treaties on the other, in saying that "it would be

Do technical assistance agreements provide new elements which would necessitate revaluation of the traditional notion "multilateral" as outlined above[54]?

The standard agreements, as well as the plans of operations contain a series of bilateral relations; reason for introducing new distinctions could be found in the number of the parties to the agreement, but not in the substance of the treaty obligations. Is it in such a case justified to make new distinctions as Bindschedler[55] does? It is submitted that it is not; for no difference in legal consequences (for example in the event of breach of treaty obligations and termination) would be covered by a distinction which merely relates to the number of the parties. The decisive criterion in introducing new classifications should be the substantial question whether the treaty in fact contains separate treaty relations or not: the question of the divisibility of obligations, because only in that event, as stated above, legal consequences will be different. It is clear, for instance, that if one organization ceased to take part in a standard agreement it would remain in force between the other organizations and the State. Likewise, most plans of operations will continue to function as experts will continue their tasks according to their job descriptions.

Concluding we may say that the traditional definition, that a multilateral treaty is a treaty in which more than two subjects of international law take part, while every party should be entitled, resp. be subject to rights and obligations towards any other party, seems satisfactory. For the substantial question whether the treaty in fact contains separate treaty relations or not is covered. The only point which is not covered by this definition relates to the formal issue whether treaty relations have been established between all the parties or not, a distinction which is not too important for the reasons stated above.

---

convenient if the terms 'bipartite' and 'multipartite' could be used to denote a treaty between two parties and a treaty between many parties, regardless of the contents of the treaty, while the term 'bilateral treaty' was reserved to denote a treaty which contains obligations, or a render and a counter-render, exchanged between two sides, and to which there may be on either or on both 'sides' only one party or several parties." Likewise, he continues, "the term 'multilateral treaty' should denote one containing three or more 'sides' or 'parties' in this sense and creating obligations between each possible pair or some of them." In this context the plans of operations will constitute multipartite bilateral treaties, the term 'multipartite' denoting the number of the parties, and the term 'bilateral' relating to the nature of the obligations assumed.

Characterizing the plans of operations as "multipartite bilateral" would in such a case be attractive, for calling them just 'bilateral' would leave aside an important element: the plurality of subjects.

[54] See p. 115 f. [55] See p. 116 f.

To fill this gap we may fall back on McNair and introduce the words "or some of them" in the definition, so that it would read as follows: "a multilateral treaty is a treaty in which more than two subjects of international law take part while a party to the treaty is entitled, resp. subject to rights and obligations towards any other party or some of them."

It will be for the drafters of a possible new convention on the law of treaties concluded by international organizations to examine the question, and to decide whether the above definition would meet the exigencies of international life.

Are the Technical Assistance Agreements International Agreements Governed by International Law?

In order to constitute an agreement governed by international law, at least one party to the agreement needs to be subject of international law and no other legal regime should have been provided for to govern its provisions.

This is not the place to deal with the international personality of international organizations, nor with their treaty-making capacity. This has been done exhaustively by other writers[56].

As stated above[57] the agreements dealing with technical assistance constitute, according to the UN Repertory of Practice[58], "essentially administrative arrangements" lacking legal character[59].

Lauterpacht, in his Second Report on the Law of Treaties[60], does not agree with this view; he submits that "the codification of the law of treaties ought to provide an opportunity not for devitalising such legal element as is contained in international instruments but for salvaging from them any existing element of legal obligation."

As to the rules governing the standard technical assistance agreements, the 'existing element of legal obligation' is easy to find if one only looks at the titles of the respective Articles mentioning the administrative and financial obligations of the organizations and the government.

---

[56] Chiu, op.cit.

Weissberg, The International Status of the United Nations, N.Y., London 1961.

Schneider, Treaty-Making Power of International Organizations, Droz. 1963.

Seyersted, International Personality of International Organizations, The Indian Journal of International Law, Vol. IV, 1964.

[57] See p. 113 f.

[58] N.Y. 1955, Vol. 5, p. 330.

[59] See Weissberg, op.cit., p. 61.

[60] UN Doc. A/CN. 4/87, p. 11 (1954).

As to the legal regime underlying the standard agreements, they refer themselves to the relevant resolutions and decisions of the assemblies, conferences and other organs of the organizations[61]. Since, moreover, no reference is made in any part of them to municipal law, one has to conclude that the proper law of the participating organizations as supplemented by the rules of general international law constitutes the legal regime governing the agreements.

Neither the uniformity of the standard agreements nor the fact that the requesting State has as a rule no bargaining position with regard to its contents encroach upon the legal validity of the agreement under international law. Similarly, the legal validity of an insurance contract under civil law is beyond doubt, although the conditions have been unilaterally set by the insurance company.

The same reasoning seems to apply to the plans of operations, although one may question whether it is appropriate to treat them as such in all cases; practice with regard to registration has already shown that efficient administration sometimes asks for different labels[62].

Giving different names, however, does in no way imply the exclusion of a group of instruments from the scope of international agreements governed by international law; if administrative practice requires a different treatment in one instance, this has no consequences whatsoever with regard to the application of the law of treaties to the remainder. This will be illustrated in the next chapter.

To What Extent Would the Convention on the Law of Treaties Apply to the Technical Assistance Agreements?

The following points seem worth mentioning:

1) One might inquire whether some sort of full powers (Articles 7 and 8 of the Vienna Convention) would be desirable in the treaty-making practice of international organizations.

With regard to the conclusion of technical assistance agreements full powers do not seem required. As stated above, it is a rule that either the Executive Chairman (c.q. Administrator) or the Resident Representative signs the agreement. Their terms of reference as laid

---

[61] See above, p. 110. Reference is also made to the application of some international treaties, such as the Convention on the Privileges and Immunities of the UN, etc. See above, p. 110 f.

[62] Another question is whether they will be considered as international treaties at the national level; again practical reasons, for instance the cumbersome procedure of approval by parliament, may cause different labeling.

down in the resolutions of the Economic and Social Council[63] are known to any requesting State, for they submit explicitly to the regime of resolutions as established by the organizations in the first Article of the standard agreement. One could very well contend that this constitutes one of the circumstances, referred to in Article 7, paragraph 1 b, of the Vienna Convention, which shows the intention of the parties to dispense with full powers. This would apply it seems, even when a non-member State of the UN or one of the specialized agencies requests technical assistance.

Then, the question arises what happens in the event the Chairman (c.q. the Administrator) exceeds his competence as circumscribed in his terms of reference. Although, according to the above, the resulting treaty would be without any legal effect (probably voidable), it is proposed to introduce here the 'manifest criterion' as used in Article 46 concerning the provisions of internal law regarding competence to conclude treaties. For can we really expect a less-developed country, which has just become a member of the UN and the specialized agencies, to go through all the resolutions underlying EPTA (UNDP) before it starts negotiating the standard agreement? Even for a country which has been a member for years, it must be quite a problem to trace the legal regime on which the technical assistance operations have been founded. Bringing in the 'manifest criterion' may give a hand in overcoming this practical difficulty: the treaty will only be without legal effect in case violation of terms of reference was objectively evident to the requesting State.

2) As mentioned above[64], TAB approved in March 1954 a new standard text of the basic agreement between participating organizations and governments for the provision of technical assistance. Since that time most recipient governments have signed the new standard agreement.

Since we are confronted here with two successive treaties dealing with the same subject-matter, the question arises to what extent Article 30 of the Vienna Convention would apply to technical assistance agreements. The standard agreements all contain a provision to the effect that they shall supersede and replace the earlier basic agreements concerning technical assistance[65]. Since, according to the general rule laid down in Article 34 of the Vienna Convention

---

[63] The Resident Representative is moreover supplied with a kind of model letter setting forth his functions, enumerating facilities and services to be provided for him by the government, etc. In effect this letter serves as his "credentials" to the government to which he is assigned. See Stoll, op.cit., pp. 514, 536.

[64] See p. 108 f.

[65] See, for instance, 227 UNTS, p. 153; 248, p. 37; 259, p. 426.

a party *only* to the earlier agreement can never be affected by such a provision, one may wonder whether the earlier basic agreement would not remain in force between the party *only* to the earlier agreement and the other parties which subsequently concluded a new standard agreement. Because of the particular nature of the technical assistance agreements—as mentioned above[66] they contain a series of bilateral relations between the participating organizations on the one side and the State on the other—the party *only* to the earlier agreement could not be but one of the participating organizations, which for one reason or another, has been left out as a party to the second standard agreement. Again because of the bilateral relations structure of the agreements, there seems to be no reason why Article 30, para. 4 (b) could not be applied in such a case to the effect that the old basic agreement would continue to function between the organization which is a party *only* to this agreement and the other parties to the basic agreement. The new standard agreement would function at the same time where it concerns the other paricipating organizations and the State.

Attractive as the construction may appear from a theoretical viewpoint, the practice of concluding new standard technical assistance agreements does reveal no instances where organizations have been dropped as parties to the new instrument. On the contrary, the growth of international contacts and the increasing need for technical assistance in various fields with the developing countries have caused a greater number of specialized agencies to join in the technical assistance operations of EPTA (UNDP), and especially the more technical agencies such as ITU and WMO have been added as participating agencies to the new standard agreements when they were presented for signature to the recipient governments.

3) The rules of interpretation as contained in the Articles 31, 32, and 33 of the Vienna Convention seem generally applicable to technical assistance agreements. The only restriction to this could possibly be Article 32 referring to the preparatory work as supplementary means of interpretation; as explained above, the term "standard" indicates already that the agreements have for the most part been drawn up unilaterally by the organizations. In this context one may question the value of such a means of interpretation.

Another point arises in connection with the interpretation of the plans of operations; in applying them one would certainly have to take into account the standard agreements, since they provide the framework for the execution of specific projects. The Vienna Con-

---

[66] See p. 116.

vention stipulates in Article 31, paragraph 3, that subsequent agreements, subsequent practice, and "any relevant rules of international law applicable in the relations between the parties" have to be taken into account as elements of interpretation together with the context of agreements. The standard agreements could certainly be considered as coming within the third category, but it seems preferable to insert a more specific paragraph in a convention dealing with the law of treaties concluded by international organizations to the effect that also earlier agreements may constitute such an element of interpretation;

4) With regard to the formal validity of treaties, we could investigate whether there exist any provisions of internal (organizational) law regarding the competence to conclude treaties. Although in many instances approval by some organ is required in order to ensure its internal validity, there do not exist any such constitutional limitations relative to the conclusion of technical assistance agreements;

5) There seems to be no reason why the provisions regarding the material validity of treaties (error, fraud, etc.) should not be equally applicable to technical assistance agreements;

6) Breach of treaty obligations being possible with regard to technical assistance agreements as well, termination or suspension of the agreements should be feasible. When the recipient government, for example, refuses to prolong its financial participation, the participating organizations are undoubtedly entitled to invoke this breach as a ground for terminating or suspending the standard agreement.

What are the legal consequences of a breach on the part of one of the participating organizations?

Article 60 of the Vienna Convention (termination or suspension of the operation of a treaty as a consequence of its breach) distinguishes between bilateral and multilateral treaties[67].

As regards the standard technical assistance agreements it has been explained above that they can be characterized either as simply multilateral, or as "semi-multilateral" treaties ("Halb-Kollektivverträge"). This, however, did not make too much of a difference since in both cases the legal consequences would be the same.

In case one of the participating organizations should violate its treaty obligations, this would certainly provide the recipient State with a valid reason for terminating or suspending the treaty with

---

[67] The fact that it does not indicate what it understands by these notions appears to be a rather serious omission, since, as has been demonstrated above, their meaning is still open to discussion.

regard to that organization, but it would very likely remain in operation between the State and the other organizations. In this context Article 60, paragraph 2 (b) seems applicable on the understanding that the State may not only suspend but also terminate the treaty[68], since the standard agreements refer themselves to the possibility of termination.

For most plans of operations the same reasoning will apply to the effect that, in case one of the participating organizations will violate its obligations, the experts provided by the other organization(s) may continue their job according to their job description. Only in case the plan of operation will constitute an organic whole[69], in the sense that one expert cannot adequately fulfil his function without the co-operation of the experts sent by the other organization(s), the position will be different. If in such a case a breach occurs on the side of the State or on the side of one of the participating organizations, the result will be a radical change in the position of every party with respect to the further performance of the treaty obligations[70]. As a consequence Article 60, para. 2 (c), would be applicable to the effect that either the organizations, in case the breach occurs on the part of the State, or the State, in case the breach occurs on the part of one of the organizations, may invoke the breach as a ground for suspending the operation of the treaty; termination does not seem appropriate in this context, because of the factual possibility that the work will be resumed after the difficulties have been settled;

7) There does not seem to be much room left for the application of Article 62 of the Convention (fundamental change of circumstances), whereas the agreements are terminable upon notice. When a party has the power to terminate a treaty, it has also the power to apply pressure upon the other party to revise its provisions[71].

Theoretically, however, invocation of the clause is certainly possible and the consequences would *mutatis mutandis* be the same as explained under point 6;

8) The consequences of the invalidity, c.q. termination of a technical assistance agreement have already been dealt with under

---

[68] In case the violation should occur on the part of the State, Art. 60, para. 2 (a), could be applied. The distinction between (i) and (ii) would in that case, however, be without any use, because termination or supension "between themselves and the defaulting State" would amount to termination or suspension as between all the parties, the relations between the participating organizations not being covered by the agreement.

[69] See p. 118 f.

[70] ILC commentary on draft Article 57, A/6309/Rev. 1, p. 83.

[71] ILC commentary on draft Article 59, A/6309/Rev. 1, p. 86.

point 6. The special problems concerning the characterization of the agreements as multilateral or bilateral together with the nature of the obligations assumed (divisibility of obligations) constitute the decisive criteria in this context.

Österr. Zeitschr. f. öffentl. Recht, Suppl. 1, 127—163 (1971)

The Capacity of International Organizations to Conclude Treaties

Gunther Hartmann
Assistant Professor of Political Science
Memorial University of Newfoundland

I. Introduction

At its first session in 1949 the International Law Commission listed the law of treaties as one of several subject matters suitable for codification[1]. The Commission's efforts culminated twenty years later in the Vienna Convention on the Law of Treaties[2]. Both the lengthy time necessary to complete this task as well as the extensive debates are indicative of the problems which the delegates faced. Mere adoption of a final text thus demonstrates that states can achieve consensus on matters which are not only basic to continued development of international law, but also central to the structure of international relations.

The Commission had originally envisaged covering the whole scope of treaty law but the end result fell far short of its intent. Although agreement on a wide range of specific provisions relating to treaty practice and progressive development of treaty law was achieved, the limited scope[3] and phraseology[4] of the Convention indicate that a comprehensive law of treaties will not become a reality in the near future. Most conspicuous by its absence in the Vienna Convention was the exclusion of international governmental organizations (IGO's) from its scope[5]. This is especially surprising since all

[1] GAOR, 4th Sess., Supp. No. 10 (A/925).

[2] UN Doc. A/Conf. 39/27 of 23 May 1969 (hereafter Vienna Convention).

[3] Cf. the Introduction to the Vienna Convention, especially definition of treaty and applicability of the Convention.

[4] Haak, "Escape Clauses and Similar Clauses," 27 ZaöRV, 1967, pp. 540—561.

[5] International Organizations are excluded pursuant to Article 1. Specific references to IGO's or constituent instruments are found in Articles 2, 5, and 20, and indirectly in Article 3.

four Special Rapporteurs had included international organization as proper treaty-making partners which should fall within the scope of the Convention[6]. In its final draft, however, the Commission decided conclusively to eliminate IGO's from the Convention because "treaties concluded by international organizations have many special characteristics; and the Commission considered that it would unduly complicate matters and delay drafting of the present articles if it were to attempt to include in them satisfactory provisions concerning international organizations[7]."

---

[6] The four Special Rapporteurs: Mr. Brierly, Sir Hersch Lauterpacht, Sir Gerald Fitzmaurice, and Sir Humphrey Waldock included the following articles in their drafts:

Brierly: "All States and international organizations have capacity to make treaties, but the capacity of some States or organizations to enter into certain treaties may be limited." UN Doc. A/CN. 4/23 of 14 April 1950, Article 3.

Lauterpacht: "Treaties are agreements between States, including organizations of States, intended to create legal rights and obligations of the parties." UN Doc. A/CN. 4/63 of 24 March 1953, Article 1. With an eye towards possible revision of this Article, Lauterpacht in UN Doc. A/CN. 4/87 of 8 July 1954 suggests that the following paragraph might be added: "In the absence of evidence to the contrary, an instrument finally accepted by both parties in the customary form of an international undertaking and registered with the United Nations in accordance with Article 102 of the Charter shall be deemed to be an instrument creating legal rights and obligations."

Fitzmaurice: "The provisions of the present Code relating to the powers, faculties, rights and obligations of States relative to treaties, are applicable, *mutatis mutandis*, to international organizations, and to treaties made between them, or between any of them and a State, unless the contrary is indicated or results necessarily from the text." UN Doc. A/CN. 4/101 of 14 March 1956, Article 1. In Article 9 (1) he goes on to state that "Treaty-making and all other acts connected with treaties are, on the *international plane*, executive acts, and the function of the executive authority. Whatever legislative processes have to be gone through in order to make such acts effective on the domestic plane, on the international plane they are authentic."

Waldock: "Capacity in international law (hereafter referred to as international capacity) to become a party to treaties is possessed by every independent State, whether a unitary State, a federation or other form of union of States, and by other subjects of international law invested with such capacity by treaty or by international custom." UN Doc. A/CN. 4/144 of March 1962, Article 3 (1). "International capacity to become a party to treaties is also possessed by international organizations and agencies which have a separate legal personality under international law if, and to the extent that, such treaty-making capacity is expressly created, or necessarily implied, in the instrument or instruments prescribing the constitution and functions of the organization or agency in question." Article 3 (4).

[7] GAOR, 21st Sess., Supp. No. 9 (A/6309/Rev. 1), p. 20. It should be noted, however, that even the Vienna Convention does not claim that international organizations are not subject to international law or that they do not have treaty-making capacity, cf. Article 3.

This decision, partially based on expediency, has some merit. State treaty-practice has over the years evolved certain common rules which aided the Commission in drafting specific provisions. Since the fledgling international organizations do not yet have such a tradition, two drafting difficulties could arise. Insufficient data concerning practice might result in provisions which are too general and hence lack the force of guiding principles, or provisions which only enumerate the specific organizational practices resulting in not only a cumbersome but also inflexible convention[8]. It may thus be agreed that, given the lack of sufficient data, exclusion of international organizations within the scope of the Vienna Convention was for the present justified. Concerted effort by international organizations and the experts of the International Law Commission should nevertheless be able, within a reasonable period of time, to identify the most common trends and use these as the basis for codification.

Implied in the Commission's report, and the proceedings of the Conference, however, is that the factual problem was not the sole reason for excluding international organizations[9]. Rather, philosophical and political motivations also contributed. The underlying and unresolved question is to what extent and in what capacity international organizations *should* be able to participate as equal units within the international legal system.

Both the International Law Commission and the Vienna Conference were thus concerned with two analytically distinct problems. One was the philosophical determination of the Convention's jurisdictional bounds; the other, the resolution of factual questions concerning procedures to be followed within the established bounds[10]. Terminology of articles dealing with procedure was objectively determinable for States because identification of these rules lay predominantly in the realm of practice. Agreement on boundaries was possible because certain *a priori* assumptions of legal philosophy and given *Weltanschauungen* were able to converge within the realm of

---

[8] Instances where organizational practice may differ from that of states are: (1) competent organs and internal procedure; (2) negotiation and conclusion of treaties; (3) forms of treaties; (4) dispute settlement procedure; and, (5) revision and termination.

[9] UN Doc. A/Conf. 39/11 of 26 March—24 May 1968. See especially the comments of Tornaritis, p. 12; Khlestov, p. 13; and, Smejkal, p. 16. See also Kearney and Dalton, "The Treaty on Treaties," 64 AJIL, 1970, pp. 495—561.

[10] Contrast, for example, the prescriptive (boundary-setting) nature of Articles 1—6, 26, and 53 with the descriptive (factual) thrust of Articles 9—16. It is not my intent to open the theoretical controversy of the relationship between description and prescription here, but merely to suggest that an analytic distinction can aid us in understanding the difficulties of drafting a Vienna Convention.

theory. In drafting a future law of treaties for international organizations[11] an interplay between these two analytically distinct factors must also take place. For a future convention to be effective a delicate balance between practice and theory must be achieved.

It is the purpose of this paper to explore alternatives as to how such a balance can be achieved. Specifically, the task will be to draft an article on organizational capacity to conclude treaties comparable to Article 6 of the Vienna Convention[12]. Should a comparable article be identical, different, how and why? It would be futile to claim that a definitive answer will be the outcome of this presentation but after weighing various alternatives, reasonable suggestions may emerge.

Before we analyze the various contentions dealing with the capacity of international organizations to conclude treaties, several methodological notes are in order.

1. In this paper the problem of organizational capacity is not viewed as a "purely" legal one, but as an interplay between various interpretations of international law *within* an historical context of international relations. An attempt will thus be made not only to explore the internal logic of a given legal contention but also to assess its relevance to the corresponding historical system.

2. Theories of law and politics are devised for two primary purposes—either to prescribe or to describe. The main purpose underlying prescriptive theories is to give "reality" a new twist and remake the world in its own image, or to maintain a given set of norms as superior to an alternative one. Style and method of supporting arguments can usually only be understood within the terms of reference that have been posited as premises. Prescriptive theories place an emphasis on internal and logical consistency. Methodological emphasis of identification, systematization, and explanation of contemporary society is the mainstay of descriptive theory. Because descriptive theories are oriented toward the here and now, they are more likely to adapt to changing reality. In this paper neither of the two types of theories is viewed as being superior, but they are seen as "persuasive tools" each striving against the other for the adoption of its correctness. Just

[11] The Conference recommended that the General Assembly request the ILC to study the question of treaties concluded by IGO's. UN Doc. A/Conf. 39/26 of 23 May 1969.

[12] The 1966 Draft Convention had included a paragraph on constitutional provisions regarding members of federal unions, GAOR, 24th Sess., Supp. No. 9 (A/6309/Rev. 1), pp. 11, 24—25. At the Vienna Conference some members felt the article on capacity to be so self-evident as to warrant its exclusion from the Convention. United Nations Conference on the Law of Treaties, 1st Sess. (A/Conf. 39/11), p. 59 ff.

as there is an interplay between international law and international relations, so on a different level of analysis, there is an interplay between prescriptive and descriptive theories.

3. Analysis of organizational capacity can be viewed in analogy with a three dimensional chess game. Justifications of various approaches do not confine themselves to one level of analysis, i.e., "purely" legal or "purely" practical, but draw on several levels at one and the same time. Proofs of capacity must thus be seen in terms of the whole "game" including analysis within and between levels. The result being that prescription, description, international law, international relations, and time-periods are closely enmeshed. In varying degrees they are present in all approaches[13].

4. Three main concepts—personality, constitution, and custom[14] —are identified in the literature as the basis for organizational treaty-making power. Establishing the validity of a nexus between these concepts and organizational capacity will be a primary aim of this presentation. As the levels-of-analysis problem suggests, however, these concepts do not lead to distinct and independent modes of analysis. Instead they all deal with the same problem—organizational treaty-making capacity—from different perspectives. Within the total logic of this paper an overlap of data, argumentation, and conclusions will, of necessity, be evidenced.

II. Personality

Personality theories of international organizations can be grouped within three categories: (1) Those which deny an independent personality of IGO's; (2) those which equate organizational personality with that of states; and (3) those which ascribe an independent personality for organizations but limit their scope of action[15]. The first and second type of theories are the extremes which, in order to maintain internal consistency, must not only unwaveringly support their basic premises but also carry these to their logical conclusions. The third group includes the "peacemakers" who realize legitimate values in both extremes and thus stop short of logical consequences.

[13] Singer, "The Levels-of-Analysis Problem in International Relations," 14 World Politics, 1961, pp. 77—92.

[14] Although the constitutional and customary approaches appear to be of primary importance, the concept of personality as affecting treaty-making capacity is sufficiently prevalent in the literature as to warrant inclusion.

[15] The first two categories view personality and capacity as a cause-effect relationship whereas some authors of the third group rely more heavily on constitutional legal explanations. See p. 143 below.

Upon what basis do these theories rest, what is their logic, and how can their conclusions be explained? It is contended that argumentation for all three theories flows from the same source—the side-by-side historical development of international relations and law[16]. Divergencies of conclusions have come about because each theory utilizes a different historical starting-point and interprets basic legal concepts differently.

International relations, broadly conceived, has passed through numerous systemic changes[17]. The various systems are distinguishable by the quantity and quality of their basic units as well as the rules that were established to regulate their mutual activities. We can identify systems in which either bands, tribes, empires, kingdoms or states were considered to be the dominant actors and thus in the forefront of developing and changing both the international political and legal systems. Scarcity of actors coupled with relatively infrequent and limited interaction of pre-state systems resulted in general stability without either political polarization or a strict universal legal system. With the rise of the territorial state as the predominant unit of international relations, and the resultant "glorification" of this abstract entity, a pronounced systematization began which has evolved into the contemporary political and legal systems[18].

Growth of the territorial state in the 17th and 18th centuries was facilitated because this unit permitted power to be used most effectively in achieving desired ends. Industrialization, technology, and education contributed further to the development of a unique social ethos. Statehood and the locus of the international system were predominantly Europe based thus evidencing European political values and traditions. Continued evolution of rules governing unit interaction required that they reflect and regulate political realities. Transformation of the international political system thus meant that the legal system also required adaptation. Such adaptation could come

---

[16] Nussbaum, A Concise History of the Law of Nations, 1954; Barkun, Law without Sanction, 1968; Röling, International Law in an Expanded World, 1960; Verzijl, International Law in Historical Perspective, 1968.

[17] For the concept of system see Easton, A Framework for Political Analysis, 1965; Kaplan (ed.), New Approaches to International Relations, 1968; Kaplan, Systems and Process in International Politics, 1957; Friedmann, The Changing Structure of International Law, 1964; Jessup, Transnational Law, 1956; Röling, International Law, 1960; Schwarzenberger, The Frontiers of International Law, 1962.

[18] The Peace of Westphalia did lead to a new international system, but it is doubtful that the break with the past, both as concerns politics and law, was as great as is assumed in texts of international law, e.g., Jacobini, International Law: A Text, 1968, p. 16; Fenwick, International Law, 1965, p. 14; Tung, International Law in an Organizing World, 1968, p. 9.

about either through the reinterpretation of traditional legal concepts or the establishment of new guidelines.

A norm hierarchy for this emerging legal system was not very difficult to establish. From a subjective point of view the tradition of monarchical family relationships gave rise to the "family of nations." Although conflicts between units were not to disappear the subjective bond viewed the units as equals. Objective analysis of practice, as well as the power configuration within the world pointed to the state as a distinct class. The territorial states, rather than any other unit in the world, effectively carried out policy and interacted peacefully and violently. In the interest of all participants, it was these relationships which required ordering.

It was up to legal theory to bring the subjective bond and objective reality into unity. Theory extracted three criteria which distinguished states from other units: territory, population, and independent government[19].

Although population and territory were present in other units, it was only the state which evidenced "effective" independence. This latter criterion went through several fine revisions eventually attaining attributes of sovereignty. And, the newly transformed notion of state sovereignty became the governing norm of international law. The political system showed states to be supreme within their territorial domain; the legal system prescribed that this should be the case. On the international level states were designated as legally equal, i.e., each having a common personality according to the precepts of sovereignty.

Legal ascription furthermore implied that sovereign entities were somehow superior to other units, that they were in a class of their own, and, that they had distinct spheres of action which other international units did not possess. One of these special considerations was the explicit development of international law, e.g., only proper entities possess the capacity to conclude treaties. Since other units of the world, e.g., colonies, played no directing role in world politics or in the continued development of the legal system, rules applicable to them were relegated to a lower or secondary level of the legal complex with the consequent result of not being permitted, by legal definition, to explicitly participate in the law creating process.

By the turn of the twentieth century the international political system began to evidence a second transition. International govern-

---

[19] The Montevideo Convention on Rights and Duties of States includes a fourth criterion. "Art. 1. The State as a person of international law should possess the following qualifications: a) a permanent population; b) a defined territory; c) government; and d) capacity to enter into relations with other States."

mental organizations began to appear. Collectively these units exhibited some characteristics of states, and yet, they did not possess all necessary attributes required by legal theory. What was to be their status under international law? What criteria were to be applied? Solutions to these questions did not become crucial until the mid-twentieth century when IGO's had begun to proliferate and actually outnumber states. Consideration by the ILC of these questions attests to the immediacy of the problem.

To find clear-cut answers today is more difficult, however, than it would have been two hundred or even fifty years ago. Since the first transition of the 17th—18th centuries, and the second transition of the twentieth, the international legal system has become sufficiently stratified and rule rich that from both a legal and political point of view it could, depending upon intent, support almost any conclusion.

The historical evolution of the international legal system reveals that argumentation linking personality to organizational treaty-making capacity rests on two theoretical legal prototypes—the "open" legal system as it existed prior to the first transition of the 17th—18th century, and the "closed" legal system as it existed approximately to the second transition of the twentieth century. The open and closed legal systems can best be illustrated by analyzing the arguments of the two extreme views of personality.

The contention which denies the personality of international organization[20] relies almost exclusively on the second stage of legal development for its proof. Its assumption is that the legal system not only accurately reflects political realities but also that the established hierarchy of norms is essentially correct. The state is, and should be, at the highest level, and any other unit wishing to aspire to this rung must, in accordance with the rules of the legal system, demonstrate identical attributes as the state. If any other interpretation is permitted either the ground rules, and hence the legal system itself, are changed or the state is toppled from its accustomed pedestal. Both alternatives open the way not only for dictating state action on the international sphere but most likely also domestically[21].

Testing the congruence of organizational and state attributes, the argument goes, is a simple matter: one need only compare the essential

[20] Akademia Nauk SSSR, International Law, 1962; Schirmer, Universalität völkerrechtlicher Verträge und Internationale Organisationen, 1966; Rubinstein, The Soviets in International Organizations, 1964; Triska and Slusser, The Theory, Law and Policy of Soviet Treaties, 1962.

[21] One area, for example, is the UN Human Rights Program. Cf. Lauterpacht, International Law and Human Rights, 1950; Moskowitz, Human Rights and World Order, 1958; Chafee, "Federal and State Powers Under the U.N. Covenant of Human Rights," Wisconsin Law Review, 1951, pp. 389, 623.

criteria of statehood. Since organizations possess neither territory nor population two criteria are quickly eliminated[22]. But might not independence of action be the only relevant criterion? Here proponents of the contention revert to an earlier state of legal development[23] by arguing that organizations are dependent in their actions upon the will of the members. An international organization is thus viewed as an appendage for state action[24] or as a non-institutionalized, non-directing entity. Both of these latter alternatives do not demonstrate the ability to act independently. Since the essential attributes of states, however, determine their personality[25], and IGO's lack identical attributes, they do not possess the same type of personality as states do. Not possessing a congruent personality therefore means that no claim to independent treaty-making capacity can be made.

From a theoretical perspective the international legal system is seen as being logically closed—no entities except those exhibiting the same characteristics as states can, by this interpretation of the system's rules, enter the legal order on the same footing as states. If it is correct that a legal order is immutable, while the international political system is dynamic, this prescription of personality is viable. From a broader perspective of law and politics, however, this interpretation appears to be untenable.

An open legal system, on the other hand, is presumed by those who place personality of organizations on the same footing with states. Justifications come from two related fronts—definition of international organization and theoretical proof from a more primitive international legal order.

Seyerstedt, the most vociferous proponent of this view, is willing to grant, from a factual point of view, that international organi-

[22] Although it may be argued that Headquarters Agreements imply territory and population of international organizations are existant, it is doubtful that the same construct should be applied. See for example Section 9 and 15 of the Headquarters Agreement between the UN and US, 61 Stat. 3146, Treaties and Other International Acts Series 1676. Also, Preuss, "The International Organizations Immunity Act," 40 AJIL, 1946, p. 332.

[23] Cf. the section on constitutional development p. 145 below.

[24] Heydte, "Von der Rechtssubjektivität und Rechtsperson im Völkerrecht," Grundprobleme des Internationalen Rechts. Festschrift für J. Spiropoulos, 1957, p. 247.

[25] It should be noted here that there is an element of circularity in this contention. At times attributes and personaliy appear to be equated, other times attributes appear to define personality, and at still other times personality appears to define the attributes. At any rate it is held that only states by virtue of their position in the hierarchy of legal norms have complete freedom in treaty-making matters. The difficulty of designing an acceptable proof for this contention has led some writers to bystep the problem. See p. 140 below.

zations are different than states but assumes that from a "legal" point of view they are not[26]. He is thus willing to accept different criteria for states and IGO's with only the concept of sovereignty linking them. To be a general subject of international law and hence possessing capacity

[a]ll that is required, is that [the subject] possesses the objective characteristics of a State, or Organization, respectively. These *necessary and sufficient characteristics* are, in the case of States, generally considered to be: Territory, population and sovereign government. In the case of intergovernmental organizations the facts required are submitted to be: Intergovernmental organs (i.e. organs established by two or more sovereign States), which are not all subject to the authority of any one State or other organized community (but only to that of the participating States acting jointly through their representatives on such organs), which perform "sovereign" and/or international acts in their own name and which are not authorized by all their acts to assume obligations (merely) on behalf of the several participating States[27].

This definition not only serves in identifying international organizations but also contains the link for interpreting personality via pre-state international law. The IGO's of today may be compared to other units of the international system before the dominance of states —those units which actively participated in the system, e.g., the basic units of the Holy Roman Empire. The major participants of the political system, presumably possessing capacity for independent action, are by virtue of their activity "necessary" subjects who can attain their personality not only by agreement of existing persons, but also in view of general international law merely because they do in fact exist[28]. In other words, legal personality, with its subsequent sphere of action, is present whenever an entity becomes a participatory unit in the international political system—the fact of its existence *ipso facto* establishes personality.

---

[26] Seyerstedt, Objective Personality of Intergovernmental Organizations, 1963, p. 112.

[27] Ibid., pp. 46—47. For other definitions see Detter, Law Making by International Organizations, 1965, p. 17; Zemanek, Das Vertragsrecht der Internationalen Organisationen, 1957, pp. 9—15; Seidl-Hohenveldern, Das Recht der Internationalen Organisationen einschließlich der Supranationalen Gemeinschaften, 1967, p. 4; Seyerstedt, "International Personality of Intergovernmental Organizations: Do Their Capacities Really Depend Upon Their Constitutions," 4 Indian Journal of International Law, 1964, p. 53.

[28] Mosler, „Die Erweiterung des Kreises der Völkerrechtssubjekte," 22 ZaöRV, 1962, pp. 46—48. Seyerstedt, "International Personality," pp. 39—40. This view can be contrasted with that of Seidl-Hohenveldern and Zemanek below.

Heydte, by implication, goes even further in asserting the personality and role of international organizations in claiming that classical international law recognized derived international organizations such as commissions and arbitration tribunals which were neither above nor equal to states, but simply their tools; and, that the task of the modern international organizations established by multilateral treaties, is to execute a legal or political control over sovereign states[29].

Acceptance of this view requires that the legal system is seen as open within the whole historical context of international relations. Any unit which actively and independently participates on the political level is automatically co-opted into the legal system. The political and legal systems thus exist in a parallel relationship where participants in one system are also actors in the other. Openness of the legal system is demonstrated by the fact that entrance and departure of units does not depend, necessarily, upon acceptance of pre-existing membership but merely upon proof of existence. Both systems are therefore fluid depending upon time and circumstance. Theoretically then, any unit, sufficiently powerful may of its own volition enter the legal system. Other actors may in practice, of course, attempt to counteract this process[30].

A compromise position concerning personality of international organizations is reached by most writers. These authors agree that IGO's are different from states and do not seek to justify congruent personality. They rather view IGO's as subjects participating with states in international relations and law. Furthermore, they generally agree that personality and treaty-making power is limited to the functional operations or constitutional prerequisites of the organization.

Limited personality can come from either general international law or through a constitutive treaty. Seidl-Hohenveldern, for example, puts forth the following criteria for the identification of international organizations:

1. Sie müssen grundsätzlich auf *Dauer* berechnete Gebilde darstellen.
2. Sie müssen durch eine *völkerrechtliche Willenseinigung* geschaffen sein.
3. Partner dieser Willenseinigung sind *Staaten* bzw. Staaten und andere Völkerrechtssubjekte.

---

[29] "... die Aufgabe haben über die souveränen Staaten eine richterliche oder politische Kontrolle auszuführen." Heydte, p. 248.

[30] In this view the political and legal system are interrelated. Seyerstedt implies that the usual movement is from the political to the legal level. And, the Soviets see the two systems as operating independently of each other.

4. Die Partner stehen sich dabei auf Basis der Gleichheit gegenüber und bewahren ihre Souveränität.

5. Die Partner wollen gemeinsam ein vom Völkerrecht erlaubtes Ziel erreichen, das, wenn es ein einzelner Staat im Rahmen seines innerstaatlichen Rechtes verwirklichen wollte, nach Ansicht der beteiligten Staaten nicht dessen Fiskalbereich zuzurechnen wäre.

6. Sie ermöglichen es diesem Gebilde, *einen eigenen Willen* zu haben, der sich nicht notwendigerweise mit dem Willen jedes seiner Mitglieder deckt.

7. Sie statten es zu diesem Zweck mit mindestens einem *Organ* aus, das den auf die Erreichung des gemeinsamen Zieles gerichteten besonderen Willen dieses Gebildes zu vertreten berechtigt ist[31].

The two key criteria for Seidl-Hohenveldern are the mode of establishment and independence of action, i.e., a will different from the collective membership. Personality is *established* because states, for duration of their membership, surrender a part of their sovereignty, even if this is only an infinitesimal part, which the organization correspondingly adopts[32]. Independence of action flows from the newly attained sovereignty, and since it is not an inherent sovereignty but a derived one, which may be withdrawn by the members individually or collectively, the personality remains limited. Another argument which serves to demonstrate independence of organizations is voting procedure. If unanimity of the plenary organ were required for all action, one might argue that the decisions are no more than the express instructions of states, precluding independence of the organization. Practice, however, has evolved towards the majority principle and even members who voted against a given

---

[31] 1. The entity must basically exhibit *permanency.*

2. The entity must be created via an *international agreement.*

3. The partners of this agreement are *States,* i.e., States and other Subjects of international law.

4. The partners interact according to the principle of equality and retain their sovereignty.

5. The partners desire to mutually achieve a legally sanctioned goal, which, in the opinion of the member States, could not be realized by each State acting independently.

6. The partners enable the entity to possess a *will of its own* which does not necessarily correspond to the wills of the individual members.

7. At least one *Organ* is empowered to represent the entity in attaining the mutual goal and in realizing the particular will of the entity. (Simplified translation supplied.) Seidl-Hohenveldern, Das Recht der Internationalen Organisationen, p. 181.

[32] Ibid., p. 5.

action are bound, in the name of the organization, from a legal point of view[33].

Seidl-Hohenveldern has one further argument based more strictly on legal premises. He distinguished between two types of rights—primary and secondary (primäre und sekundäre Gemeinschaftsrechte). Primary rights are those which belong to the proper international legal system and are the basis of the constituent instrument. Secondary rights are those which the organization itself can create[34], but these, by definition, must conform with the primary ones contained in the constituent instrument. For any given organization there are two "law sets" forming a closed legal system which is applicable to member states and those non-members who have recognized the organization[35].

Zemanek has the same general view as Seidl-Hohenveldern but a different explanation. To him general international law contains no norms governing the relations and capacity of international organizations. Hence these norms must be created by those entities which are both subjects as well as law creating sources of the legal system. He thus views the legal system as open and closed at the same time: "Keine Erscheinung der Tatsachenwelt ist *a priori* Person im Rechtssinn. Sie werden es dadurch, daß eine bestimmte Rechtsordnung sie als solche bezeichnet[36]."

The system is closed in the sense that no entity, of its own volition, may enter the legal complex[37]. It is open in the sense that preexisting participants can "create" additional units. Once these new entities have joined the legal order, they may interact on the basis of legal equality with previous members. This does not mean, however, that the newly joined entities have absolute equality—the original member's prerogative may stipulate limiting conditions as prerequisites to acceptance within the legal system[38].

Rosenne demonstrates Zemanek's notion on the organizational level by arguing that "[i]t is rare for a State to have an absolute right to become a member of an international organization. Usually, membership in an organization is only open to States which meet

[33] Another example that can be cited is that when a new state joins the United Nations, it also accepts the previous commitments and rules of the Organization, rather than individually negotiating the applicability of each item.

[34] Seidl-Hohenveldern, Das Recht der Internationalen Organisationen, p. 181.

[35] Ibid., pp. 182—4.

[36] No phenomenon (entity) of the real world is *a priori* a Person in the legal sense. It becomes a Person because a particular legal system designates it as such. Zemanek, Das Vertragsrecht, p. 20.

[37] Contrast this with p. 136 above.

[38] See for example The Agreement Establishing the Inter-American Development Bank in Peaslee, pp. 826—853. Of interest here are Articles 1, 3, and 11.

certain conditions, and admission consists of a dual process: (a) an application by the interested State submitted in due form, followed by (b) a determination by the qualified organ of the Organization that those conditions are fulfilled[39]."

How do these views on personality clarify organizational capacity to conclude treaties? For the two extreme positions personality plays a central role—an attempt is made to establish a cause-effect relationship. If any entity possesses personality, then it may also conclude treaties. The proof of capacity thus centers around the proof of personality. To prove this cause-effect relationship appears to be as futile an exercise as resolving the chicken and egg puzzle.

Necessary for treaty-making capacity is that a minimum of two entities are prepared to enter into a contractual relationship and able to carry out their respective obligations. The notion of personality, per se, has no direct bearing on capacity.

The futility of proving a necessary nexus between personality and capacity has led most contemporary authors to treat proof of personality as irrelevant to treaty-making power[40]. Even the proof of the compromise contention discussed above relies not so much on showing a relationship between personality and capacity, as determining capacity solely on the basis of constitutional or general law prerequisites[41]. It is around these latter two justifications that we should focus our main attention.

III. Constitutions

A constituent instrument for international organizations, just as a constitution for states, is a founding instrument which defines the general framework within which the organization may act. It usually contains two types of provisions: general and specific. General norms and organizational structure prescribe the skeletal or directional tenor towards which the entity should strive and by which rules it should be governed in order to maintain itself. Specific provisions are devised to establish a hierarchy of norms, to explicitly emphasize rights and obligations deemed to be of special importance by the drafters, and to provide certain limitations of competence on specific sub-units or

---

[39] Rosenne, "Is the Constitution of an International Organization an International Treaty: Reflections on the Codification of the Law of Treaties," 12 Communicazioni e Studi, 1966, p. 54.

[40] Detter, Law Making, p. 21; Chiu, The Capacity of International Organizations to Conclude Treaties, 1966, p. 29; Schneider, Treaty-Making Power of International Organizations, 1959, p. 17; Jenks, "The Legal Personality of International Organizations," 22 BYIL, 1945, p. 271.

[41] Zemanek, Das Vertragsrecht, p. 25.

subject matters. It is the general provisions which usually provide for sufficient flexibility enabling the entity to meet future contingencies[42].

Since the founding instruments are not designed to explicitly provide for all contingencies, situations may arise whereby the legality of a given action is challenged. It is then incumbent upon some interpretive body to weigh the various constitutional provisions and reach a decision. Both general and specific provisions provide the guidelines. International organizations in view of a future law of treaties now face such legal questions as to which organizations may conclude treaties and what type of relationships they may enter into.

Some constituent instruments are explicitly concerned with treaty-making capacity. This capacity may be expressed either in terms granting the organization general powers, or enumeration of specific instances in which treaties may be concluded. Within this latter grouping competence may be delegated to the organization generally or to specific organs. Finally, some constituent instruments do not contain any treaty-making provisions[43].

---

[42] This flexibility is found in most constitutions in the principles of self-organization and the establishment of subsidiary organs.

[43] On treaty-making provisions see Neuhold in this volume. Also, Rohn, "A Legal Theory on International Organizations," 5 Turkish Yearbook of Intl. Law, 1964, analyzes twenty IGO's and develops ten indeces to measure and compare constitutional powers.

An exhaustive study of IGO constituent provisions has not yet been undertaken, nor was it attempted in this study. Partially this is due to a time factor, and partially due to determining the "extents" of a constitution in distinction from a constituent instrument. For the present I would thus hold with Schneider in stating that: "The legalistic approach that of trying to find a constitutional provision for every activity of an organization, must be abandoned as unrealistic. In a number of cases constitutions have been drawn up in haste and evident oversights can be found ... It is not necessary to review the practice of each individual organization, because a perfunctory investigation already brings to light the wide gap between the constitutional authority and the actual practice which exists in a great number of agencies." Schneider, Treaty-Making, pp. 69—70.

Numerous studies, however, have been undertaken in regard to the more "dominant" IGO's, e.g., Bowett, The Law of International Institutions, 1963; Seidl-Hohenveldern, Das Recht der Internationalen Organisationen, 1967; Schneider; Zemanek, Das Vertragsrecht, 1957; Kelsen, The Law of the United Nations, 1950; Weissberg, The International Status of the United Nations, 1961; Erler, Rechtsfragen der ICAO, 1966; Szasz, The Law and Practice of IAEA, 1968; Lörcher, Der Abschluß völkerrechtlicher Verträge nach dem Recht der drei europäischen Gemeinschaften, 1965.

It should be pointed out that for the more "recognized" organizations there seems to be no doubt, that according to the constituent instrument they may enter, at the minimum, into some treaty relationships. Although there are no explicit treaty-making provisions in the constituent instruments of the following organizations, they have entered into agreements: Hague Conference on Private Inter-

The variety of constituent provisions thus enable a variety of interpretations, each possibly serving as a future general norm concerning organizational capacity. It could be made logically plausible, for example, that international organizations have only enumerated powers and thus only that extent of capacity explicitly provided for in the constituent instrument. The accepted assumption would only have to be the derived nature of organizations[44]. Three customary trends on the state level, however, lend a strong counter-argument. Since constitutions are general guidelines not providing for all contingencies, circumstances may arise necessitating an action not foreseen by the drafters. Failure to take the specific action could constitute dissolution of the state. Such a situation is unlikely to arise, however, since the purpose of constitutions is exactly to avoid such dilemmas via its generality. Secondly, it is a generally accepted rule that government may exercise all types of implied powers that are not explicitly prohibited, i.e., negative constitutional provisions. Thirdly, lack of treaty-making provisions has not deterred some organizations from concluding international agreements[45]. It may therefore be assumed that explicit provisions are not sufficient reason for capacity.

The functional approach provides a second possible interpretation. A constituent instrument is drawn up for the realization of certain

national Law: "The Permanent Bureau may correspond ... with the competent international organization" (Art. 6); League of Arab States: "The Council shall be entrusted with the function of realizing the purposes of the League and supervising the execution of the agreements concluded between the member States..." (Art. 3), "[The Council] shall also have the function of determining means whereby the League will collaborate with the international organizations..." (Art. 3); COMECON: In order to achieve principles and aims the Council shall "take any other measures necessary to achieve its aims" (Art. 3 (1) (c)), "The Session of the Council shall ... exercise such other functions as it deems necessary to achieve the aims of the Council" (Art. 6 (5) (c)), "... may establish and maintain relations with economic organizations of the United Nations and other international organizations" (Art. 11), "The Council shall have within the territory of each member the legal personality..." (Art. 13); South Pacific Commission: "The Commission may discharge such other functions as may be agreed upon by the participating Governments" (Art. 4, P. 7), "The Commission may make such administrative arrangements as may be necessary for the exercise of its powers and the discharge of its functions" (Art. 4, P. 8), "... Commission will be recognized in [participating Government] territories as possessing such legal capacity ... as are necessary for the independent exercise of its powers and discharge of its functions" (Art. 4, P. 10); Organization of Central American States: "The Economic Council shall perform the functions assigned to it by the Meeting of Ministers of Foreign Affairs..." (Art. 14); All instruments quoted from Peaslee, International Governmental Organizations, 1961.

[44] See p. 139 above.

[45] This also includes categories of treaties not mentioned in constituent instrument, e.g., Headquarters Agreements. See also footnote 43.

purposes or functions which the organization is to implement. The scope may be limited to one main function or to several related functions[46]. In order to realize this purpose, action and intercourse with other units on the international plane is required. Tradition dictates that these interactions be "formalized" via "contractual" relations. It may thus be claimed that simply because of the "functional imperative" international organizations have treaty-making capacity. Paraphrasing Morgenthau's syllogism[47] it can be stated that (1) International organizations must perform certain functions; (2) In order to perform these functions, treaty-making capacity is necessary; (3) Therefore, international organizations possess treaty-making capacity.

Other provisions of the constituent instrument not to the contrary then, international organizations, at the minimum, have some treaty-making power by necessary implication. The case for implied powers can be made stronger if we follow Rosenne's contention that "constituent" instruments fall within two categories—those whose central object is to purposely create an international organization and those where the organizations is only peripheral to the objects and purposes of the treaty[48]. Given this distinction one might draw a tentative "working" definition between "true" IGO's and "administrative" IGO's[49]. True IGO's by virtue of intent of creation and by virtue of their functions, in acting on the international plane, attain a will of their own. The implied capacity notion, by definition, would be uniformly applicable and because of this universal applicability actually inherent in true IGO's.

A third interpretation grows out of the compromise of the personality approach which recognizes but limits the treaty-making capacity of international organizations. In order to find a legal basis for including IGO's as independent units of the international system, Zemanek, for example, puts forth the proposition that these new units must be accepted into the international order by existing participants, and more importantly, that in this manner the scope of organizational capacity may be limited. IGO constituent instruments,

---

[46] See Bowett's, The Law of International Organizations, 1963, and his distinction between organizations of general and limited competence. Also, Rapisardi-Mirabelli, "Théorie Générale des Unions Internationales." 2 RCADI, 1925, pp. 345—390; Schwarzenberger, "Formen und Funktionen Internationaler Organisationen der heutigen Welt," Europa-Archiv, 1957, pp. 10299—10304.

[47] Morgenthau, Politics Amoung Nations, 1965, Ch. 1.

[48] Rosenne, "Is the Constitution," p. 57; Rohn, "A Legal Theory," pp. 33—34 distinguishes between three types of intent: *animus contrahendi, animus constituendi,* and *animus foederandi.*

[49] Following Heydte, "Von der Rechtssubjektivität," pp. 247—248.

it is argued, provide one manner by which these limitations can be determined.

These three interpretations rely heavily on a constitutional approach to establish either qualified or unqualified treaty-making power of international organizations. It may be questioned, however, whether the constitutional approach in whatever variation has a *direct* bearing on organizational capacity to conclude treaties.

IV. Constitutions: An Alternate Interpretation

The cornerstone of the constitutional approach is an analogy which, instead of using the concept of statehood as a basis for comparisons as in the personality approach, utilizes a state's constitution. *Although the constitutional analogy is applicable to international organizations in their relation to international law, it is doubtful that it has a direct bearing upon the capacity to conclude treaties.* Rather, a different construct, than the one presented by the constitutional approach, can be developed; a construct which, in the long run, is claimed to be the more valid.

To develop this construct it is first necessary to trace the arguments of the constitutional approach. And, in doing so, it is necessary to keep in mind a distinction between time and levels of analysis. By time is simply meant the historical growth of constitutions, and priority of domestic constitutional development. For purposes of distinguishing levels of analysis we can hypothesize over time a general legal system which, purely for analytic purposes, can be broken down into domestic and international sub-systems; each developing its own peculiar variation of general law. Given this dichotomy to what extent are constitutions and constituent instruments similar under general law and to what extent may historical variations have brought about a qualitative distinction between the two types of instruments?

Since we are at this stage of explication not yet concerned with the relationship of the two sub-systems nor the hierarchy of norms established by each, but only the process by which constitutions are brought about, in what manner is a constitution in both of these sub-systems established? The parallels are obvious and striking. The only morphological difference between the two is constitutional membership—individuals in the one, states in the other. As far as purpose and process go the distinction is not one of substance but one of definitional form, i.e., individuals are members of the national system and states of the international system.

Beginning with the domestic constitution it can be demonstrated that this instrument is the formal basis of the state and its governmental functions. Norms and structures contained therein provide the mechanisms by which societal interaction is regulated[50].

Within the realm of the domestic system it is accepted that the basic unit is self-determining, i.e., whatever concerns the domestic unit is decided within it[51]. From this rule flow subsidiary ones such as that the entity has the right of self-organization, that when dealing with other units it has an unfettered right to decide with whom, in what areas, and to what extent it will interact. A corollary rule is that other basic units are not to interfere with this self-determination. Although basic units in their external relations are theoretically free to interact to whatever extent they wish, constitutions and internal political process can limit actual interaction. These limitations, according to legal interpretation, are not the concern of international law, but that of the domestic system. A strict separation is thus brought about between domestic and international legal systems, and constitutions fall within the domestic sphere.

For international organizations, however, it is argued that only partial self-determination is permitted, the extent of which is deduced from the constituent instrument. Thus, self-organization, choice of entities with which IGO's wish to interact, and the subject matter with which the organization may deal are limited by the constituent instrument. Up to this point there appears to be little differentiation between the function of a constitution and a constituent instrument; and, if, the manner of limitation were to end here, the parallel with the domestic system would be continued. It does not. Rather proponents of the constitutional approach argue that these limitations should be codified under international law. In short, it is claimed that the constitution of other units, i.e., states, is essentially different from that of international organizations.

On what basis is this distinction made, and how defensible is it? As long as international political action was primarily carried on

[50] The notion expounded here is akin to that of the social contract. Although it may be claimed that the original contract has universal applicability, it is also possible to identify numerous specific contracts applicable only to the "signatory" society. Specific provisions and mode of establishment may differ, but the intent of ordering and regulating are uniform. It may be posited that the fictional original contract and the historically specific contract lead through time to two types of legal orders. On the one hand domestic law which through the logical function of basic unit became a self-contained system with its primary instrument being the constitution. On the other hand, interaction of these basic units were regulated by a second sub-system of general law—international law.

[51] This is not to say that the domestic unit cannot limit its sphere of actions via an external contract. Such a decision, however, is made within the unit.

between basic units of the same structural type, the distinction between domestic and international systems was functional. A theoretical line was drawn between the internal and external actions of the basic units of international relations. With participation of organizations a new unit had to be accommodated within the existing framework, and a fundamental question which could have been extensively discussed was: should IGO's be treated in analogy to the State system or do they fall within the international order. Since IGO's were composed of states, it was accepted that organizations also fell within the international legal system. International organizations, however, also had some attributes analogous to states, e.g., constituent instruments (constitutions) and the capacity for external action. Furthermore, the desire to limit the organizational scope of action was also present. How could the attributes of stateness and the desired limitation be fitted into the international legal system?

As often before, international law sought an analogous phenomenon in the domestic legal order, and found it in the "legal person." Within the domestic system the legal person is under the law "equal" with real persons but does not necessarily have the same rights, e.g., a corporation does not cast a ballot in national elections. Furthermore, the corporation's scope of action can be regulated by statute. The legal person is thus a "second-rate" citizen controlled by the real persons and the international legal systems. The analogy of the legal person, thus permitted the logical consequence within the international legal system for (1) placing the constituent instrument of an international organization directly under the scrutiny of international law, (2) limiting the scope of action of organizations via international law.

However, the constitutional analogy begins to break down with the introduction of the legal person. A subtle shift in proof takes place. Whereas constitutions and constituent instruments were compared a shift has taken place to comparing the state unit with the IGO unit, and the IGO unit *by definition of the domestic legal system* has *ipso facto* been relegated to a subservient role. And, only by defining the units in a hierarchical relationship are the constitutions and constituent instruments hierarchically related.

It would thus appear that a more logical avenue of inquiry and a more logical construct is the analysis of states and IGO's as political and juridical units within a total environment.

The basis of this construct is a broader conception of international law than generally accepted, as well as overlapping legal relationships regulating internal and external action.

Boundaries of a general legal system can be posited encompassing levels of legal systems, which, by commonality of designation, presumably all regulate interaction between identifiable entities. Excluding several historical units for purposes of simplification we can identify the following entities: individuals, states, international organizations, see Figure 1. Each of these entities by virtue of reality may have two types of relationships—an internal and an external—and regulation of these relationships give rise to corresponding rules of legal systems.

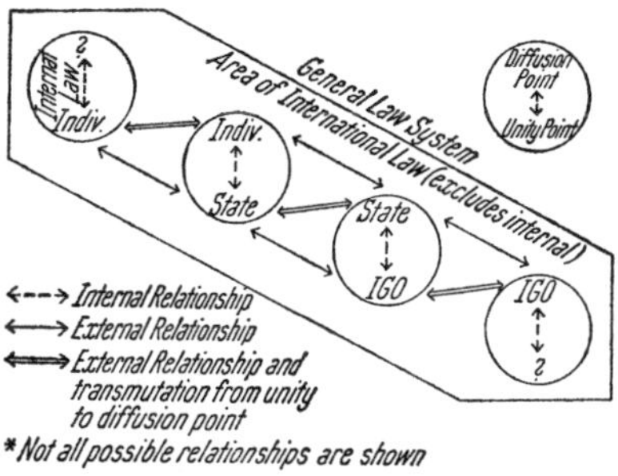

Fig. 1. Levels of international law

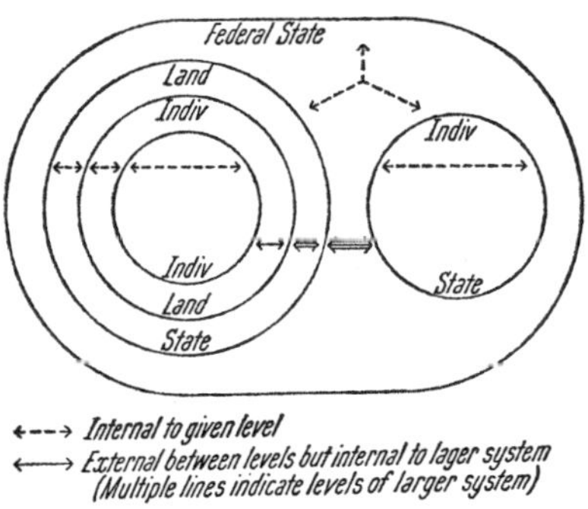

Fig. 2. Levels of relationships within federal system

Within any internal relationship there can be identified at least two reference points which are of primary concern and whose mutual regulation is of central importance to the legal system—the diffusion point and the unity point[52]. Historically the diffusion point has been

[52] The diffusion point is a collective term representing the subsystems of any system, e.g., the individual members of a family, stockholders in a corporation, members of an organization. The unity point stands for the theoretical system itself, e.g., the individual, the corporation, the state; or for the spokesman of the practical system, e.g., the head of the family, the board of governors, the government.

Any unity point exhibits a threefold capacity. First, in regard to its subsystems which is defined as the internal relationship. Second, in regard to other

hierarchically subordinate to the unity point with the interaction of the two being governed by a rules system. In the case of the state level, the rules system is the constitution. This rules system regulating the internal aspect has also, historically, been applicable only to those entities falling within the unity point. The internal system may, furthermore, have within it several hierarchical and/or coequal systems, see Figure 2. Whatever the size, number of levels, or type of structure, the unity point always delineates the bounds for legal purposes. But even more so, the unity point of the legal system is identical with the concept of basic unit for the analysis of any given level of the political system.

An entity's external relationships concern those activities which are carried on between basic units or entities having different unity points. History again demonstrates that these activities are governed by a somewhat different rules set termed the international legal system. Tautologically the prime purpose of international law (more descriptive would probably be the term "interunit law") is to regulate relationships between basic units. Basic units, however, need not be of the same type but may be differentiated structurally.

The internal and external aspects are not independent, however, neither theoretically nor practically. Political and legal development have both identified the unity point of any system playing a dual role. On the one hand it provides the super-structure of one organizational and legal system, while on the other it acts within a second legal system and may provide the infra-structure (diffusion point) of another organization. In this manner the unity point provides continuity for the whole system.

By becoming the diffusion point of a more encompassing system it cannot be assumed that the totality of any one diffusion point is automatically subordinated to a new unity point. It is at this stage that it becomes necessary to revert to the importance of constitutions for it is they that set forth extent of the regulating process as well as the mutual rights of diffusion and unity points. In the case of federal states, for example, the degree of hierarchical structural relationship may be greater than for confederations, while for an IGO it may be low. In any event, the degree to which a new unity point establishes a hierarchical relationship should be measurable on a continuum[53].

---

unity points which is defined as its external relationship. And finally, in its capacity to transform itself into one part of a diffusion point whenever it participates in creating a new unity point.

[53] For organizations certain criteria could be measured to test integration, see Rohn, "A Legal Theory of International Organizations," 5 Turkish Yearbook of Intl. Law, 1964, pp. 19—54.

Thus, whenever an additional unity point (or expanded basic unit) is brought into being, another legal level is created, and the new relationships, depending upon previous agreements, compounds possible relationships. The differential of basic unit development in its unity point encompassment furthermore permits differing structural types to act on the international level. Thus, it is possible in the first instance for a state to interact with an insurgent group. Theoretically, interact on the international plane with a state, or in the second instance for a state to interact with an insurgent group. Theoretically, of course, it is possible for any unit, no matter what its relationship to a unity point, to interact with any other unit.

What does it have to do with constitutions and organizational capacity to conclude treaties? Firstly, the constitutional analogy seen within a total context demonstrates that the rise of international organization, or for that matter the reality of any other type of basic unit, is neither novel nor unexpected given the historical development of international systems. This being the case, IGO's have in fact, interacted as independent units with other types of international entities, and will continue to do so. Secondly, it can be demonstrated that configurations of possible interactions multiply with each addition of another level or layer of relationships. Extent and degree of interaction may be restricted by previous commitments but these restrictions operate on the internal process. Thirdly, it can be demonstrated that constitutions are the instruments which regulate internal process. Since constitutions regulate the relationships between diffusion and unity points only, they are inner-oriented and fall within the scope of the domestic rather than the international legal system. Fourthly, it can be demonstrated that since the unity point has a dual role, whenever it is transmuted into a diffusion point on a different level, it may have a high degree of regulatory function within one organizational system, a participatory function in another system, and again depending upon the type of relationship established between the two levels, independent spheres of action. In any event, the governing rules are always internally oriented to a specific organization and to a specific level. Finally and most importantly, nowhere in the process of Figures 1 and 2, nor in historical development of basic units has it been demonstrated that treaty-making capacity emanates strictly or can be determined legally from a source outside of the unity point. In fact capacity must be seen as a *sine qua non*—otherwise there would be no legal system. On the practice level, regardless of international legal prescription, capacity will be determined by the mutual decision of two units, whatever their structure and designation, to interact. Only when they have interacted, or are in the process of doing so, is the relationship governable by the international legal system.

The preceding argument attempts, on a theoretical level, to provide a new construct whereby certain specific problems facing a draft on organizational treaty law may be resolved. One problem, for example, is to determine the proper role of constituent instruments. The Vienna Convention mentions them in four articles[54] and evidently treats them as a *lex specialis*. Constituent instruments are, on the one hand, considered to be treaties falling within the scope of the Convention; yet, recognizing their special characteristics, they are also treated as something else[55]. Thus, in Article 5 the constituent instrument as a whole falls within the scope of the law of treaties for states. Article 20 (2) places acceptance of reservations under organizational discretion. What the drafters of the Vienna Convention failed to do was to distinguish between time and levels of legal relationships. There is no reason why a constituent instrument, just as a state constitution, cannot fall within two different categories at different time periods. Before the international organization becomes operative as a juridically functioning unit, the constituent instrument can be considered as an international treaty. At the moment the IGO becomes operative the instrument becomes a constitution. Simply because the organization is called to life a qualitative change takes place in the functioning of the instrument.

Once the organization is established it is governed by its constitution, and since a constitution is internally oriented, constitutional considerations of any type are not directly subject to the external legal system of international law. This being the case, there is no theoretical or legal basis for the inclusion of constitutional provisions within the sphere of a future convention.

Finally, the analogy provided here can serve to sharpen the focus between "capacity" and "competence." Capacity to conclude treaties, it may be argued, is itself not a legal concept rather it is a *sine qua non*, or *a priori* assumption that must be made in order for legal relationships to be subsequently established. In this sense, capacity, just as the unity point, of the political system, can be seen as the nexus between legal levels. And in this sense it can furthermore be seen as giving rise to relationships which have external organizational effects. Capacity for external action is thus present whenever two unity points interact. From an external point of view capacity to conclude treaties is thus technically and theoretically unlimited as to scope and type of entity.

[54] See footnote 5.

[55] Rosenne, "Is the Constitution," p. 46.

Capacity thus depends upon the "willingness" of two units to interact. This willingness, however, is procedurally circumscribed by the internal procedure of any given unit. In the case of established entities the procedure is provided by the constitution which may distribute powers, priorities, or limitations on external actions. Such distribution delineates the competence of any given organ to act in the name of the organization as a whole. Given this latter distinction, it should become clearer that the organization as a whole possesses capacity, while competence may be possessed limitedly or generally by an organ. Following the reasoning of the Vienna Convention, the validity of a treaty is determined primarily by capacity and secondarily by competence of an organ[56].

In summary then, the description of the foregoing contention is to remind us that international law and precedents set by some provisions of the Vienna Convention[57] should not be viewed as regulating interaction only between states but also between basic units. If international law is limited to states primarily, international realities will bypass the legal system built on this basis. It will, eventually result in a possibly irreversible gap between the norms and reality of the legal superstructure. The model provided here has attempted to provide for continuity and transition by taking into account the process of change and the appearance of new political units. It is not claimed that this rudimentary alternative takes into account all practical problems which have arisen in conjunction with organizational capacity to conclude treaties, but it is contended that it can provide a basis for a system of theoretical thought which will accommodate probable change much more easily than the thoughts underlying the Vienna Convention.

V. Custom

Custom enables us to explore another perspective from which it is claimed that capacity of international organizations can be determined. Custom may be defined as an habitual way of doing things, and because of repetition and uniformity establishing norms which are incorporated into a legal system either directly or implicitly. The intent or manner of action determining usage is of secondary importance, of primary relevance is repetitiveness of the end result if accompanied by *opinio juris*[58].

---

[56] Article 46 of the Vienna Convention.

[57] Article 5 of the Vienna Convention.

[58] Compare the arguments of The Paquete Habana and The Lola, 175 U.S. 677, and the Lotus, P.C.I.J., Ser. A, No. 10 (1927).

Justification for customary actions establishing capacity of IGO's are general observations of how states and international organizations act, and they are also legal in nature in the sense of ICJ 38/1/6: international organizations have concluded treaties, i.e., have entered into some forms of relationships with states and other IGO's; states have not challenged this practice either as members of an organization or as treaty partners; even when an IGO's explicit constitutional provisions have been expanded beyond the intent of the framers, such action was sanctioned not only by the member states of the organization but also by the IGO's treaty partners. Thus, for all practical purposes, organizational treaty-making capacity is "accepted as law" by the states of the world[59].

The fact that "it is being done" suffices as a premises for a realist theory. However, the question "why" may linger, and proponents of the customary approach attempt to answer it. As with personality and constitutional arguments, it is claimed that organizations have certain functions to perform, and to realize these must enter into relationships with other entities. More importantly, however, the reserve is also true: the organization has something to offer which is desired by another entity. Together a meeting of minds is achieved and a bargain struck. It is the desire and will of the two entities which is the basis of a treaty: a mutual desire to receive, share, or give a certain good (object) and the knowledge, belief, or hope that the object will actually be delivered[60]. Thus, whenever two entities realize both a need and mutual opportunity for the satisfaction of that need, action via treaty is taken. It is for this reason that Seyerstedt argues that simply because organizations at this time do not have certain needs, they have not entered into the same kinds of relationships as states, but this does not preclude their doing so when needs and opportunities arise[61].

Even if the argument of custom with the tenet of "it is being done" is accepted, custom is not a panacea which automatically resolves all practical questions related to a law of treaties for IGO's. Specifically, it may be asked (1) when has practice sufficiently developed to be accepted as law? (2) can a general rule on organizational capacity be agreed upon given the diversity of IGO structures and treaty-making practices; and (3) despite customary rules, to what extent can (should) an agreed-upon prescriptive rule challenge practice?

[59] Chiu; Schneider; Rosenne, "United Nations Treaty Practice," 86 RCADI, 1954, pp. 275—444.

[60] It is also practice which determines the extent to which given states observe their contractual relations.

[61] Seyerstedt, "Objective Personality," p. 28; But neither have all states exercised all the powers that they actually could.

In dealing with custom we are at the outset faced with questions of fact as to actual practice. The two central factual questions revolve around the definition of treaty and the identification of international organizations. Traditionally, it has been claimed that no matter what the form or name of an international agreement, its legal nature is the same. This view has of late been challenged[62]. Whatever the solution agreed upon, it will have a significant bearing on the legality of organizational contracts. A great variety of views have also been expressed as to relevant criteria for the identification of international organizations[63]. In both instances confusion abounds because either no prescriptive criteria have been agreed upon, or because practice and interpretation of practice has become so complicated as to make a clear over-view impossible.

An attempt will be made here to demonstrate that practice of international organizations has available criteria, and that application of these criteria can lead to practical alternatives. It, again, is not the intention that either the data or the criteria presented are to be considered as absolute and the only relevant ones, but it is hoped that the method and over-all profile presented will result in a clearer picture concerning IGO and state treaty practice.

Since neither a universal nor commonly accepted definition of international organization exists, for reasons of availability, and in regard to a certain amount of practical experience, we can adopt the Union of International Association's distinction between inter-governmental and non-governmental organizations:

> Any international organization which is not established by inter-governmental agreement shall be considered a non-governmental organization[64]. [Non-governmental organizations also include] organizations which accept members designated by governmental authorities, provided that such membership does not interfere with the free expression of views of the organization[65].

---

[62] The actual problem might be whether or not a certain type of instrument should be treated in the same manner as a treaty. Parry, "The Treaty-Making Power of the United Nations," 26 BYIL, 1949, pp. 108—149; Jones, "International Agreements Other than 'Inter-State Treaties'—Modern Developments," 21 BYIL, 1944, pp. 111—121; Lejnieks, "The Nomenclature of Treaties: A Quantitative Analysis," 2 Texas International Law Forum, 1966, pp. 175—188. The question can also be raised whether "administrative" agreements, cf., footnote 41, or parallel resolutions, cf., Schneider, p. 31, should be treated as being the same as treaties.

[63] See footnote 27.

[64] ECOSOC Res. 288 (X) of 27 February 1950 concerning the implementation of consultative status.

[65] Resolution 1296 (XLIV) of 25 June 1968 amplified on Res. 288 (X).

The UIA having taken its criteria from these resolutions states in the 1966—67 Yearbook that

[i]dentifying eligible governmental organizations therefore presents no problem. All organizations established by agreement to which three or more states or parties have been included. Following adoption of Resolution 334 (XI) of 20 July 1950 it was agreed with the U.N. Secretariat in New York that bodies arising out of bilateral agreements should not be included in the Yearbook[66].

Again because of availability of data and reliability, treaty will be defined as an instrument registered or filed with the United Nations[67]. For purposes of explaining the treaty profile of international organizations it is assumed that a representative picture is presented in the Treaty Series. This assumption is made notwithstanding Article 2 (a) of the Vienna Convention, and knowing that not all treaties are registered in accordance with Article 102 of the Charter[68].

In the 1966—67 Yearbook of International Organizations 199 intergovernmental and 2,134 non-governmental organizations are listed. Of the inter-governmental organizations 25 belong to the United Nations "family," nine were attributed to the European Communities, and 165 were listed as "other." These 199 entities are the universe of international organizations. How many of these IGO have concluded treaties, and what is the nature of these treaties?

---

[66] Yearbook of International Organizations, 1966—67, p. 11. The Treaty Information Project defines an IGO as composed of two or more states. Cf. footnote 70.

[67] Data for organizational treaties came from the Treaty Information Project which is a computerization of UNTS and other treaties. For background see 12 International Studies Quarterly, 1968, pp. 174—195. The format of the Project is so designed as to give not only a total profile of treaty-making practice but also a comparative profile of distinct entities. The data is furthermore organized in such a manner that statistical operations can be performed to identify trends of treaty practice which can serve as foundations for specific premises. For a novel analysis of IGO's in treaties see Rohn, Institutions in Treaties: A Global Survey of Magnitudes and Trends from 1945 to 1965, 1970.

Rohn, Treaty Profiles, pre-publication copy at the Hague Academy of International Law, 1969.

[68] For a comparison of UN registered v. unregistered treaties see Rohn, "Canada in the U.N. Treaty Series: A Global Perspective," 4 Canadian Yearbook of Intl. Law, 1966, pp. 102—130, and Rohn, "Turkish Treaties in Global Perspective," 6 Turkish Yearbook of International Relations, 1965, pp. 119—160. Failure on the part of states or organizations to register (file) all international instruments may also be indicative of practice regarding definition of treaty. See for example the comment of the Australian government in Reports of the International Law Commission, GAOR, 21st Sess., Supp. 9 (A/6309/Rev. 1), p. 106.

For the twenty-year period 1 January 1946 to 31 December 1965, 7,885 bilateral and "quasi-bilateral[69]" treaties were published in the United Nations Treaty Series volumes 1—598. Of this total states only were parties to 6,199 treaties while international organizations were party to 1,686 treaties or 27%. The organizational treaties included 1,493 of a bilateral nature and 193 of a quasi-bilateral. Specific breakdowns are presented in Tables I—IV.

Table I. *Organizations Which Have Concluded Treaties*

Organization	No. of Treaties			Organization	No. of Treaties		
	Tot.	Sts.	IGO		Tot.	Sts.	IGO
BRD	455	450	5	IRO	3	2	1
JN	248	201	47	IMF	2	0	2
VHO	182	172	10	OAU/STRC	2	0	2
JNICEF	120	120	0	E Af Comm Ser O	2	0	2
JNDP	111	103	8	NATO	2	2	0
DA	82	81	1	SPC	2	0	2
AEA	71	58	13	SEATO	2	2	0
LO	59	35	24	OAU	2	0	2
CAO	22	18	4	ELDO	2	2	0
NESCO	16	9	7	IFC	1	0	1
ELUX	15	15	0	UPU	1	0	1
AO	12	3	9	APO	1	0	1
N	9	0	9	BIS	1	1	0
URATOM	7	6	1	CERN	1	1	0
VMO	6	2	4	Hague Priv IL	1	1	0
llied Mil Occ	6	6	0	IDB	1	1	0
MCO	5	0	5	IANEC	1	0	1
OMECON	5	5	0	LAFTA	1	0	1
CSC	5	4	1	League Arab St	1	0	1
AS	5	4	1	OECD	1	0	1
SRO	4	4	0	OCAS	1	0	1
EC	4	3	1	OPEC	1	1	0
TU	3	0	3	PAHO	1	0	1
of Europe	3	1	2	OCAM	1	0	1
ENELUX	3	3	0	Danube Sav Rail	1	1	0
				Sub-Total	1493	1317	176
State and 2 IGO					10	10	0
State and Multi IGO					135	135	0
ulti State and 1 IGO					47	47	0
dd					1	1	0
				Total	1686	1510	176

[69] For definition of "quasi-bilateral" see Rohn, Users Manual for Treaty Profiles, 1969, p. 2, and Scott, "Doubtful Laterality in Treaties," 1969, unpublished research paper, Treaty Information Project, University of Washington.

Table II. *Organizations Which Have Concluded Treaties with both States and Organizations*

UNTS PROJ No.	YBIO No.	Organization	No. Memb. 68/9 YBIO	No. Instruments			Subject Matter*										Regist. by Party		Non Memb. Sig.
							ADM/ DPL		SOC/ COOP		ECO/ COOP		AID/ IGO		MILI-TARY				
				Tot.	with Stat.	with IGOs	S	I	S	I	S	I	S	I	S	I	S	I	
206	1180	IBRD	107	455	450	5					1		449	5			449	2	
201	1010	UN	124	248	201	47	14	8	23	3	3		145	36	16		191	44	5
205	1140	WHO	127	182	172	10			45	2	2		125	8			169	4	
221	1890	UNDP		111	103	8	1		1		1		100	8			1		
207	1240	IDA	98	82	81	1							81	1			80		
216	1650	IAEA	98	71	58	13	1		9		1		47	13			54	8	
202	1020	ILO	118	59	35	24		1	2	4			33	19			33	19	
210	1280	ICAO	116	22	18	4			2				16	4			18		
204	1100	UNESCO	122	16	9	7	1		4				4	7			2	1	
203	1060	FAO	117	12	3	9							3	9				1	
473	8350	EURATOM	18	7	6	1			2				4	1					1
213	1400	WMO	120	6	2	4							2	4			1	1	
471	8150	ECSC	6	5	4	1	1				2		1	1					1
365	7320	OAS	23	5	4	1							4	1					1
472	8250	EEC	6	4	3	1					3			1					1
274	3320	Cl of Europe	18	3	1	2					1	2					1		
403	6249	IRO		3	2	1	1							1	1				
		Total		1291	1152	139	19	9	88	9	14	2	1014	119	17	0	999	80	9

* For topics of subject matter see footnote 74
S = Treaties with states
I = Treaties with organizations

Table III. *Organizations Which Have Concluded Treaties with States only*

UNTS PROJ No.	YBIO No.	Organization	No. Memb. 68/9 YBIO	No. Instruments			Subject Matter										Regist. by Party		Non Memb. Sig.
				Tot.	with Stat.	with IGOs	ADM/ DPL		SOC/ COOP		ECO/ COOP		AID/ IGO		MILI- TARY				
							S	I	S	I	S	I	S	I	S	I	S	I	
219	1830	UNICEF	30	120	120	0	1		4		2		113						
404		BELUX		15	15	0					14		1						10
451		Allied Mil Occ		6	6	0					5				1				
273	3280	COMECON	9	5	5	0					5						5		
294	3860	ESRO	10	4	4	0							4				4		1*
381	2640	BENELUX	3	3	3	0							3						2
359	7140	NATO	15	2	2	0							1		1				
378	7660	SEATO	8	2	2	0			1				1						
496	3880	ELDO	7	2	2	0							2				2		
257	2580	BIS	26	1	1	0							1						
293	3780	CERN	13	1	1	0							1						
296	3980	Hague Priv IL	23	1	1	0							1						
305	4420	IDB	21	1	1	0							1						
368	7360	OPEC	9	1	1	0							1						1
497		Danube Sav Rail		1	1	0							1						
		Total		165	165	0	1	0	5	0	26	0	131	0	2	0	11	0	14

* Observer

Table IV. *Organizations Which Have Concluded Treaties with Organizations only*

UNTS PROJ No.	YBIO No.	Organization	No. Memb. 68/9 YBIO	No. Instruments Tot.	No. Instruments with Stat.	No. Instruments with IGOs	Subject Matter ADM/DPL S	ADM/DPL I	SOC/COOP S	SOC/COOP I	ECO/COOP S	ECO/COOP I	AID/IGO S	AID/IGO I	MILITARY S	MILITARY I	Regist. by Party S	Regist. by Party I	Non Memb. Sig.
401	6949	LN		9	0	9		8						1					
214	1440	IMCO	67	5	0	5								5					
212	1360	ITU	134	3	0	3								3					
209	1200	IMF	107	2	0	2								2					
265	7280	OAU/STRC	38	2	0	2						2							
278	3480	E Af Com Ser O	3	2	0	2				1				1					
377	7680	SPC	6	2	0	2								2					
480	7260	OAU	38	2	0	2		1						1					
208	1220	IFC	86	1	0	1								1					
211	1320	UPU	137	1	0	1								1					
255	2540	APO	12	1	0	1				1									
308	4540	IANEC	23	1	0	1								1					
355	6840	LAFTA	11	1	0	1								1					
357	6920	League Arab St	14	1	0	1				1									
361	7220	OECD	21	1	0	1								1					
366	7340	OCAS	5	1	0	1								1					
369	7380	PAHO	26	1	0	1				1									
430	2940	OCAM	14	1	0	1								1					
		Total		37	0	37	0	9	0	4	0	2	0	22	0	0	0	0	0
IGO with States and IGO				1291	1152	139	19	9	88	9	14	2	1014	119	17	0	999	80	9
IGO with States only				165	165	0	1	0	5	0	26	0	131	0	2	0	11	0	14
IGO with IGO only				37	0	37	0	9	0	4	0	2	0	22	0	0	0	0	0
		Total		1493	1317	176	20	18	93	13	40	4	1145	141	19	0	1010	80	23

Of the 199 organizations listed in the Yearbook[70], 50 or one-fourth were signatories to at least one treaty. Fifteen of these organizations, however, concluded the bulk of bilateral treaties—1,421 (95%). Twelve of these organizations belong to the UN "family," while two are no longer active members of the international community[71].

A treaty profile may also be seen in terms of the type of entities with which organizations concluded agreements. Table II includes organizations which have concluded instruments with both states and other organizations. Seventeen IGO's fall within this category with a total of 1,291 or 87% of all organizational treaties. The predominant number of instruments (1,152) were signed with states, and the UN "family" as well as the European Communities are represented. Organizations which have concluded treaties with states only (Table III) number 15 with a total of 165 instruments. UNICEF, whose independent organizational status may be questioned[72], accounts for 120 of these, and if eliminated from the grouping would reduce the final sum to 45 instruments. Primary functions of these organizations include alliances, research, economic, and financial matters. With the exception of UNICEF, the UN "family" is not represented. The third grouping (Table IV) represents the IGO's which have signed only with other organizations. These number 18 with 37 agreements. As to function this group is most diversified in that specialized agencies, research, and economic organizations are represented.

If we were to assume that the type of partner with whom an organization enters into relationship has a bearing on its capacity, the numbers indicate that a future article should be limited to organizations which have conclude or may conclude treaties with both states and IGO's. On the other hand, it could also be deduced that an article on capacity should be limited to treaties with states only in view of the fact that 1,317 (88%) of organizational treaties were concluded with states.

The size of an organization's membership does not appear to affect its treaty-making capacity. Organizations which have signed treaties range in membership from 137 (UPU which has signed only with IGO's) to 3 (East African Common Service Organization also signing with IGO's only). The range of membership of organizations

[70] Included in the Tables are the Belgium-Luxembourg Economic Union, the Allied Military Commission, and The Danube-Save-Adriatic Railway Company, which are not listed in the Yearbook of International Organizations.

[71] See Table I.

[72] The Yearbook of International Organizations gives UNICEF a distinct code from the UN even though the organization should probably be listed under the UN directly.

which have relationships with both states and IGO is 127 (WHO) to 6 (ECSC). Practice thus indicates that capacity is not dependent upon size of membership.

In regard to subject matter[73] organizations cover the same range of topics as states. Overwhelmingly predominant, however, is the Aid-IGO category with 86%, followed by social co-operation with 7%. Organizations taken together may thus deal with the same range of subject matters as states[74].

As concerns registration, a high percentage of IGO treaties have been filed and accepted by the Secretariat. If we take the first registrant as criterion we notice that IGO have filed 92% of all their mutual treaties, and 76% of all those with states. As in other examples above, the UN "family" has been the most active; however, treaties have also been registered by the Council of Europe, COMECON, ELDO, and ESRO.

Finally, it has been argued that in evaluating capacity, it might be functional to distinguish between treaties with members and non-members. As the Tables indicate most organizations entered into relationships only with their own members, and it should be logically evident that the greater the membership, e.g., UN, the less the possibility to sign with non-members. There are several instances whereby non-members have recognized organizational capacity to conclude treaties. As in the case with states it can be assumed that entering into treaty-relationship indicates recognition of the independence of the organization[75].

The above statistics give us indications as to treaty-making capacity and generally support arguments made by proponents of the customary approach.

VI. Conclusions

On 23 May 1969 the Vienna Conference on the Law of Treaties recommended to the General Assembly that the International Law Commission study the question of treaties concluded by international

[73] Rohn, Manual, pp. 4 and 12: ADM DIPL = administrative and diplomatic matters; SOCIO COOP = health, education, culture and welfare plus communications and transportation; ECON COOP = economic matters; AID + IGOS = aid and international organizations; MILITARY = all military matters.

[74] See Tables II—IV.

[75] On recognition see Heydte, "Von der Rechtssubjektivität," p. 254; Seidl-Hohenveldern, "Die völkerrechtliche Haftung für Handlungen internationaler Organisationen im Verhältnis zu Nichtmitgliedstaaten," 11 ÖZföR, 1961, pp. 497 to 506; Valki, "The Juristic Personality and Treaty-Making Power of International Organizations," Questions of International Law, 1968, pp. 285—308.

organization. The implication of this recommendation is that organizations possess treaty-making capacity, and this will most likely become the ILC's working premise. Neither this working hypothesis nor the empirical fact of the existence of organizational treaties, however, will satisfy all members of the Commission. And, even if the working hypothesis is not challenged on the theoretical basis, difficulties are likely to arise in specific application. Problems to be resolved will include the place of IGO's in the modern world and its international legal system, the explicit determination of what an IGO is, the extent of capacity that an organization can exercise, and the types of instruments that are to be regulated by the convention. In each instance, given certain premises, the range can be limited or all-inclusive. The final choice will depend upon balancing differing interests until a workable consensus is achieved. Justifications for each view point will be derived from those philosophical, political, legal, and practical considerations which best support a given view.

The aforementioned approaches to organizational capacity have demonstrated that various alternatives are available in resolving specific problems, and although each perspective has validity and merits, each also brings new problems with it. This is probably to be expected in view of divergent purposes. Taken together, however, could difficulties be resolved and a viable alternative presented by finding common ground on which most approaches could agree?

Organizational capacity has three alternative conclusions: (1) exclusion from the law of treaties (as in ILC 1966 and Vienna 1969); (2) limiting capacity and defining this limitation; and (3) full inclusion in, or analogous to, Article 6 of the Vienna Convention.

Excluding an article on capacity in a future Convention would in all likelihood not affect the convention as a whole. As statements at the Vienna Conference and in the International Law Commission evidence, Article 6 states the obvious, and the only logical reason for its retention was to reaffirm the *raison d'être* of the Convention. Since it is generally accepted that organizations also possess treaty-making capacity, exclusion would have the same effect on a future convention. In view of the relatively recent appearance of so many IGO's it might nevertheless be helpful to explicitly reaffirm their capacity.

It has been demonstrated adequately by writers that constitutions of international organizations are varied and do not contain provisions for all treaties that IGO's have concluded. Since explicit constitutional provisions have not served actual treaty-practice, the notion of implied powers has been forwarded to compensate. Implied powers, it is argued, are necessary for any organization to fulfill the purposes for which it was established. Implied powers leading to the idea of functional imperative and subsequent limitation by convention, however, have two major drawbacks.

First, "function" is a term which permits almost any interpretation one wishes to give it. It is so inclusive that one would be hard pressed in trying to exclude anything from its scope. Even if function could be defined, e.g., in the health area, the problem of "related functions" remains. It is quite possible that an ingenious person could make a good case for relating all worldly phenomena to the area of health thus enabling WHO, for example, to deal with all possible functions. Since the inter-relationship of the modern world does not permit clear-cut functional distinctions, an additional section on limitations would lead only to disputes concerning organizational jurisdiction. More problems would be created than resolved.

Secondly, and more importantly, it is doubtful that a limitation on organizational capacity is properly included in an international convention. Under the constitutional approach an attempt was made to demonstrate the necessity of applying international law to external situations only while leaving constitutional limitations and interpretations to internal consideration. Within an organization a vast majority of members might wish to change or enhance functions explicitly through constitutional amendment or through more informal means. Given a limiting provision in a convention, however, a dissenting state could argue that any change in "violation" of the original constituent provisions is illegal. Such a possible interpretation would tend to stifle development of organizations. Furthermore, a limiting provision would also permit both member and non-member states wishing to conclude a treaty with an IGO (and possibly even third states) to interpret constitutional provisions from an external perspective. In practice this would also give rise to numerous disputes. Here too, the arguments against including constitutional interpretation within a convention are similar to those presented for the deletion of Article 5 (2) from the 1966 Draft Treaty.

In any event, the hard empirical fact which remains is that IGO's are concluding treaties in ever greater numbers. And, they are doing this regardless of theoretical considerations or possible constituent instrument limitations. Thus, both logically and sensibly, the ILC should be less concerned with determining whether or not IGO's possess treaty-making capacity than with providing guidelines for the resolution of conflicts which may arise out of organizational treaties.

It is therefore suggested that a comparable article to the Vienna Convention should read:

> Every inter-governmental organization possesses the capacity to conclude treaties.

No limitation or amplification is necessary. Because treaties primarily are related to signatory entities only, each entity is free to determine whether or not it recognizes a unit as an IGO. The organizational treaty profile presented above indicates that this is in fact the manner in which states and organizations operate. If there are to be limitations of treaty-making powers for IGO's, these can be handled by the internal process of the organization just as this is the accepted practice for states.

Finally, within the constitutional approach a rudimentary framework was presented to indicate that organizational participation in the international legal and political system need not be considered detrimental, but is simply part of societal adaption to contemporary needs. Thus, seen within the context of dynamic international politics and law, the proposed article is based on the hope that a future contention in providing for contingencies will not stifle progressive development of international law by unnecessary and unworkable limitations on organizational capacity.

Österr. Zeitschr. f. öffentl. Recht, Suppl. 1, 165—193 (1971)

The Concept and Forms of Treaties * Concluded by International Organizations

Chris Osakwe
Research Student at the Faculty of Laws, Moscow State University, Moscow, USSR

Introduction

The role of treaties and, in fact, of international agreements as a whole in international relations is constantly on the increase. Both sovereign states and international organizations have found it necessary to make constant resort to the conclusion of treaties and other forms of international agreements as a means of developing peaceful co-operation among themselves. The conclusion of a Convention on The Law of Treaties[1] in the Spring of 1969 is a partial recognition of this fact.

Prior to the adoption of the Vienna Convention on The Law of Treaties—a Convention which is still at the stage of ratification by states—there had been previous private attempts to codify The Law of Treaties[2].

Whereas all codification efforts so far attempted to give a definition of a treaty[3], none of them thought it necessary to dilate on the essential constituent elements of a treaty. This latter task is probably left to doctrinal law. The inevitable result is that there is no generally accepted meaning of the term "treaty," and less so is

* The term "treaties" in this title employed without prejudice to the subsequent technical application of the same term in our analysis below.

[1] The Convention on The Law of Treaties which was signed at Vienna on 23rd of May, 1969 applies anly to treaties concluded between states. However, nothing in the present Convention prevents international organizations from applying some of the provisions of the Convention to treaties concluded by them, subject to the law of the organizations concerned.

[2] A glaring example of such private effort is The Havard Draft Convention. Vide infra.

[3] Vide infra.

there any unanimity among text-book writers as to which elements constitute a treaty. The attitude of any international lawyer towards this question is determined by a combination of factors—the specificity of his municipal legal system, his ideological and political posture. In this report which is in two parts we shall try to examine in part I two inter-related questions. First, we shall try to delimit the term "treaty" from an international agreement and international engagement; and, second, we shall attempt a legal analysis of the elements which constitute a treaty. In part II we shall get down to the forms of international agreements concluded by international organizations. On the basis of the conclusions reached in the above analysis we shall try to juxtapose our findings with the relevant provisions of the 1969 Vienna Convention on The Law of Treaties with an eye on finding out, first, the degree of applicability of the provisions of this Convention to treaties concluded by international organizations inter se or with sovereign states, and, second, we shall attempt to put forward some suggestions on any future Convention on The Law of Treaties concluded by international organizations.

Part I

A. The Meaning of the Term "Treaty," "International Agreement," and "International Engagement." Problem of Delimitation

In international jurisprudence the term "treaty[4]" has no settled meaning. This term has been employed differently by different authors to mean the same thing and at times to mean different things.

The uncertainty surrounding this term is yet heightened if one and the same author or text freely interchanges it with other terms which have quite different meanings. When Lord McNair wrote his groundwork on The Law of Treaties[5] he probably intended, in the title of this book, to give this term a generic connotation. Whereas in The Vienna Convention on The Law of Treaties the term "treaty"

---

[4] In Soviet Municipal law the term "dogovor" which literally means "treaty" is not exactly the same thing as "treaty" as applied in international jurisprudence. The term "dogovor" in Soviet Civil Law is probably the same thing as "contract" in the Anglo-American Conflict of Laws. In order to avoid any possible misinterpretation Soviet doctrinal International Law employs the term "mezhdunarodnyi dogovor" to designate treaties concluded on the international plane and intended to be governed by international law. Vide infra.

[5] McNair, The Law of Treaties, Oxford 1961.

is employed to denote a species in Lord McNair's genus. Furthermore, whereas the Vienna Convention on The Law of Treaties maintained this technical application of the term "treaty" in its subsequent articles[6], Lord McNair later on in the same book resorted to a double-standard[7].

Art. 18 of the Covenant of the League of Nations was perhaps the first deliberate attempt to employ the term "treaty" in a discriminate manner. This article provides: "Every treaty or international engagement entered into hereafter by any member of the League shall forthwith be registered with the Secretariat and shall as soon as possible be published by it. No such treaty or international engagement shall be binding until so registered." In no part of the Covenant is the distinction between these two acts explained.

However, in an Interpretative Memorandum proposed by the Secretary-General of the League and approved by the Council of The League in May, 1920 reference in Art. 18 of the Covenant to "every treaty and international engagement" was interpreted as follows: "Not only every formal treaty of whatsoever character and every international convention, but also other international engagement or act by which nations or their governments intend to establish legal obligations between themselves and another state, nation or government[8]."

In other words this Interpretative Memorandum understands a treaty to be a "formal treaty or international convention" concluded by states or their governments and aimed at establishing legal relations with other states, nations or their governments.

The usefulness of such an interpretation for our immediate purpose is minimal. This Interpretative Memorandum only tells us that a treaty is "a formal treaty or an international convention" and that an international engagement is, by deduction, "an informal treaty." Such an explanation only beclouds the question which it sought to resolve and it leaves the reader more confused than he was before ever reading it.

During the drafting of the 1945 Charter of an International Organization which was conceived to replace the League of Nations, the term "international engagement" as contained in the Covenant of the League of Nations probably did not appeal to the San-Francisco draftsmen. Subsequently, in Art. 102 of the UN Charter the term "international engagement" was replaced by a new one—"inter-

---

[6] Vide Art. 2-1-a of the Convention.

[7] Ibid., p. 4.

[8] Vide I LNTS, p. 9.

national agreement." Art. 102-I of the 1945 Charter provides: "Every treaty and every international agreement entered into by any member of the UN after the present Charter comes into force shall as soon as possible be registered with the Secretariat and published by it."

This same distinction between a treaty and an international agreement was maintained in paragraph 2 of Art. 102.

At the UNCIO it should be recalled that no generally accepted definition of international agreement was arrived at. But we often find references to what has now evolved as an Interpretative Statement by Committee IV/2 which was the Committee responsible for drafting Art. 102 of the Charter.

The Rapporteur of Committee IV/2 advocated the abandonment of the term "international engagement" since the latter may fall outside the strict meaning of the word "agreement." He went on define what he meant by 'agreement' in the following words: "The word 'agreement' must be understood as including unilateral engagements of an international character which has been accepted by the state in whose favour such an engagement has been entered into[9]."

It is interesting to note that even in 1945, when the general consensus was to drop the term "international engagement," attempts to distinguish a treaty from an international agreement still found it necessary to retain the term which they sought to do away with.

This distinction between the terms "treaty" and "international agreement" was also maintained in the GA Regulations intended to give effect to Art. 102 of the UN Charter[10].

Art. 1-I of these Regulations provides: "Every treaty or international agreement, whatever its form and descriptive name, entered into by one or more members of the UN after 24th October 1945, the date of the coming into force of the Charter, shall as soon as possible be registered with the Secretariat in accordance with these Regulations."

One finds it difficult to understand to what antecedent the pronoun "it" in the second phrase refers to in the above article. At any rate the use of the loose conjunction "or" in the first phrase signifies that the pronoun "it" in the second phrase refers either to "treaty" or "international agreement." This is hardly conceivable so long as the difference between treaty and international agreement, as shall be shown below, is essentially one of form[11].

---

[9] Vide 13 UNCIO Docs., p. 705.

[10] Vide UN-GA Regulations on the Registration and Publication of Treaties and International Agreements adopted by the UN-GA on 14th Dec. 1946 and subsequently amended in 1949 and 1950 respectively. Vide II YILC, 1962.

[11] Vide infra.

A treaty has only one form—the written form, whereas an international agreement is "a treaty in an unwritten form[12]." Therefore, to speak of "... treaty ... whatever its form ..." is, to say the least, highly inconsistent.

Granted that this technical deficiency in the drafting of Art. 1-I of these Regulations is rectified, the latter hardly throws any light on the basic distinction between a treaty and an international agreement.

The 1969 Vienna Convention is perhaps the most up-to-date and, in our opinion, the most lucid attempt to draw a line of difference between a treaty and an international agreement. Art. 2, parag. I-a provides: "'Treaty' means an international agreement concluded between states in written form and governed by international law, whether embodied in a single instrument or in two or more related instruments and whatever its particular designation." Thus, according to the reasoning of the Vienna Convention, a treaty is an international agreement in a written form and an international agreement is any international act concluded in an un-written form and intended to operate under international law[13].

Considering the direct involvement of the UN in the conclusion of this Convention, and bearing in mind that the Convention comes after the 1945 Charter of the UN and the 1946 UN-GA Regulations intended to give effect to Art. 102 of the UN Charter, one would not hesitate to say that Art. 2-I-a of the 1969 Vienna Convention is the latest pronouncement within the framework of the Law of the UN on the subject[14].

Thus in the Law of the UN—by which expression we mean, for the purposes of this report, the Charter of the UN, the UN-GA Regulations of 1946 intended to give effect to Art. 102 of the Charter, and the 1969 Vienna Convention on the Law of Treaties—a treaty is an international agreement in a written form and an international agreement is a treaty in an un-written form. It follows, therefore, that

---

[12] The use of the phrase "treaty in an un-written form" in this context is in line with the current definition of an international agreement in contemporary international jurisprudence. Vide supra.

[13] However, not all international acts come within the context of an international agreement. For example, an international engagement is essentially an international act but, as has been demonstrated above, international engagements embrace a much wider connotation than international agreements. Vide supra.

[14] The Preamble to the Vienna Convention speaks of some sort of organic links between the Convention and the UN Charter, and even though these two instruments constitute entirely different legal norms, UN organs are bound to operate under the permanent shadow of the Vienna Convention until an effective alternative is found.

the distinction between these two acts is only formal. Both are international acts intended to operate under international law and their legal force and international validity are basically the same.

The Harvard Draft Convention on the Law of Treaties in Art. 1 defines a treaty as follows:

a) A formal instrument by which two or more states establish or seek to establish a relation under international law between themselves;

b) A treaty does not include an agreement affected by Exchanges of Notes;

c) The term "treaty" does not include an instrument to which a person other than a state is or may be a party.

The word "formal" in its ordinary application means "in accordance with an established form." Applied, *mutatis mutandis*, to the Law of Treaties, one really wonders if there is any established form for concluding an international agreement. Except if by the phrase "formal instrument" the drafters of the Convention intended to mean an instrument in a written form, it is submitted that parag. (a) of Art. 1 of this Draft Convention is of no significant interpretative value.

Parag. (b) of this same Art., in our opinion, refers to an Exchange of Notes as an "informal instrument" and grants that, *ipso facto*, such Exchanges of Notes are not treaties. This may be correct given that by an informal instrument this paragraph means "an international instrument in an un-written form."

Art. 2 of The Inter-American Convention on The Law of Treaties concluded in 1928 stipulates that the written form is a fundamental prerequisite for any treaty[15].

So far we have discussed attempts by organized bodies—intergovernmental and private national institutions—to delimit a treaty from an international agreement. We shall next turn to the views of text-book writers on the question.

Lord McNair in his Law of Treaties[16] defines a treaty as "a written agreement by which two or more states or international organizations create or intend to create a relation between themselves operating within the sphere of international law."

Sir H. Lauterpacht in his 1953 Report on The Law of Treaties to the ILC defines a treaty as "an agreement between states, including organizations of states, intended to create legal rights and obligations of the parties" (Art. 1); and in Art. 2 he adds that "Agreements

---

15 Sexta Conferencia International Americana. Acta Final. Habana 1928.

16 McNair, The Law of Treaties, Oxford 1961, p. 4.

defined in Art. 1 constitute treaties regardless of their form and designations[17]."

In an alternative version of Art. 2 Sir H. Lauterpacht states that agreements as defined in Art. 1 constitute treaties regardless of their form or designation and regardless of whether they are expressed in one or more instruments, and that a treaty obligation may be created by a unilateral instrument accepting an offer or followed by an acceptance[18].

It is interesting to note, however, that in Part II of his Report (this part of the Report is dedicated to alternative proposals on the Law of Treaties *de lege ferenda*) Sir H. Lauterpacht proposes in Art. 17 that "an agreement is void as a treaty unless reduced to writing[19]."

Prof. F. I. Kozhevnikov, writing in 1951 stated: "There is no compulsory form for all international treaties. However, it is typical to consider treaties as being in a written form[20]." It should be noted that almost all Soviet writers on this topic hold this view as expressed by Prof. F. I. Kozhevnikov[21].

We could continue *ad infinitum* to bring examples of such doctrinal pronouncements on the distinction between treaties and international agreements but meanwhile we might try to analyse the definitions already quoted above. Most of these definitions dwell, *inter alia*, on the capacity of the parties to conclude treaties, the bases for the validity of the treaties so concluded etc. These factors do not come within the province of this report and therefore we shall try to limit ourselves only to those elements which have a direct bearing on the subject matter of this part of our report.

A perusal of the definitions given above presents us with the following general picture: a treaty is an international agreement con-

---

[17] Vide ILC Docs. A/CN. 4/63. 24th March, 1953.

[18] Ibid. [19] Ibid.

[20] Vide Kozhevnikov, International Law, M. 1951, p. 399 (in Russian).

[21] Vide Tunkin, Questions of the theory of International Law, M. 1962; Talalaev, The legal nature of an international treaty, M. 1963; Shurshalov, The bases of the validity of International treaties, M. 1957; Lukashuk, The structure and form of International treaties, Saratov 1960; by the same author—"On the significance of forms of International treaties." "Pravovedenie," 1958, No. 3. Lukashuk, in a manner which is characteristic of Soviet doctrinal International Law, states that the choice of the form of treaty is determined in the long run by the socio-economic structure of the parties to such a treaty. In his opinion, a socialist state, by which he understands a society where the interest of the state coincides with that of the masses, prefers "the most clearly expressed and most accessible form," whereas the capitalist states prefer ambiguous and cloudy forms for treaties concluded by them. Vide Lukashuk, The structure and form of International Treaties, pp. 8—17.

cluded, in principle, by subjects of international law, in a written form and intended to create legal relations between such parties. An international agreement is a treaty in an un-written form. Attention should be drawn to the fact that in our definition the phrase "un-written form" should not be understood too literally.

An international engagement is a much looser term than a treaty or an international agreement. An international engagement can possibly be defined as a common commitment by the parties on an international plane. Such a commitment shall not be deemed as precipitating any legal relations between the parties thereto. Whereas a treaty or an international agreement is an act in the law, an international engagement is probably not. A classical example of an international engagement is perhaps the Atlantic Charter by which the parties pledged themselves to certain common values. Whereas international engagements are registrable under Art. 18 of the Covenant of the LN, their registrability under Art. 102 of the UN Charter is highly debatable. It should be mentioned, however, that the registrability of an international act either under Art. 18 of the Covenant or under Art. 102 of the Charter is not a sufficient proof of the legal nature of such an act.

Whereas only subjects of international law can be parties to bilateral treaties[22], nothing precludes a subject of international law, for example, an international organization, from entering into an international act with a non-subject of international law and by subsequent agreement with such an entity confer on such an act the regime of a treaty. In such cases the proper law of the act concerned shall constitute a *'lex specialis'* only to derogate the *'lex generalis'* under which such a non-subject of international law shall not be deemed capable of participating in such treaties. Where, however, such a regime is not specifically confered on such an act, the presumption is that it as an act in some municipal law. In the case of a dispute arising either from the interpretation or the application of such acts, the judicial organ competent to settle the dispute shall apply, in the absence of a choice of law clause, any one or more of the following laws—municipal law, the internal law of the organization, international law, or the general principles of law[23]. Thus we find that

[22] The participation of non-subjects of international law in multilateral treaties is by now a familiar spectacle. Such participation neither alters the essential nature of such treaties nor does it confer upon such non-subjects of international law the character of a general international person.

[23] The author of this report holds the view that "general principles of international law" constitute a different legal system from the other three mentioned above. This same view is held by Seyersted vide "Applicable law in relations between Intergovernmental Organizations and private parties." Lecture at The

whereas, under general international law, only subjects of international law can be parties to bilateral international agreements, nothing prevents the parties to an international act from exercising their autonomy through the incorporation into the proper law of such an act a "*lex specialis*" which confers on the latter the regime of an international agreement. In such circumstances the capacity of the non-subject of international law to participate in such a bilateral treaty is '*ad hoc*.'

From the above discussion we can see that it is essential that before any act can be considered an act in international law, any disputes arising from it must necessarily be justiciable, i.e. any obligations from such an act shall be judicially determinable. In other words, it is not sufficient that the parties should reach an agreement on any subject matter. It is essential that by so doing they shall show sufficient proof that they intend to create legal relations *inter se*.

This automatically leads us to the next question in our analysis—what are the essential elements of an act in the law, what elements make up an international agreement? In this context we shall try to supply an answer to a question that has hitherto lingered around: If two parties undertake on the international plane to create for themselves extra-legal, e.g. moral or political, obligations shall such an act be binding under international law; shall such an act constitute an international agreement in the light of Art. 102 of the UN Charter?

B. The Constituent Elements of an International Agreement

According to the principle of "*Ex consensu advenit vinculum*" the foundation of treaty obligation is consent, coupled with the fundamental principle of law that consent gives rise to obligation. For the obligation to exist the consent must be true consent. However, in certain circumstances consent is an inference from the facts and a state may not deny the reality of its consent apparently regularly given.

A treaty or an international agreement presupposes a consensus, i.e. a meeting of the minds of the parties. This meeting of the minds presupposes the existence of the elements of offer and acceptance without which an internationally contracted instrument cannot belong to the genus of international agreements.

Hague Academy of International Law, July, 1967. For other views on this subject, vide Jenks, The Proper Law of International Organizations, L. 1962; see also Zemanek, Das Vertragsrecht der Internationalen Organisationen, Wien 1957, pp. 55, 135.

When two or more parties set out to conclude an international agreement it is quite natural to expect that each of them holds to an original position which may not necessarily coincide with that of the other party or parties. Such coincidence, however, is not to be absolutely ruled out. In the course of the tough bargaining which follows, the parties eventually co-ordinate their original positions into what, in Soviet legal doctrine, is referred to as the "co-ordinated will" of the parties[24].

According to Prof. G. I. Tunkin, this process of the "co-ordination of the wills" of the parties is manifest in two stages: the first stage is the co-ordination of the wills of the parties with regard to the subject matter of the treaty, and the second—the co-ordination of the wills of the parties with regard to the subsequent recognition of the resultant agreement as a norm of International Law[25]. In such a process one party offers his own terms for the treaty and the other party, acting on his own free will, either accepts such an offer with or without modifications or rejects it outright. In the latter case the rejecting party may offer fresh terms as the basis for renewed negotiations. Not until this offer is accepted by the other party can we really speak of a sufficient meeting of the minds of the parties concerned as to constitute an international agreement.

In an international engagement it would appear that the first element of Prof. G. I. Tunkin's two-stage process of the co-ordination of the wills of the parties is present, i.e. an international engagement marks the co-ordination of the wills of the parties with regard to the subject matter. However, the second element—the co-ordination of the wills of the parties with regard to the subsequent recognition of such an international engagement as a norm of international law—is lacking. In traditional language an international engagement does not yet show sufficient proof of the intention of the parties thereto to create legal relations *inter se*.

Judge Read, in a Dissenting Opinion in the Status of South-West Africa Case, stated: "It is sufficient for the present purpose to state that an arrangement agreed between the UN and the Union of South Africa necessarily included two elements—a meeting of the minds and an intention to constitute a legal obligation[26]."

In international agreements, unlike in private contracts, it is not always easy to determine which party is offering, and which is accept-

---

[24] Vide Tunkin, Questions of the theory of International law, M. 1962 (in Russian); also his '40 years of co-existence and International law' in The Soviet Yearbook of International law, 1958 (also in Russian).

[25] Tunkin. Ibid.

[26] Status of South-West Africa Case. ICJ Reports, 1950, pp. 170—1.

ing the terms of the agreement. It is not even necessary to try to establish such facts. All we need to establish is that there is a consensus of the parties because every such consensus is a complex combination of a series of offers, counter-offers and acceptances but such that in the very long analysis the process stands out as an offer followed by a subsequent acceptance. It may happen that an acceptance precedes the offer. This is the case when a party declares a public acceptance of hypothetical terms and invites suitable offers from any other party or parties. In such circumstances a treaty obligation may be created by a unilateral instrument accepting an offer or followed by an acceptance. However, not until such a unilateral offer or acceptance is subsequently responded to by another party, we can hardly talk of any treaty obligation. Prior to the acceptance of such a public offer, the offering party may withdraw or modify his original offer[27].

The elements of offer an acceptance, which necessarily result in a consensus of the parties, are essential elements of any international agreement. The mere meeting of the minds of the parties is not, *per se*, sufficient to create legal obligation between such parties. It is equally necessary that the parties should direct their intention at creating legal relations between themselves. Any international engagement that does not lead to legal obligations between the parties is hardly an act in the law. An obligation cannot be properly called a legal obligation unless its existence and extent are judicially determinable, i.e. according to the general principles of law[28].

The principle of '*Nemo judex in re sua*' is a general principle of law. If, therefore, the agreement has provided in advance that the

---

[27] Under some municipal legal systems a public offer may not be withdrawn by the offering party until a suitable acceptance is found. It is highly doubtful, however, if such a rule can be applied in International Law, except if the principle of 'Estoppel' can be successfully evoked.

[28] Another essential difference to be drawn between a contract in municipal law and an international agreement is that whereas in the former it is necessary to prove the element of consideration before such an agreement can be considered enforceable at law, this is not necessarily true of an international agreement. If, for example, state 'A' offers to train thirty engineers, free of any charges and 'without any strings attached' for state 'B' and the latter accepts the offer, the agreement shall be assumed to have been concluded between the parties at the time the offeree accepts the offer and is, *ipso facto*, enforceable at international law if the parties intended by this act to create a legal relation *inter se*. However, in the law of contract such an act does not yet constitute a contract, in other words, it is not enforceable at law because it lacks the essential element of consideration. As a matter of fact most technical assistance agreements lack this element of consideration *stricto sensu* but yet have been upheld as enforceable at international law given all other circumstances.

parties are to be judges each for himself, then the question arises as to whether such obligations are judicially determinable. Such arrangements would leave a recalcitrant party with a loophole for rejecting the jurisdiction of a tribunal or even for outright rejection of any decision by the latter. It may be equally true that an agreement is drafted in such a manner that only the extent of the obligation and not its very existence is removed from the field of judicial review.

However, there are cases when parties to an international agreement employ phrases which tend to blur their intention to create judicially determinable obligations. Such phrases like "subject to the law in force," "the parties shall take all possible measures," "the parties shall use any such action as they deem necessary" etc. only leave it to the parties to determine the degree of legal obligations upon themselves.

Whenever we are confronted with any international act the natural question we should ask is—did the parties intend that the agreement should create or declare legal rights and obligations between them? It is an essential element of a contract or an agreement that there should be an intention to create legal rights and obligations between the parties. If this intention is lacking, there is no act in the law, though there may still be an agreement in the eyes of the moralist or sociologist. The intention to create legal relations is an intention to create rights and obligations which may be declared or enforced in a court of law. There is a presumption that parties, who have expressed their agreement consistently with the rules for the formation of contracts, intend to create legal relations between themselves.

This is not the same thing as advocating for a compulsory jurisdiction of the ICJ over disputes arising from international agreements. The ICJ is just but one of many avenues for the judicial determination of obligations arising from such international agreements.

Before we come to the conclusion that the parties to an international act intended to create legal relations *inter se* we shall apply the following tests:

a) Have the parties included in the agreement any provisions for the settlement, by compulsory juridical process, of disputes arising out of such an agreement? Such a settlement clause may not necessarily incorporate the law to be applied by the organ called upon to settle such disputes. The choice of law clause does not necessarily coincide with the settlement of disputes clause.

b) Have the parties (if they are all sovereign states) accepted the jurisdiction of the ICJ under Art. 36 of the Statute in terms which would give the Court jurisdiction over any such disputes?

c) Has the agreement been registered under Art. 102 of the UN Charter or Art. 18 of the Covenant of the League of Nations?

d) Is there an intention, declared or to be deduced from the subject matter of the agreement, that the agreement or particular provisions of it are to be governed by public international law, by the internal law of an international organization, by a specified system of municipal law, or by the general principles of law?

The first test is decisive. Any dispute arising either from the interpretation or application of the agreement must be judiciable at the instance of any of the parties and such a decision shall be binding on the other party. The mode of settlement shall be left to the parties concerned but practice shows that constant resort is being made to negotiation, conciliation, arbitration, and adjudication. Given that the parties are free to provide in the settlement of disputes clause any mode of pacific settlement that they prefer, it should be stressed, however, that it is essential that the parties should not be left to determine for themselves the existence and extent of such obligations. Any disputes arising from such agreements shall be justiciable so long as the obligations therefrom are legal.

In the absence of any settlement of disputes clause in the agreement itself we shall apply the second test. We must mention, however, that test two is not a very effective one because, in the first place, only states can accept the optional clause of the ICJ Statute, and besides, some states formulate their acceptance in such a manner that the jurisdiction of the Court in such matters boils down to zero. Secondly, a wide range of international organizations are excluded from such mode of settlement—a restriction which renders the otherwise valuable institution of international adjudication by the ICJ regrettably useless.

The third test is of dubious value. Under Art. 102 of the UN Charter every treaty and every international agreement entered into by any member of the UN after 1945 shall as soon as possible be registered with the UN Secretariat and published by the latter. The only repercussion for non-registration of such treaties and international agreements is that no party to any such treaty or international agreement which has not been registered with the UN Secretariat may invoke the treaty or international agreement before any organ of the UN.

Similarly, under Art. 10 of the UN-GA Regulations intended to give effect to Art. 102 of the UN Charter, treaties and international agreements entered into by the UN or by any one or more of the UN Specialized Agencies shall be filed and recorded with the UN Secretariat. Obviously the legal repercussion for refusal to file and record with the UN Secretariat any such treaties and international agreements is the same as that for non-registration under Art. 102 of the UN Charter. The fact that the UN Secretariat accepted to register or file and record a treaty or an international agreement does not confer on such an act the character of an international agreement. Acceptance by the UN Secretariat to register or file and record an international act does not convert the latter into an international agreement, *stricto sensu,* if the former was not one before it was submitted for such registration or filing and recording.

Under Art. 18 of the Covenant of the LN the legal repercussion for non-registration is that no such treaty or international engagement shall be binding until so registered. The value of such provision is only psychological except if, by implication, it shall be construed as confering on the Secretariat of the LN the task of determining the legal validity of such acts before registering them. In which case registration shall be a proof of the fulfilment of all the essential prerequisites of a treaty.

Test 4, like test 1, is decisive. If the parties to an international act intended it to be an act in International Law, or in the law of any given international organization, or in the municipal law of any particular state, or, finally, to be governed by the general principles of law, then the presumption is that any dispute arising from such act shall be justiciable.

The principles of '*Pacta sunt servanda*' and '*Bona fides*'—principles which legal metaphysicians describe as hierarchically superior norms—shall apply only to such acts which, by intention or implication, create legal obligations between the parties. A '*pactum*' is essentially an act in the law. The twin principles of '*Pacta sunt servanda*' and '*Bona fides*' exhort parties to a '*pactum*' to keep their legal obligations.

It should be noted, however, that these twin principles cannot render agreements legally enforceable which are not made so by their own terms. This does not mean, however, that political obligations should not be kept. Such commitments should be kept not on the basis of the principle of '*Pacta sunt servanda*' but because they represent hypothetical imperatives which, if international public order is to be maintained and extended, should be fulfilled in sufficiently good faith.

Having established that an international agreement or a treaty presupposes a consensus of the parties and the intention of such parties—expressed or implied—to create legal relations *inter se,* we shall then go on to discuss very briefly the third constituent element of any international agreement—the capacity of the parties to enter into such relations.

For any treaty to be binding upon the parties it must be validly contracted. Validity is the condition necessary to give a treaty operative force and effect in law, and consists in the fulfilment of the aggregate of these requirements prescribed by the law in order that a treaty may have such force and effect[29].

Validity comprises formal validity, essential validity and temporal validity—all of which must be present at any one given time[30].

For any treaty to be essentially valid, the parties to such a treaty must show sufficient proof of their capacity—general, particular, or ad hoc—to conclude such treaties. Sovereign states possess general treaty-making powers, subject only to such restrictions as might be imposed by generally recognized norms of international law or by the state itself on the exercise of such powers. Intergovernmental international organizations, qua corporate entities, possess such treaty-making powers the exercise of which is essential for the effective discharge of their aims and objectives so long as their constituent instruments do not expressly prohibit the exercise of such powers. Such treaty-making power is hereby referred to as particular treaty-making power. Private entities, i.e. entities that are neither states nor a combination of states, can possess *ad hoc* treaty-making powers for the specific purpose of any one given treaty or international agreement. This happens when a subject of international law—a sovereign state or an international organization of states and/or of international organizations[31]—enters into a relation *jure gestionis* with a private entity and both parties incorporate into the proper law of the act contracted by them an agreement to accord such an act the regime of an international agreement. The conferement of such *ad hoc* treaty-making power upon the weaker party shall be applicable only and

---

[29] Vide Fitzmaurice, Report on the Law of Treaties of 14th March, 1956, Doc. A/CN. 4/101. Art. 10—1.

[30] The term 'formal validity' denotes validity in point of form, with reference to negotiations, conclusion, and entry into force; 'essential validity' denotes validity in point of substance, having regard to the requirements of contractual jurisprudence; 'temporal validity' denotes validity in point of duration, having regard to legal considerations governing the termination of a treaty, whether in itself or for any particulare state. Vide Fitzmaurice. Ibid.

[31] There is already an example of sovereign states teaming up with another international organization to constitute another international organization. A typical example of such an international organization of states and an international organization is the Middle Eastern Regional Radio Isotope Centre in Cairo in which the IAEA, alongside with certain Arab states, is a full member. For the constituent instrument of the Centre, see 494 UNTS, p. 220.

The time is not far away when three or more international organizations would team up to create a tertiary '*corpus seperatum*' possessive of particular international personality.

exclusively to this particular agreement. This right of the parties to choose the law applicable to their contract—the so-called principle of "the autonomy of the parties" is a general principle of the Conflict of laws[32].

Thus, when entities possessive of treaty-making-powers arrive at a consensus *inter se* with an intention to create legal relations among themselves we shall have before us all the essential elements necessary to make such resultant acts treaties or international agreements.

If these three elements are present in a treaty as well as in an international agreement, we might wonder where the distinction between these two categories of international acts lies. This leads us to the next question in our analysis—the forms of international acts concluded by international organizations.

Part II

Forms of Treaties Concluded by International Organizations

International law itself does not prescribe the form for the making of an international instrument although the constitutional laws of certain states do. In international law the question of form is a matter of convenience, however, there are cases when intolerable vagueness in form can cast some doubt on the substance of the entire agreement. This is probably why Sir Hersh Lauterpacht in his Law of Treaties *de lege ferenda* proposes that "An agreement is void unless reduced to writing[33]."

By form we specifically mean the "aspect exterieur d'un acte juridique[34]." In ordinary language "form" merely means a sort of

[32] It is expressly laid down in the Polish Act on Private International Law of 12th Nov. 1965, no. 46, in Art. 25 that:

Parag. I: En matière d'obligations contractuelles, les parties peuvent soumettre leur rapport juridique à la loi de leur choix, pourvu qu'elle ait une relation avec ledit rapport.

Parag. II: Néanmoins, lorsqu'une obligation concerne un immuable, il est appliqué la loi de l'Etat où cet immuable est situé.

Vide Seyersted, Applicable Law, The Hague, July, 1967 (Lecture).

[33] Report to the ILC on The Law of Treaties, March, 1953. Lukashuk also maintains that the choice between the written and the oral form is not entirely left to the parties as this shall be influenced by the aims and substance of the treaty being concluded. In his opinion, some international agreements are inconceivable unless reduced to a written form, e.g. the Universal Postal Convention. Vide Lukashuk, The structure and Form of International Treaties, Saratov 1960, p. 18.

[34] Vide Dictionnaire de la Terminologie du Droit International, p. 290.

"window decoration" or "external garb" over the real substance. A well-dressed international agreement is a treaty.

There is, however, some close relationship between the substance of a treaty and its form. The latter is a means of expressing the former. There can't be a form without a corresponding substance, and *vice versa*. Subsequently, there should be some intimate interaction between form and substance. Whereas the form of a treaty is relatively stable, the substance of a treaty is permanently dynamic. As has been shown above, time will come when the substance of a treaty might call for a new form in order to give full expression to the new developments which have taken place in the substance. Such tendencies lead to treaty revision or its amendment, i.e. a revision or amendment of the form of expression of the original substance to tally with the new substance. In other words the relationship between the form and the substance of a treaty is dialectical.

As has been shown above the difference between an international agreement '*lato sensu*' and a treaty '*stricto sensu*' is in the form, and this does not necessarily affect the legal effect of any of such acts. Whereas Art. 2-I-a and Art. 1 of the Vienna Convention on The Law of Treaties limits the application of the Convention to treaties '*stricto sensu*,' Art. 3-a stipulates that the above provisions do not in any way derogate from the legal force of any such agreements that do not come under the definition of "treaty" as given in Art. 2-I-a of the Convention.

In the Legal Status of Eastern Greenland Case in 1933, the PCIJ upheld that "The Court considers it beyond all dispute that a reply of this nature [i.e. in reference to an oral statement made by the Norwegian Foreign Affairs Minister to his Danish opposite number in the course of an interview between them] given by the Minister of Foreign Affairs on behalf of his government in response to a question falling within his province is binding upon the country to which the Minister belongs ... It follows that as a result of the undertaking involved (l'engagement impliqué) in the Ihlen declaration of July 22nd, 1919 Norway is under an obligation to refrain from contesting Danish sovereignty over Greenland as a whole and, *a fortiori*, to refrain from occupying a part of Greenland[35]."

States, as well as international organizations, have often resorted to various nomenclatures to designate treaties concluded by them. Some of such nomenclatures include: treaty, convention, protocol, act, final act, general act, additional articles, compromis d'arbitrage, agreed minutes, instrument, agreement, arrangement, avenant, com-

---

[35] PCIJ Series. A/B No. 53, pp. 71—3.

promis, lettres réversales, modus vivendi, statute, covenant, pact, concordat, articles of agreement, pactum de contrahendo, etc.

Other forms of inter-state activity or conduct which may create or affect legal rights and obligations are unilateral declaration, estoppel, notification, protest, recognition, renunciation, acquiescence, etc.

Forms of informal agreements include: oral statements, written declarations, proces verbal, memorandum of understanding, exchange of notes, parallel (corresponding) resolutions by the various competent organs of international organizations, etc.

International agreements concluded by international organizations come under the following general categories:

a) Headquarters agreements—these cover the status of the headquarters, as well as the offices of the regional and *ad hoc* organs of the organizations, diplomatic privileges and immunities of the organizations.

b) Operational agreements—these include all agreements aimed at executing the functions of the organizations concerned, e.g. technical assistance agreements, loan agreements, etc.

c) Peace-keeping agreements—mainly by the UN.

d) Relationship agreements—these include relationship agreements between the specialized agencies and the UN and between the specialized agencies *inter se,* co-operation agreements with other organizations and agencies outside the UN family of organizations, agreements on co-ordination, etc.

e) Private contracts—these include all acts in the municipal law of any state or in the internal law of the organizations concerned, e.g. the acquisition, transfer, or disposal of property, labour relations, insurance policy, etc.

f) Miscellaneous agreements—these cover all other extraordinary agreements that might be concluded by international organizations. These include such agreements as the UN agreement on the Memorial Cemetry in Korea.

Of all the designations of international agreements mentioned above, we shall single out only a few for detailed examination in the light of contemporary practices by international organizations.

1. *International Agreements.* Most of the international acts concluded by international agreements are designated "international agreements." Such agreements include the Relationship agreements concluded between the UN and the various Specialized Agencies of the UN; Inter-Agency agreements on co-operation and co-ordination; most Headquarters agreements between the Organizations and their host states; Technical Assistance and Loan Agreements.

In view of the interim nature of some of such agreements, some of them are appropriately designated as Interim Agreements, e.g. the Interim Agreement between the UN and The Swiss Federal Council on the privileges and immunities of the UN signed in 1946[36].

2. *Arrangement.* This is a term which is not very current in UN practice but yet it was used to describe the agreement concluded between the LN and the UN on the practical execution of transfer of LN Assets to the UN[37].

3. *Protocol.* This is a term which found much application in the early days of UN treaty practices particularly in connection with the inheritance agreements between the UN and the LN. Examples of agreements which were designated as Protocols include: the two Protocols on the execution of transfers of LN assets to the UN[38]; LN/UN Protocol on the transfer of the Leon Bernard Fund to the UN[39]; LN/UN Protocol on the transfer of the Administration of the Darling Foundation from the LN to the UN[40]; the Protocol between the UN, LN, and the UNRRA[41]; Protocol between the UN and the ILO on the entry into force of the agreement between the UN and the ILO of Dec. 1946[42].

4. *Memorandum of Agreement.* This was entered into between the UN and the ILO on 17th Feb. 1949[43].

5. *Exchange of Notes.* There was an Exchange of Notes between a representative of the ICJ and the Dutch Foreign Minister on the status of the Peace Palace—the location of the ICJ—in The Hague[44].

6. *Parallel (Corresponding) Resolutions by the Competent Organs of Different International Organizations.* Whereas states often resort to such unilateral acts like unilateral declarations, negotiation, protest, recognition, renunciation, acquiescence, etc., the roughest equivalent in the practices of international organizations to the adoption of simultaneous acts by states as a form of concluding an international agreement is the adoption of parallel resolutions by organs of two or more international organizations. The legal effect of such unilateral acts on the international plane is highly debatable. Of recent we find international organizations, especially the UNICEF, concluding internationally binding agreements through the mere adoption of corresponding resolutions. It should be stated right from the beginning

[36] Vide I UNTS, p. 163.
[37] 1 UNTS, p. 119.
[38] 1 UNTS, pp. 131, 135.
[39] 5 UNTS, p. 389.
[40] 5 UNTS, p. 395.
[41] 1 UNTS, p. 139.
[42] 1 UNTS, p. 183.
[43] 26 UNTS, p. 323.
[44] In 1946—47 the UN concluded an agreement with the Carnegie Foundation on the use of the premises of the Peace Palace. This Agreement, by necessary intendment out of its proper law, is governed by the general principles of law rather than by the law of any particular state.

that corresponding resolutions of organs of international organizations, *per se*, do not constitute an international agreement. Unless such corresponding resolutions are sufficiently formulated in such a manner as to give the intention of the parties to enter into legal relations *inter se*, and unless one of such resolutions shall be construed as constituting an offer and the other—an acceptance, and unless the organ adopting such a resolution is competent, under the internal laws of the organizations, to bind the organization on the international plane, in short, unless these corresponding resolutions satisfy the essential tests for an international agreement, they shall not be construed as such. Such corresponding resolutions must necessarily converge, i.e. they must lead to a consensus of the parties. Secondly, they must show sufficient proof of the intention of the parties to create legal relations *inter se*. Thirdly, such resolutions must emanate from the competent organs of the organizations concerned. In short, such resolutions must show sufficient proof of any claim to international validity and this includes formal, substantive and temporal validity[45].

7. *Convention*. The term "Convention" is generally associated with multilateral agreements between states, for example the Vienna Conventions of 1961 and 1963 on Diplomatic and Consular relations, the Geneva Conventions on the law of the sea, the Postal and Telegraphic Convention, etc. But of recent we have all been witnesses to the spectacle of international organizations being parties to certain international conventions.

The Convention on the privileges and immunities of the Specialized Agencies[46], which was approved by the UN-GA on Nov. 21, 1947 provides in Sect. 37 of Art. X and in Sect. 41 of Art. XI that it (i.e. the Convention) will be submitted to the Specialized Agencies for their acceptance and to members of the UN and to any other state which is a member of one or more of the Specialized Agencies for their accession. Although the Convention establishes different procedures for the acceptance by the Specialized Agencies and by states, there appears no doubt that the Specialized Agencies are parties thereto. A close analysis of the list of accessions[47] to this Convention shows that most of the Specialized Agencies have deposited instruments of accession and, *ipso facto*, are parties to the Convention[48].

---

[45] Vide supra.

[46] 33 UNTS, p. 621.

[47] For a list of the accessions, see 33 UNTS, p. 262.

[48] Shibaeva, however, contends that the Specialized Agencies of the UN are not parties to this Convention, but rather are its object. Vide Autoreferat of her doctoral dissertation, M. 1969, p. 27 (in Russian).

The General Convention on the privileges and immunities of the UN was approved by the UN-GA on Feb. 13, 1946. Since then, the UN has neither signed nor formally accepted the Convention. As a result the position of the UN vis-à-vis the Convention remains a controversial question. There are at least three points of view on the issue.

The first of such views is to consider the Convention as not amounting to a treaty. Thus the question as to who are the parties to it does not arise[49].

The ground for this view is the contention that Art. 105 of the UN Charter is self-executing, and that the Convention of 1946 merely determines the details of the application of that Article and cannot, therefore, constitute a separate legal act.

One finds it difficult to subscribe to such an argument. In the first place, the contention that Art. 105 of the UN Charter is self-executing is highly controversial. In our opinion, the privileges and immunities so vaguely referred to in Art. 105 are not automatically acquirable by the UN. They need to be concretized in a separate legal act.

Even if we for a moment accept the submission that Art. 105 of the UN Charter is self-executing, that does not in any way derogate from the legal status of any separate instrument that shall be signed in order to determine the details of it. Such a subsequent instrument still remains an international act, and, under such circumstances, Art. 105, at best, represents an agreement to agree at a later date.

Thirdly, the contention that the General Convention only detalises the provisions of Art. 105 is not completely true, given the fact that the Preamble to the Convention itself mentions specifically Arts. 104 and 105 and not just Art. 105 alone as this point of view contends.

Another possible reason for this view is that the Convention has no original parties to it. The Preamble, it is often contended, only stipulates that the UN-GA shall propose the Convention to member-states for their accession. This argument too is hardly convincing.

In the general law of treaties accession to a treaty precipitates the same rights and obligations as original participation. Art. 15 of the Vienna Convention on The Law of Treaties stipulates that the consent of a state to be bound by a treaty is expressed by accession under three conditions one of which is that the treaty or an amendment to it provides that such consent may be expressed by the states by means

---

[49] Vide Parry, 26 BYIL, 1949, at p. 108.

of accession. This was the case with the General Convention on the Privileges and immunities of the UN. We, therefore, submit that the contention that the General Convention is not a treaty and that the question of participation does not arise, is basically wrong.

The second view is that the UN is a third-party beneficiary to the General Convention. In its judgement of 7th June, 1932 on the Free Zone Case, the PCIJ stated, *inter alia,* "It cannot be lightly presumed that stipulations favourable to a third state have been adopted with the object of creating an actual right in its favour. There is, however, nothing to prevent the will of sovereign states from having the object and this effect. The question of the existence of a right acquired under an instrument between other states is, therefore, one to be decided in each particular case. It must be ascertained whether the states which have stipulated in favour of a third state meant to create for the state an actual right which the latter has accepted as such[50]."

One can hardly accept the view that the UN is a third-party beneficiary from this Convention. The UN-GA adopted the Convention and proposed it to member-states for their accession. Section 35 of the Final Article of the Convention provides that "this Convention shall continue in force as between the UN and every member which has deposited an instrument of accession for so long as that member remains a member of the UN . . ."

This provision can be construed to mean that the obligations resulting from accession exist directly between the UN and the acceding member. In actual fact, the Convention, even though formulated in one act, is a series of agreements between the UN and the various acceeding members. The relationship is not that of member-member, but rather of member-UN and in this context one can hardly speak of UN being a third-party beneficiary.

The third point of view, and, in fact, in our opinion, the only correct view, is that the UN is a party to the General Convention. This conclusion seems to flow out of the provisions of Sections 30, 32, 35, and 36 of the Convention.

A relevant factor, though not an independent proof in itself, is the fact that the Secretary-General of the UN registered the Convention *ex officio* although the Convention does not specifically authorize such a step. The Regulations for the registration or filing and recording of treaties and international agreements provide for *ex officio* registration by the UN Secretary-General either when such registration is authorized by the treaty itself or when the UN is a

---

[50] PCIJ Series A/B, No. 46, at p. 147, 1932.

party to the treaty. The fact that the Convention was registered by the UN Secretary-General *ex officio* can only indicate that the UN, at least, considers itself a party to the Convention[51].

As regards the procedure of acceptance by the UN, Shabtai Rosenne argues that "If the process of treaty-making is broken into its essential elements of offer followed by acceptance, then the adoption of the text of the General Immunities Convention is the offer by the General Assembly and the individual states' acts of accession are the acceptance by these states[52]."

On this same point Lauterpacht stated that "whenever there exist in fact the elements of an offer and an acceptance thereof—a recorded instrument or succession of combination of recorded instruments—there may fairly be held to exist a treaty[53]."

In our opinion, the UN qua organization, can be construed as participating in this Convention. There is sufficient evidence in the Convention to justify the assertion that obligations arising out of this instrument are in existence only between the UN and the member-states and not between the member-states *inter se.* Section 30 of Art. VIII of the Convention stipulates that "... if a difference arises between the UN on the one hand and a member on the other hand ..." This construction presupposes that the Convention will operate as between the UN and a particular given member.

And Section 35 of the Final Article provides that "This Convention shall continue in force as between the UN and every member which has deposited an instrument of accession for so long as that member remains a member of the UN and until a revised General Convention has been approved by the General Assembly and that the member has become a party to this revised Convention."

As regards the procedure of accession by the UN to the Convention the act of adoption of the text of the Convention by the GA serves this purpose. The UN-GA, by adopting the Convention, makes a *de facto* offer to the member-states, and the latters' acts of accession shall be tantamount to an acceptance of this general offer by the UN. If this element of offer and acceptance is present as between the UN and the various acceding states, then we can safely conclude that the Convention is a treaty and the UN is a party to it.

---

[51] This view is equally expressed by: King, The privileges and immunities of the personnel of international organizations, 1947, p. 146; Rosenne, UN Treaty practice, 86 RCADI, 1954-II, at pp. 281, 322; Weissberg, The international status of the UN, 1961, at p. 63.

[52] Rosenne, 86 RCADI, 1954-II, at p. 323.

[53] See Report on The Law of Treaties, 1963-II, 90 YILC, p. 103. UN Doc. A/CN. 4/63, 1953.

Section 36 of the Final Article of the Convention tends to throw more light on this reasoning in its provision that "The SG may conclude with any member or members supplementary agreements adjusting the provisions of this Convention so far as that member or those members are concerned. These supplementary agreements shall in each case be subject to the approval of the GA." The technique of *inter se* modification is applicable only to multilateral treaties and such modification shall be tenable only between the parties to such treaties.

Participation in, as Against Sponsorship of, International Agreements by International Organizations: Theoretical Examination

It is necessary to draw a line of difference between participation in a treaty and the sponsorship of a treaty. Participation presupposes the creating of rights and obligations for the participating entity vis-à-vis other participants, a fact which is absent in sponsorship.

A party to a treaty is an entity which by its own wilful act accepts to be bound by the provisions of a treaty vis-à-vis other parties to the same treaty. This is not the same thing as "third party" beneficiary —a misnomer for a non-participant who enjoys certain rights created by the regime of a treaty between other entities.

Similarly, a sponsoring entity is not the same thing as a participant in a treaty. It is possible to sponsor a multilateral treaty without necessarily being a party to it, or even without being a third-party beneficiary from such a treaty.

Recasting, *mutatis mutandis,* the provision of section "g," parag. I, Art. 2 of the Final Draft Articles on The Law of Treaties, a party to a treaty means a state or an international organization which has consented to be bound by a treaty or for which the treaty is in force. This is differenciated from a third-party-section "h," parag. I, Art. 2—which means a state or an international organization not a party to the treaty; and Art. 4 of the same Final Draft Articles speaks of "treaties which are adopted within an international organization."

The Classification of International Agreements into Multilaterial, Bilateral, Multipartite, and Bipartite

The multilaterality or bilaterality of an international agreement shall not be determined exclusively on the basis of arithmetical considerations. A bipartite treaty is different from a bilateral treaty in the sense that in the former there are two parties, whereas in the latter there are two sides (from the latin word—"*latus*") and each or both of such sides may contain more than one party. Similarly, a multipartite treaty is different from a multilateral treaty in the sense that the multipartite treaty has many parties to it, whereas a multilateral treaty has many sides out of which one or all the sides may have many parties. The classification of treaties into bipartite and multipartite, however, has more of formal connotation, and since these terms are not domiciled in international law we shall be restrictive in our application of them.

Without prejudice to such classification as given above, it is essential that the sides to a multilateral treaty should be anything from three upwards. The contention that it takes more than three sides to make a multilateral treaty is not very correct. A treaty with three sides could be described as trilateral and trilateral treaties are essentially multilateral.

A treaty may remain essentially bilateral even though more than two states or entities participate in it. This happens when several states or entities act as one side in concluding a treaty with another state or entity.

A typical example is the Indus Basin Development Fund Agreement signed at Karachi on 19th Sept. 1960 between the BANK on the one hand, and the governments of the Commonwealth of Australia, Canada, the Federal Republic of Germany, New Zealand, Pakistan, the United Kingdom, and the USA acting as the other side. Thus, irrespective of the number of parties to this agreement, it is essentially a bilateral treaty[54].

Similarly, most Technical Assistance Agreements belong to this category. For example, the Basic Agreement for the provision of Technical Assistance, signed at Djarkata on 2nd Nov. 1950 between the UN, ILO, FAO, UNESCO, ICAO, and WHO—members of the TAB—acting as one side and Indonesia[55]; or the Revised Standards Agreement between the UN, ILO, FAO, UNESCO, WHO, WMO, and ITU acting as one side and the government of the Federal Peoples' Republic of Yugoslavia concerning technical assistance signed at Belgrade on 26th June, 1956[56].

Waldock in Art. I, parag. (d) of his Report on the Law of Treaties defined a multilateral treaty as a "treaty which by its terms or by the terms of a related instrument has either been made open to participation by any state without restriction, or has been made open to participation by a considerable number of parties or either purports

[54] Vide 444 UNTS, 1962, at p. 259.
[55] 81 UNTS, 1951, at p. 160.
[56] 253 UNTS.

to lay down a general norm of international law or to deal in general manner with matters of general concern to other states as well as to the parties to the treaty[57]. . ."

Unfortunately, we cannot accept such a definition which, in our opinion, takes very many factors for granted. The definition assumes that all multilateral treaties are necessarily open. This is not necessarily true. A treaty could be multilateral and yet remain closed. This depends on the provision of the treaty itself.

Secondly, Waldock, by such a definition assumes that all multilateral treaties must be general, i.e. they must seek to stipulate norms of general international law or deal in general manner with matters of general concern to other states as well as to the parties to the treaty. This is not necessarily so. A multilateral treaty could be either general or particular, i.e. local or regional. For example, whereas the 1961 Vienna Convention on Diplomatic Relations is a general multilateral Convention, the Treaty of Rome which set up the EEC, the Constituent instrument of the COMECON, the Charters of the OAS and the OAU respectively, represent regional or local multilateral treaties. Waldock's definition of multilateral treaties applies more to general multilateral treaties and less to local or regional or closed multilateral treaties.

General Conclusions

Whereas the distinction between a treaty and an international agreement is only formal, an international engagement presupposes not only formal but also substantive distinctions from the above two international acts. Whereas the registrability of international engagements is permissible under Art. 18 of the Covenant of the League of Nations, an international engagement that fails to satisfy the basic prerequisites of an international agreement can hardly be registrable under Art. 102 of the UN Charter.

International agreements as a generic concept and treaties as a species of this genus, the difference between them being only formal, presuppose the existence of three constituent elements—a consensus of the parties (the principle of "*Ex consensu advenit vinculum*"); the intention of the parties—expressed or implied—to create legal relations *inter se*; and the capacity of the parties—either on a general, on a particular, or on an *ad hoc* basis—to enter into such legal relations. It is only a totality of these three elements that can lead to an international agreement. If two competent parties arrive at a consensus

[57] Vide UN Doc. ST/SGB/UNEF/I (1957).

on any subject matter and if such a consensus is divorced of any intention to create legal relations between the above parties, the final act of such a consensus shall not be construed as an international agreement. If the intention was to create political relations, then the final act is at best a hypothetical imperative the observance of which, however, is necessary if international public order is to be maintained and extended.

The role of informal agreements on the international plane is constantly on the increase. In view of this it is only to be regretted that the 1969 Vienna Convention on the Law of Treaties decided to place all such informal agreements outside the law. This group of international agreements still continues to be subjected to the whims and caprices of customary international law—a body of norms which hardly means anything to an intransigent party. The decision by the ILC to allow informal agreements to float on the international plane is a big blow to an otherwise marvellous codification work the ILC produced in the 1969 Vienna Convention. It is only to be hoped that this unfortunate *lacuna* shall be filled somehow sometime.

Our second remark on the 1969 Vienna Convention on the Law of Treaties is that, under pressure from the conservative members of the ILC, the Convention decided to keep international agreements concluded by international organizations out of its sphere of operation. This double standard is probably in line with the traditional division of subjects of international law into original and derived subjects. There is no inherent reason why this Convention couldn't have been open to treaties concluded by international organizations as well. Such a decision would not mean, as might be argued by the conservative members of the ILC, that international organizations shall become states or super-states.

In view of the vertical and horizontal restrictions imposed on the Vienna Convention on the Law of Treaties, it is only fair to call for one of the following remedial measures:

a) Either Art. 1 of the Convention should be amended to grant access to international organizations; or

b) A new Convention, modelled on the pattern of the 1969 Vienna Convention, should be drawn up to fill the gap.

In our opinion, the second measure will only serve as a perpetration of the conservative distinction between states as original subjects and international organizations as derived or secondary subjects of international law. Besides, it will probably take another decade of tough bargaining before any tangible compromise will be reached on any new Convention to cover the treaty practices of international organizations.

In any case, whichever method is chosen the artificial restrictions imposed by Art. 2-I-a and by Art. 3 of the 1969 Convention should be dropped. Any future Convention on the Law of Treaties should be stripped of the suspicions which have dominated the infantry and which today threaten to ruin the future of the present Convention.

A more suitable title for any such Convention, in our opinion, is perhaps "A General Convention on The Law of International Agreements." Possible alternatives are the retention of the present title of "Convention on The Law of Treaties," a phrase which is too restrictive in its application, given that the term 'treaty' only refers to a specific category of international agreements; or a "Convention on The Law of International Engagements"—a term which, in our opinion, is too vague to be of any useful purpose.

Another possible alternative to the two remedial measures given above is to leave the provisions of the 1969 Vienna Convention as they are and to apply them to the treaty practices of international organizations subject to the laws in force within the various international organizations. The advantages of such a measure are immense. In the first place, it will represent a healthy deviation from the contemporary pactomania which has permeated the entire fibre of international law. Secondly, it will save the ILC from going through the ordeal of the critical negativism which will almost dominate the sessions of the Commission. It is no secret that certain countries are highly critical of the role of universal international organizations in contemporary international relations and such states are bound to adopt a nihilist attitude towards any Draft Convention on The Law of Treaties of International Organizations, if ever the ILC succeeds in preparing one.

In an attempt to get a Convention at any cost the ILC might be forced to make such compromises that the resultant Convention will be more of a detriment to the future development of international organizations than a promoter of such growth. If international organizations are left to apply the provisions of the 1969 Vienna Convention subject to the laws in force within the respective organizations, it is our belief that these organizations shall be left with a wider degree of manoeuvrability.

A perusal of the general treaty practices of international organizations shows that they conclude all forms of international agreements ranging from the most solemn form—treaties *stricto sensu*—to the most informal agreements, e.g. Exchange of Notes. Whereas preference should be given to formal agreements, there is no reason why international organizations should not be allowed to conclude informal agreements as well if the latter provide them with efficient safety valves. The advantages of such informal agreements are numerous—they are faster to conclude, less combersome to formulate, more elastic and, therefore, more adaptable to possible changes in the original circumstances which surround their conclusion.

On the other hand, a total abandonment of formal agreements should not be encouraged. The continued retention of these two forms of international agreements, especially in the functioning of international organizations should, therefore be seen as a healthy phenomenon which should be encouraged as much as possible.

International organizations are a social organism and their growth is determined by the needs of the international society rather than by the wishes of their founding fathers. The evolution of international organizations remains a mystery of sociology as much as the birth of a physical person remains a mystery of biology. Under such circumstances states should do well to base their judgements, on the future development of these institutions, less on facts and more on the tendencies of this growth. A natural person continues to be tied to the apron strings of his parents during his infancy, but as soon as the former attains the legal age for the assumption of independent legal responsibility, he breaks loose from this biological straitjacket.

Similarly, the founding fathers of an international organization try to model the future growth of an international organization by the adoption of an instrument that is inherently archaic—the constituent instrument of the organization they seek to bring to life. But once created, the future development of an international organization shall henceforth be determined by the principles of teleological constitutionalism.

If any future Convention on the Law of Treaties of International Organizations will disrupt this slow but steady progress of international organizations towards a more respectable status in the society of nations, then we might as well do without one. Nothing can be more disruptive to the efficient functioning of international organizations than an unchecked proliferation of the contemporary pactomania which has grinded the law of nations to a virtual standstill.

The choice of forms of treaties to be concluded by international organizations should be influenced by various factors—the continued need for efficiency and alacrity in the discharge of their duties, adaptability and dynamism in their progressive development to loftier heights. These and only these factors can guarantee the continued metamorphosis of these social organisms which, for lack of a better term, are called "International Organizations."

Österr. Zeitschr. f. öffentl. Recht, Suppl. 1, 195—268 (1971)

Organs Competent to Conclude Treaties for International Organizations and the Internal Procedure Leading to the Decision to Be Bound by a Treaty
and
Negotiation and Conclusion of Treaties by International Organizations

Hanspeter Neuhold
Assistant Lecturer at the University of Vienna

I. Introduction

After the Second World War, one of the salient features of international relations and of international law, which for centuries had been regarded as inter-State law, was not only the marked increase in the number of international organizations but also of the agreements concluded[1] by them[2].

Several facts come to mind if one tries to explain this phenomenon. Agreements between international organizations and their member States bridge the gap between two contradictory trends in contemporary international relations[3]. On the one hand, governments realize that there is an increasing number of problems which they cannot solve alone but that joint efforts and co-operation are required in certain fields, especially in technological and economic matters. On

[1] There is some confusion about the scope of the term "conclude." Whereas in American treaty practice it is confined to the establishment of the text of the treaty, it includes the expression of consent by the organ possessing treaty-making power in German, Italian, and French legal terminology. It is in this second meaning that the term is used throughout this paper. See Zemanek, Das Vertragsrecht der Internationalen Organisationen (1957), p. 63—67; Dupuy, Le Droit des relations entre les Organisations internationales, 100 RCADI (1960), p. 461—584 (p. 491); Kasme, Le capacité de l'Organisation des Nations Unies de conclure des traités (1960), p. 177—179.

[2] For a general discussion of the new environment of international law see Friedmann, The Changing Structure of International Law (1964).

[3] Kasme, op.cit., p. 7.

the other hand, the Communist and the young States in particular are reluctant to renounce their sovereignty[4] unless they deem it absolutely necessary. Unwilling to confer broad competences upon international organizations and to accept majority decisions within them, member States prefer to conclude agreements with them, thus retaining a stronger position when determining their future obligations towards the organizations. As for non-member States, agreements are the obvious means for regulating their relations with an international organization with which they want or must enter into contacts.

International organizations also maintain treaty relations among themselves. Since States were and are still haunted by the specter of an emerging super-State, they have not entrusted any single organization with international co-operation but have chosen to set up a whole network of such legal entities with limited functions and powers. The system of functional decentralization[5] thus established undoubtedly offers certain advantages. On the other hand, international organizations have to co-ordinate their activities in order to avoid conflicts and overlapping in their work[6].

It is therefore somewhat amazing that the legal aspects of the conclusion of agreements have been neglected in the constituent instruments of the various organizations. This phenomenon is understandable with respect to those international organizations which were established during or immediately after the Second World War. It can be argued that at that time the issues were largely unknown or that they were overlooked, as the constituent instruments of some organizations appear to have been drawn up in a hurry.

But it is certainly astonishing that even such a complex treaty as the Treaty of Rome creating the European Economic Community, an instrument consisting of 248 articles and drawn up after long discussions, deals but inadequately with the questions to be discussed in this paper.

What is more, writers on international law have so far paid relatively little attention to this new category of international agree-

---

[4] Korowitz, Some Present Aspects of Sovereignty in International Law, 102 RCADI (1961), p. 1—113; Hinsley, Sovereignty (1966).

[5] Jenks, Co-ordination: a New Problem of International Organization, 77 RCADI (1950), p. 157—301 (p. 163).

[6] It is worth noting in this context that international organizations tend to be rather jealous of their position and therefore view newcomers to their ranks quite suspiciously. Thus the creation of IAEA in 1956 met with little enthusiasm on the part of WHO and ILO which were reluctant to abandon any of their competences or renounce their programs in matters of common concern. Balekjian, Les Rapports de l'A.I.E.A. avec les autres Organisations internationales, 69 RGDIP (1965), p. 76—100 (p. 81—82).

ments. This may have been due to the fact that these agreements were still considered something of an anomaly[7] and were, furthermore, rather difficult to come across[8].

When the International Law Commission turned to the codification of the law of treaties, the issue came to the fore. Though the Commission recognized the importance of international organizations and of the agreements entered into by them, it eventually decided, albeit hesitantly, to limit its work to treaties to which only States are parties[9].

At the beginning of the First Session of the Vienna Conference on the Law of Treaties in 1968 the question of whether to include in the Convention agreements concluded by international organizations was raised again by the delegates of the USA and the Republic of Vietnam[10]. After a lengthy debate the opinion prevailed that the discussion of this topic at the Conference would take too much time. Hence the problem was shelved again. However, a Swedish proposal to adopt a resolution recommending to the General Assembly of the UN to refer to the ILC the study of that particular category of treaties met with general approval[11]. Consequently, the questions to be discussed in this paper are of a certain actuality.

---

[7] Thus the authors of the Harvard Research Draft Convention on the Law of Treaties decided to limit the Draft Convention to treaties concluded by States. In the comment to Article 1, paragraph c this approach was explained as follows: "For the purposes of this Convention it is not deemed advisable to deal with such agreements (those concluded by other subjects of international law) because, like others which have been excluded, they have peculiar features which distinguish them from the normal type of treaty and make it doubtful whether certain of the rules of this Convention could be applied to them. 29 AJIL (1935), Spec. Supp., p. 699.

[8] Schneider, Treaty-making Power of International Organizations (1959), p. 18—25.

[9] The hesitations of the ILC are described by Chiu, The Capacity of International Organizations to Conclude Treaties, and the Special Legal Aspects of the Treaties So Concluded (1966), p. 39—43.

[10] A/CONF. 39/C. 1/L. 15 and A/CONF. 39/C. 1/L. 27.

[11] Fischer-Köck, Das völkerrechtliche Vertragsrecht im Lichte der Ergebnisse der ersten Session der Wiener Vertragsrechtskonferenz der Vereinten Nationen, 23 Österreichische Juristenzeitung (1968), p. 505—511 (p. 508); iidem, Das Recht der völkerrechtlichen Verträge nach der zweiten Session der Wiener Vertragsrechtskonferenz der Vereinten Nationen, 9 Österreichische Zeitschrift für Außenpolitik (1969), p. 274—296; Neuhold, The 1968 Session of the United Nations Conference on the Law of Treaties, 19 Österreichische Zeitschrift für öffentliches Recht (1969), p. 59—94 (p. 61); idem, Die Wiener Vertragsrechtskonvention 1969, 15 Archiv des Völkerrechts (1970/71) (forthcoming); Verosta, Die Vertragsrechts-Konferenz der Vereinten Nationen 1968/69 und die Wiener Konvention über das Recht der Verträge, 29 ZaöRV (1969), p. 654—710 (p. 672—675); Kearney and Dalton, The Treaty on Treaties, 64 AJIL (1970), p. 495—561 (p. 502—503).

The issue of the legal basis of the treaty-making capacity of international organizations should not detain us in this context. Whereas the treaty-making power of States is generally considered an attribute of sovereignty, most writers are reluctant to extend the notion of sovereignty to the realm of international organizations. A different explanation has therefore to be sought. Incidentally, this is one of the few problems arising from the conclusion of agreements by international organizations which have been dealt with at some length by a larger number of writers. However, their views diverge considerably.

One school of thought derives the treaty-making power from the constituent instruments of international organizations. Two variants have been put forth by authors defending this theory. Kelsen takes a restrictive view on the issue[12]. In his opinion, international organizations enjoy general treaty-making power only if international juridical personality is conferred on them by the constituent treaty. Otherwise the organization may enter only into those agreements which it is authorized to conclude under special provisions of its charter. However, this theory is clearly at variance with the treaty practice of international organizations.

Consequently, more recent writers advocate a more liberal approach by propounding some variant of the implied power theory[13]. According to this theory, the treaty-making power is not confined to the conclusion of expressly authorized agreements but covers also those which are not mentioned in the instrument but are necessary for the achievement of the purposes of the organization and the discharge of its functions as laid down by the framers of the constituent instrument.

Another school of thought refuses to regard the constituent treaty as the basis of the international personality of international organizations in general and their treaty-making power in particular. On this view, if the criteria required by international law for international organizations are met by an entity, this entity is a general

---

[12] Kelsen, The Law of the United Nations (1951), p. 329—330.

[13] Rosenne, United Nations Treaty Practice, 86 RCADI (1954), p. 281—438 (p. 294—296); Weissberg, The International Status of the United Nations (1961), p. 37—38; Bowett, The Law of International Institutions (1963), p. 278; Seidl-Hohenveldern, The Legal Personality of International and Supranational Organizations, 21 Revue Egyptienne de Droit International (1965), p. 35—72. See also the pronouncements of the International Court of Justice in its advisory opinions in the Reparation case (I.C.J. Reports 1949, p. 174—188), the UN Administrative Tribunal case (I.C.J. Reports 1954, p. 47—63), and the Certain Expenses case (I.C.J. Reports 1962, p. 151—180). For a more thorough discussion of the problem see Hartmann, this volume, p. 127—163.

subject of international law by the very fact of its existence[14]. It has the inherent (and not only delegated or implied) power to perform any act—hence also to conclude agreements—it is in a position to perform. According to this theory, the treaty-making power of international organizations is based on a norm of customary international law[15].

II. The Organs of International Organizations Competent to Conclude Agreements

1. The Organs of States Possessing and Exercising Treaty-Making Power (Art. 7 of the Vienna Convention on the Law of Treaties)

In principle international law leaves to each State the determination of the organs invested with treaty-making capacity and the details of its exercise[16]. States wishing to enter into a treaty need not rely, however, on the mere statement of another party's purported representative that he is competent under internal law. Common usage requires negotiators to produce a document known as "full powers" proving their authority. Therefore parties need not interpret each other's constitution in order to ascertain whether a representative is competent to perform acts relating to the conclusion of a treaty. Such an attempt to interpret the constitution of another party may not only prove difficult in practice, but may be considered an act of intervention by the State concerned.

Yet there are two important exceptions to the rule just mentioned. First, an increasing number of treaties are concluded in simplified form[17]. For this category of treaties full powers are usually not required. Secondly, the ILC had reached the conclusion that State practice had resulted in the emergence of a rule under which certain organs are competent to represent their State in virtue of their functions. Consequently they do not have to produce full powers. Article 6 of the Commission's final draft conferred this capacity on Heads of State, Heads of Government and Ministers for Foreign

[14] Seyersted, Objective International Personality of Intergovernmental Organizations (1963); idem, International Personality of Intergovernmental Organizations: Do their Capacities Really Depend upon their Constitutions, 4 The Indian Journal of International Law (1964), p. 1—174 (especially at p. 53).

[15] Schneider, op.cit., p. 135—139; Chiu, op.cit., p. 34.

[16] Verdross, Völkerrecht (1964), p. 159—160.

[17] Weinstein, Exchanges of Notes, 29 BYIL (1952), p. 205—226: Chayet, Les accords en forme simplifiée, 3 AFDI (1957), p. 3—13; Smets, La conclusion des accords en forme simplifiée (1969).

Affairs[18] with respect to all acts relating to the conclusion of a treaty[19]. As for heads of diplomatic missions and representatives accredited to an organ of an international organization, the scope of the presumption was limited to the adoption of the text of treaties with the authorities they are accredited to. The ILC's formula met with general approval at both Sessions of the Vienna Conference on the Law of Treaties[20].

In retrospect, one may say that it received surprisingly little attention. Only the representative of the Federal Republic of Germany thought that the scope of the presumptio juris set forth by the Commission was at variance with State practice[21]. Consequently, he introduced an amendment[22] to the effect that the rule should be confined to Heads of State, whereas the authorization of other representatives was to be determined by the internal law of each party and not by international law. The amendment was eventually withdrawn in view of the little support it had gained during the debate[23].

The main question which arises with regard to our topic concerns the possibility of applying similar presumptions to certain organs of international organizations.

2. The Organs Invested with Treaty-Making Power under the Constituent Instruments of some International Organizations

Just as in the case of inter-State treaties, international law primarily refers to the constitutions of the international organization concerned when the organ competent to conclude agreements has to be determined. Unfortunately, the constituent instruments of inter-

[18] The problem of the capacity of Foreign Ministers to represent their States was dealt with by the Permanent Court of International Justice in connection with the so-called Ihlen declaration in the Eastern Greenland case; P.C.I.J. Series A/B, No. 53, p. 22—75 (p. 73); see also Oppenheim-Lauterpacht, International Law I, eighth edition (1967), p. 764.

[19] The Text of the ILC's draft articles and the commentary thereto can be found in 61 AJIL (1967), p. 263—463.

[20] For a summary of the 1968 Session of the Conference, see Fischer-Köck, op.cit., and Neuhold, op.cit.

[21] See also Geck, The Conclusion of Treaties in Violation of the Internal Law of a Party, 27 ZaöRV (1967), p. 429—450.

[22] A/CONF. 39/C. 1/L. 50.

[23] Two other amendments which were not solely of a drafting character but of some material relevance were submitted by Hungary and Poland (A/CONF. 39/C. 1/L. 78 and Add. 1) and the USA (A/CONF. 39/C. 1/L. 90). These States wanted to see representatives accredited to international organizations as such and not only to their organs—as the ILC had suggested—covered by the above rule. These proposals were adopted.

national organizations offer but rarely a conclusive answer to this question.

Apart from containing only exceptionally general provisions on the treaty-making competence of the organization, constituent instruments do not specify, as a rule, the organ endowed with the power to enter into agreements. The same holds true of the distribution of functions with respect to the procedure leading to the conclusion of agreements. The following types of provisions can be distinguished[24]:

a) At best, constituent instruments authorize specific organs to enter into certain agreements.

b) There are also provisions which clearly envisage the conclusion of agreements although the term is not used expressly. On the other hand, the organ competent to conclude these agreements is mentioned.

c) Besides express authorization, the capacity to enter into agreements may be deduced from provisions conferring on specific organs a sphere of competence, without specifying the means for attaining the objectives in question.

d) One also comes across cases where the conclusion of specific agreements by the organization is provided for in the constituent treaty but where the organ which is to express the organization's consent to be bound by these agreements is not mentioned.

e) Other agreements can be justified only by reference to the general objectives and functions of the organization concerned; they become relevant under some variant of the implied power theory. As already indicated, constituent instruments as a rule do not name the organ in which the treaty-making power of the organization is vested. Hence the problem of the organ capable of committing the organization arises in the last two cases.

The picture becomes even more confusing due to the fact that organs not competent under the constituent instruments, especially chief administrative officers, frequently conclude agreements without any apparent authorization by the organ invested with treaty-making capacity.

A few examples shall illustrate the aforementioned possibilities of regulating the conclusion of agreements in constituent instruments of international organizations and should at the same time bear out the difficulties resulting from unsatisfactory provisions.

A) The UN

Even within the most important international organization, the UN, these problems arise. The Charter does not contain a general

[24] Capotorti, Sulla competenza a stipulare degli organi di unioni, 7 Comunicazioni e Studi (1955), p. 143—198 (p. 155—157).

provision on the treaty-making capacity of the Organization. Nor does it confer upon any organ (or organs) the general capacity to commit the UN. The Charter only provides for the conclusion of specific agreements by specific organs. Thus Article 43 calls for agreements on military assistance to be granted by the member States to the Security Council. In addition, Article 43, paragraph 3 stipulates that these agreements are to be concluded by the Security Council, which therefore undoubtedly possesses capacity to engage the UN in this particular field[25].

Article 63 deals with the so-called Relationship Agreements between the UN and the various Specialized Agencies[26]. These Agreements are to be entered into by the Economic and Social Council but are subject to approval by the General Assembly. The wording of this Article is ambiguous and can therefore be interpreted as investing the Economic and Social Council with treaty-making power. Under this theory, ECOSOC could therefore express the United Nations' consent to be bound by these Agreements. The approval by the General Assembly would have to be compared with the consent to ratification given by a national Parliament. According to another view confirmed by practice, the rôle of the Council is limited to negotiating the Agreements, whereas the UN is committed by the approval of the General Assembly[27].

In contrast, no such approval is necessary for the arrangements the Economic and Social Council may make under Article 64 with the Members of the United Nations and the Specialized Agencies. Under these arrangements, the other parties are to submit to the Council reports on the steps taken to give effect to its own recommendations and to recommendations on matters falling within its competence made by the General Assembly. This provision of the Charter clearly empowers the Council to bind the Organization, albeit in a sphere of minor importance[28].

There are other provisions in the constituent instrument of the UN which do not expressly refer to agreements but which more or less clearly envisage their conclusion and also mention the competent organ.

---

[25] As is known, no such agreement has hitherto been entered into, as the system of collective security conceived by the framers of the Charter never came into being.

[26] Jenks, op.cit., 205—237; Weissberg, op.cit., p. 41—50; Chiu, op.cit., p. 122 to 138.

[27] Zemanek, op.cit., p. 65—66; Capotorti, op.cit., p. 159—161.

[28] It may be added that no such arrangements were concluded in practice as the matter was included in the Relationship Agreements under Article 63. Goodrich-Hambro, Charter of the United Nations (1949), p. 380—381.

Examples include Article 28, paragraph 3 permitting the Security Council to hold meetings at such places other than the seat of the Organization as in its judgment will best facilitate its work. This seems to require an agreement between the Council and the State whose territory the Council chooses for its meeting, at least on the Council's legal status there[29].

Article 32 authorizes a non-member State which is a party to a dispute under consideration by the Security Council to participate, without vote, in the discussion relating to the dispute, provided it accepts the conditions for participation laid down by the Council. The determination of these conditions and their acceptance by the non-member State undoubtedly constitute an agreement in the broad sense of the term[30].

Another instance of an offer of the UN to be accepted by a non-member State is contained in Article 93, paragraph 2, which allows such States to become parties to the Statute of the International Court of Justice on conditions to be determined in each case by the General Assembly upon recommendation of the Security Council[31].

Similarly, the admission of new members in accordance with Article 4 can be construed as an agreement and not merely as accession to a multilateral treaty[32]. For the State in question does not simply accept the conditions posed by the original parties to the treaty and express its consent to be bound by it by a unilateral act. The procedure of admission also requires action on the part of the UN, the General Assembly having to vote in favor by at least a two-thirds majority upon a positive recommendation of the Security Council[33].

In the last two instances, the question of the organ competent to bind the UN arises. Capotorti holds the view that the General Assembly alone engages the Organization, the recommendation of the Security Council being only of internal relevance. An argument

---

[29] Kasme, op.cit., p. 38.

[30] There were several cases where this part of Article 32 was applied during the period where the permanent members of the Security Council were unable to agree upon the admission of new members. Those disputes involved Albania and Bulgaria in the Greek Civil War in 1946, Indonesia in its struggle against the Netherlands in 1947, Albania again in 1947 on the occasion of the Corfu incident and Jordan in 1950 as a party to the Palestine dispute. Kasme, op.cit., p. 38—39.

[31] Switzerland, Liechtenstein, and San Marino have made use of this opportunity.

[32] Morelli, Nozioni di diritto internazionale (1947), p. 194—195; Capotori, op.cit., p. 158; Kasme, op.cit., p. 45.

[33] The instruments of accession are registered ex officio by the UN Secretariat which regards them as elements of an international treaty. Kasme, op.cit., p. 45.

of considerable weight in support of this thesis is the establishment of the will of the UN at the moment the General Assembly endorses the recommendation previously adopted by the Security Council[34].

On the external plane, it is indeed the Assembly which definitely expresses consent. It is submitted, however, that the exercise of the treaty-making power should be distinguished from its possession. It may be useful to distinguish between the internal competence and the external capacity of the organs of international organizations too and not to limit this distinction to States. In practice the organ exercising treaty-making capacity is often not identical with the organ possessing competence. Other parties should neither be expected nor permitted to interfere with the internal law of an international organization by attempting to interpret it. The difference between capacity and competence may become relevant if it is manifest that the organ exercising capacity lacked direct constitutional competence as well as authorization by the organ possessing treaty-making power. In this case the agreement will be invalid. It may be assumed that the absence of agreement between the two main organs of the UN will be manifest to a State applying for admission.

It is therefore important to know whether the Assembly possesses the treaty-making power alone. The theory of a joint competence of the Council and the Assembly should not be lightly rejected. Arguments advanced against it which are based on analogies with the constitutional law of States are in reality of little value in this context. For the participation of the Security Council cannot be compared to the consent of a legislative organ to ratification as is required by many constitutions. As the International Court of Justice has clearly pointed out in its advisory opinion on the Competence of the General Assembly for the Admission of a State to the United Nations, the initiative for the admission of new members rests with the Council[35]. If it does not take the first step, the Assembly is legally barred from acting at all.

Moreover, whereas under Article 63 the Economic and Social Council is in a subordinate position vis-à-vis the General Assembly, so that the Assembly may negotiate Relationship Agreements itself or delegate the Council's functions to some other organ[36], the Security Council and the General Assembly are placed on a footing of equality in the cases under consideration. To say the least, the question remains therefore controversial.

---

[34] Capotorti, op.cit., p. 158—159.
[35] I.C.J. Reports 1950, p. 4—10.
[36] Capotorti, op.cit., p. 160—161.

Furthermore, many agreements were concluded in the practice of the UN for which no direct authorization could be found in the Charter. Nevertheless, the constitutionality of these agreements was generally not contested. The theories of implied powers[37] or functional extension have been invoked to provide them with a legal basis.

The following results can be inferred from this brief analysis: under the Charter of the UN, three organs are expressly authorized to commit the Organization. Two of these organs, the Security Council and the Economic and Social Council, possess treaty-making power within more or less narrow limits.

However, Article 24 can probably be interpreted as authorizing the Security Council to conclude a wide range of agreements not expressly provided for in the Charter, whenever the maintenance of international peace and security seems to necessitate the conclusion of agreements. As regards the Secretary-General, it is debatable whether his functions empower him to enter even into purely administrative arrangements with the chief administrative officers of other international organizations without the consent of any other organ. This would mean that he enjoys at least an implied treaty-making capacity within his sphere of competence.

As regards other agreements covered by some implicit authorization, the structure of the UN suggests that it is for the General Assembly to express consent to be bound in cases of doubt. The argument that under Article 10 of the Charter the Assembly may only discuss matters within the scope of the Charter and make recommendations but not binding decisions on them and therefore cannot bind members by entering into agreements on these matters is not convincing. It stands to reason that in the absence of a clearly established competence of another organ, it is the plenary organ on which all member States are represented which should commit the organization[38].

B) The Specialized Agencies of the UN

So far as the Specialized Agencies of the UN are concerned[39], a detailed analysis of the relevant provisions of each constituent instrument would be beyond the scope of this paper. May it therefore suffice to state that these constituent instruments vary considerably

---

[37] Rosenne, op.cit., p. 295—296.

[38] See below, p. 222—227.

[39] For a general presentation of these Agencies see Labeyrie-Menahem, Des institutions specialisées (1953); on some particular legal aspects, see Ahluwalia, The Legal Status, Privileges and Immunities of the Specialized Agencies of the United Nations and Certain other International Organizations (1964).

as regards the precision with which the organs invested with treaty-making power and its exercise are determined. This is all the more surprising as most of the instruments in question were drawn up at approximately the same time and by the same parties. The constituent instruments of FAO, WHO, and WMO, for example, contain rather detailed provisions on the matter under discussion. On the contrary, the statutes of ILO and UPU deal with the conclusion of agreements only briefly and vaguely.

However, a few common features emerge even from a brief analysis. The constituent instruments do not confer general treaty-making power on any Agency. Within the organizations, the general competence to enter into agreements seems to be usually vested in the plenary organ on which all member States are represented. Moreover, as a rule the statutes of the Specialized Agencies provide only for agreements with other international organizations, but this fact has not prevented treaty relations with States. Sometimes a limited treaty-making power in specific fields is entrusted to the restricted executive organ, so that the plenary organ does not always enjoy exclusive competence to conclude agreements[40]. Moreover, Article XIII, paragraph 2 of the constituent instrument of FAO even authorizes the Director-General to enter into specific agreements with other inter-governmental organizations[41].

Here the chief administrative officer is expressly granted a share of the treaty-making power. He is to exercise it, however, subject to any decision of the plenary organ.

There is one exception among the Specialized Agencies of the UN to the possession of general treaty-making power by the plenary organ of the organization. It may therefore be worthwile to discuss the case of UNESCO[42] in greater detail. In fact, Article X of the Charter of UNESCO (which presents the "classical" tripartite structure)[43] provides for a Relationship Agreement with the UN. The Agreement is to be approved by the General Conference, the plenary organ of the Organization[44].

[40] Thus the Council of ICAO is given rather broad compentences under Articles 55 and especially 65 of the constituent instrument of the Organization.

[41] These agreements are to provide for the maintenance of common services and for common arrangements in regard to recruitment, training, conditions of service and other related matters, and for interchange of staff.

[42] As regards UNESCO in general, see Kipp, UNESCO, Recht, Sittliche Grundlage, Aufgabe (1957); Thomas, UNESCO (1962); Shuster, UNESCO, Assessment and Promise (1963).

[43] Zemanek, op.cit., p. 31—42.

[44] The Agreement envisaged in Article X was entered into in 1946 and came into force on its approval by the UN General Assembly in conformity with its Article XXII. 1 UNTS, p. 238—258.

Furthermore, Article X of the statute of UNESCO was construed as covering agreements with subsidiary organs of the UN as well[45].

Under Article XI, paragraph 2, the General Conference is also competent to enter into another specific category of agreements. By virtue of to this provision, the Director-General, subject to the approval of the Conference, may make arrangements on the transfer of resources and activities from other international organizations, whose purpose and functions lie within the competence of the UNESCO, to the latter Organization.

On the other hand, Article XI, paragraph 1, given the general terms in which it is couched, confers a much broader authority upon the Executive Board. The Board has to approve all the formal agreements on co-operation with other specialized intergovernmental organizations and agencies[46] whose interests and activities are related to the purpose of UNESCO[47].

Although the UNESCO-Charter remains silent on the Organization's capacity to conclude agreements with States, such agreements are nevertheless quite frequent in practice[48]. They were approved either by the General Conference or the Executive Board. Other agreements concerning the establishment of regional centers of

---

[45] Thus at its eight session the General Conference authorized the Director-General to enter into an agreement with the UN Relief and Works Agency for Palestine Refugees in the Near East which was signed in 1952. A similar agreement was signed with the Special Fund of the UN in 1959 pursuant to another resolution adopted by the General Conference. As regards the agreement with the UN Korean Reconstruction Agency signed by the Director-General in 1957, it is interesting to note that he was authorized to sign by the Executive Board and not by the General Conference, which seems to be hardly compatible with Article X and the subsequent practice of the Organization. Smets-Mertens, Le "treaty-making power" de l'U.N.E.S.C.O., 70 RGDIP (1966), p. 916—960 (p. 930—933).

[46] On inter-agency agreements in general, see Jenks, op.cit., p. 237—243.

[47] The Organization entered into such agreements, both with other Specialized Agencies, for example ILO, WHO, FAO, and IAEA, with which it concluded inter-agency agreements as well as working arrangements, and other intergovernmental organizations (for example with OAS and the Council of Europe). Smets-Mertens, op.cit., p. 938—943.

[48] Of particular interest is the Headquarters Agreement with France. It was approved by the Executive Board, but only after this power had been delegated to it by the General Conference, as the latter's approval was requested by the Agreement. The Conference also authorized the Director-General to sign the Agreement. Fischer, U.N.E.S.C.O., Accord relatif au siège, I AFDI (1955), p. 393—406. For a general discussion of headquarters agreements see Cahier, Etude des accords de siège conclus entre les organisations internationales et les Etats où elles résident (1959) and Bota, The Capacity of International Organizations to Conclude Headquarters Agreements and some Features of these Agreements, this volume, p. 57—104.

UNESCO were only exceptionally approved at all[49]. The general trend towards shortening the procedure of treaty conclusion can also be observed in the practice of UNESCO. Thus in many cases the Director-General expresses the Organization's consent without any special authorization by another organ. This practice may be justified by pointing out that he acts within the framework of the general program laid down by the competent organs which thus constitutes a "global" or implicit authorization[50].

In the final analysis, UNESCO is far from presenting a uniform picture so far as the organ endowed with treaty-making power is concerned. Its constituent instrument charges two organs with the conclusion of agreements, the Executive Board undoubtedly receiving the lion's share. The General Conference is only competent to enter into specific agreements. Practice is ambiguous as regards agreements with States which are not provided for in the statute of UNESCO, since they were concluded and approved sometimes by the General Conference and sometimes by the Executive Board. Furthermore, many agreements were entered into by the chief administrative officer of the Organization without the approval of either collegiate organ.

Thus the results of this brief investigation are rather confusing and admit no clear-cut answer to the central question under consideration. It is safe to say, however, that no single organ of UNESCO is invested with treaty-making power.

C) The European Communities

In view of their economic and political importance and their particular legal features, the European Coal and Steel Community (ECSC), the European Economic Community (EEC), and the European Atomic Energy Community (Euratom) deserve at least a brief mention in this context[51].

One of the striking aspects of the three Communities is again the extent to which their constituent instruments differ in the precision with which they deal with the conclusion of agreements. Furthermore, even among these closely related regional organizations, there are no uniform rules on the internal distribution of the treaty-making competences among the various organs.

This phenomenon is most probably due to the fact that the objectives and powers of both ECSC and Euratom are limited to

[49] Smets-Mertens, op.cit., p. 948—950.

[50] Ibidem, p. 959.

[51] Reuter, Organisations Européennes (1965), p. 173—430; Ganshof van der Meersch, Organisation Européennes (1966); Robertson, European Institutions (1966), p. 135—204; Cartou, Organisations Européennes (1967), p. 89—425.

certain economic sectors and well defined. This fact resulted in a rather strong position of the independent organ, the High Authority of ECSC[52] and the Commission of Euratom vis-à-vis the other "directive" organ[53], representing the individual interests of the member States, viz. the Council of Ministers.

EEC, on the other hand, pursues a much more ambitious aim. It is to bring about the economic and possibly the political integration of Europe. Given the complex subject matter and in order to avoid differences of opinion on specific issues, which may have compromised the Treaty of Rome as a whole, its authors chose to lay down only broad principles to be further defined by the organs of the Community[54]. Since the six member States were reluctant to give a kind of blank check to the independent organ, the Council composed of the representatives of States occupies the dominant position within EEC.

These basic considerations are reflected in the provisions governing the conclusion of agreements.

a) As to ECSC, treaty-making capacity is once more not expressly conferred upon it by the constituent Treaty. Nor are the organs generally competent to enter into agreements mentioned there. Yet the treaty-making power of the Community can obviously be deduced from the broad formula used in Article 6, paragraph 2 of the Treaty of Paris[55].

Writers are generally agreed[56] that this vague provision includes the capacity to conclude agreements, even if they are not expressly envisaged by the ECSC Treaty, provided that they are necessary for the attainment of the objectives of the Community[57].

---

[52] A treaty of 9 April 1965 created a single Commission for the three Communities.

[53] Reuter, op.cit., p. 218.

[54] The EEC was therefore entrusted with important legislative functions too. Consequently, its constituent instrument has been referred to as "traité-ordre" or "traité de procédure." Loercher, Der Abschluß völkerrechtlicher Verträge nach dem Recht der drei Europäischen Gemeinschaften (1965), p. 114.

[55] Article 6, paragraph 2 reads as follows: "In international relations the Community shall enjoy the legal capacity necessary to perform its functions and achieve its ends."

[56] Catalano, La Comunità Economica Europea e l'Euratom (1959), p. 72; Cassesse, Le relazioni internazionali della Comunità economica europea, 15 La Comunità Internazionale (1960), p. 471—486 (p. 471); Loercher, op.cit., p. 71. This view is not shared by Riphagen, De juridische structuur der Europese Gemeenschap voor Kolen en Staal (1955), p. 32—33.

[57] In this connection Article 3 (a) and (f) whose objects affect third States are worth mentioning.

(i) Apart from this general formula, the Treaty authorizes the conclusion of specific agreements. Some provisions also name the organ competent to conclude them[58].

(ii) While specifying the competent organ, other provisions do not refer to agreements expressly, but their conclusion seems to be covered by the more or less broad wording[59].

(iii) A third variant is the reference to a particular agreement with a given party without determining the organ competent to act on behalf of the Community[60].

As to the organ or organs in which the treaty-making power of ECSC is vested, it has already been mentioned that the Treaty contains no general provision. The Articles which seem to provide an answer to this question are on the one hand Article 6, paragraph 4, according to which "the Community shall be represented by its institutions each within the limits of its competence." Article 8, on the other hand, charges the High Authority with "the duty to ensure the attainment of the objects set out in this Treaty, under the conditions laid down herein."

Some authors have mainly relied on this second provision. They have concluded that the High Authority, which they regard as the executive of the Community, enjoys a monopoly in the field of external relations including the exclusive possession and exercise of ECSC's treaty-making power[61]. It is submitted, however, that the principle of the separation of powers, which in the case of States is the product of a more or less accidental evolution, should not be applied to ECSC by simple analogy.

---

[58] Thus Article 52, Paragraph 2 empowers the High Authority to enter into agreements with the member States concerned or the appropriate authorities on the transfer of funds. Furthermore, Article 14 of the Protocol on the Privileges and Immunities of ECSC authorizes the High Authority to enter into supplementary arrangements with the member States.

[59] Article 49, paragraph 1, for example, empowers the High Authority to contract loans. Article 47 confers upon the High Authority the capacity to "take any measures in accordance with this Treaty" in certain cases of discrimination in the field of commercial policy. There appears to be general agreement that the measures referred to include the conclusion of agreements. Similarly, Article 93 speaks of "all appropriate relations" to be entertained by the High Authority with the UN and OEEC. Likewise, Article 98 which deals with the accession of other European States to ECSC implies the conclusion of an agreement between the Council (and not the High Authority this time!) and the respective candidates.

[60] This applies to Article 94 which reads as follows: "Relations shall be maintained between the Community's institutions and the Council of Europe under the terms of a Protocol annexed hereto."

[61] Reuter, La Communauté Européenne du Charbon et de l'Acier (1953), p. 124; Sperduti, L'unione degli Stati partecipanti alla Comunità Europea del Carbone e dell'Acciaio, 8 Comunicazioni e Studi (1956), p. 81—118 (p. 117).

Article 6, paragraph 4 ought rather to be construed as lex specialis to Article 8[62]. It would follow that each organ is to represent the Communities within its sphere of autonomous competence. This includes the conclusion of agreements. True enough, the High Authority will be competent in most cases. It should be stressed, however, that there are instances where the Council is empowered to act on behalf of the Community on the external plane, notably in the important matter of the admission of new members, but possibly also under Article 72.

b) The founding fathers of EEC opted for a solution different from that of ECSC, both from a substantial and technical point of view. The Treaty of Rome does not set forth a general provision endowing the Community with treaty-making power. However, Article 228 lays down rules concerning the organ possessing this power and the procedure to be followed in its exercise.

As already mentioned, the Council plays the dominant rôle within EEC. This holds true of the conclusion of agreements under Article 228[63]. This Article does not constitute in itself, however, a sufficient legal basis for concluding any agreement[64]. It is but a

[62] Riphagen, op.cit., p. 38; Hallier, Die Vertragschließungsbefugnis der Europäischen Gemeinschaft für Kohle und Stahl, 17 ZaöRV (1956—57), p. 428—447 (p. 433); Carstens, Die Errichtung des gemeinsamen Marktes in der Europäischen Wirtschaftsgemeinschaft, Atomgemeinschaft und Gemeinschaft für Kohle und Stahl, 18 ZaöRV (1957—58), p. 459—525 (p. 517—518); Steindorff, Europäische Gemeinschaft für Kohle und Stahl, Wörterbuch des Völkerrechts I (1960), p. 458—466 (p. 464); Pescatore, Les relations extérieures des Communautés européennes, 103 RCADI (1961), p. 9—238; Loercher, op.cit., p. 99; Melchior, La procédure de conclusion des accords externes de la Communauté économique européenne, 2 Revue belge de droit international (1966), p. 187—215.

[63] Article 228 reads as follows:

"1. Where this Treaty provides for the conclusion of agreements between the Community and one or more States or an international organization, such agreements shall be negotiated by the Commission. Subject to the competence conferred upon the Commission in this respect, such agreements shall be concluded by the Council after the Assembly has been consulted where required by this Treaty.

The Council, the Commission or a Member State may obtain beforehand the opinion of the Court of Justice as to extent to which a contemplated agreement is compatible with the provisions of this Treaty. An agreement which has been the subject of an adverse opinion by the Court of Justice shall only come into force under the conditions laid down in Article 236.

2. Agreements concluded in the manner laid down above shall be binding on the institutions of the Community and on Member States."

This distribution of functions between the three organs on the external plane reflects their respective rôles within the Community. Melchior, op.cit., p. 189.

[64] Wohlfahrt-Everling-Glaesner-Sprung, Die Europäische Wirtschaftsgemeinschaft, Kommentar zum Vertrag (1960), p. 590; Loercher, op.cit., p. 119—120.

procedural provision whose application depends on some separate authorization in the Treaty[65].

This, of course, does not give rise to any problems whenever the constituent instrument expressly refers to the entering into of agreements[66].

Article 6, paragraph 2 of the Protocol on the Privileges and Immunities of EEC[67], albeit of little material relevance, is of particular interest in this connection because it empowers the Commission (and not the Council) to enter into agreements for the passports issued to members and servants of the institutions of the Communities by the presidents of these institutions to be recognized in the territory of third countries as valid travel documents.

Like the High Authority of ECSC, the EEC-Council does not possess exclusive treaty-making power, however dominant its position vis-à-vis the other organs.

Furthermore, the question arises whether the express references to the making of agreements in the constituent instrument of EEC are exhaustive or whether Article 228 is also applicable if the conclusion of agreements is covered by a less precise provision or may be justified only as a means for attaining an object put forth in general terms by the draftsmen of the Treaty.

Writers are again divided on this problem of interpretation[68]. It is submitted that the question ought to be answered in the affirmative. Several Articles of the Treaty of Rome can be quoted in support of this thesis[69].

---

[65] This view is contested by Cahier, op.cit., p. 168, and Catalano, op.cit., p. 72.

[66] The following examples may be quoted in this context: Articles 111, paragraph 2, and 113, to be read together with Article 114, envisage tariff and trade agreements with third States, both during and after the transitional period. Another explicit reference to agreements is set forth in Article 238 dealing with association agreements with third countries, unions of States or international organizations.

[67] Article 7, paragraph 2 of the new Protocol of 8 April 1965.

[68] Catalano, op.cit., p. 74—75; Cassesse, op.cit., p. 473—474; Wohlfahrt-Everling-Glaesner-Sprung, op.cit., p. 590—593; Pescatore, op.cit., p. 100—101; Loercher, op.cit., p. 120—121; Melchior, op.cit., p. 188—189.

[69] For example, Articles 59, paragraph 2, 75, paragraph 1, 116, paragraph 1, and 229—231 seem to fall into this second category where the authorization to enter into agreements can more or less clearly be inferred from the wording of the provisions. Article 229 is particularly noteworthy. It entrusts the Commission with ensuring the maintenance of all appropriate relations with the organs of the UN, those of the Specialized Agencies and of GATT, as well as with all other international organizations. If it is admitted that the maintenance of these "appropriate relations" implies that the Commission may conclude those agreements which form the necessary basis for the relations concerned, the apparent monopoly of the Council in the field of treaty relations is broken again. It may be added that

To sum up, in comparison with the constituent instrument of ECSC, the EEC-Treaty offers one decisive advantage: once the authorization to conclude an agreement has been established under its material provisions—in cases of implicit authorization, the legal basis may not always be free from doubt—it is evident which organ is invested with treaty-making power and how the power is to be exercised. This certainly is a step towards the security of treaty relations. Finally, it may be recalled that no single organ is endowed with the competence to enter into agreements on behalf of EEC.

c) It is the constituent instrument of Euratom, however, which sets forward the best solution to the problem at issue. Like Article 6, paragraph 2 of the Treaty of Paris, Article 101, paragraph 1 contains a general authorization to conclude agreements. This time, however, the authorization is express. This aspect ought to be emphasized, for as a rule one looks in vain for a clear-cut provision conferring treaty-making power on an organization[70].

Consequently, whenever the tasks of the Community and the measures to be taken with a view to fulfilling these tasks, as enshrined in Articles 1 and 2 of the Euratom-Treaty, seem to justify the conclusion of an agreement it can be entered into[71]. True enough, the problem of whether the conclusion of a particular agreement in a given situation is covered by the tasks and powers of the Community may give rise to difficulties.

It is worth noting that several Articles of the Euratom-Treaty expressly provide for the conclusion of agreements, but are certainly not exhaustive in view of Article 101, paragraph 1[72].

---

in practice the Commission did profit from this implicit authorization. Writers advocating a restrictive interpretation point to the introductory phrase of Article 228: "Where this Treaty provides for the conclusion of agreements..." Melchior, op.cit., p. 188—189. However, it does not conclusively result from this wording that the Treaty of Rome must *expressly* provide for the entering into of agreements. Cf. footnote 63.

[70] Article 101, paragraph 1 reads as follows:

"The community may, within the limits of its powers and jurisdiction, enter into obligations by concluding agreements or conventions with a third country, an international organization or a national of a third country."

[71] Loercher, op.cit., p. 175; Raux, La procédure de conclusion des accords externes de la Communauté européenne de l'Energie atomique, 69 RGDIP (1965), p. 1019—1050 (p. 1022).

[72] Articles 29 on agreements for the exchange of scientific or industrial information on nuclear matters, 64 dealing with agreements on the supply of ores, source material or special fissile material, 106 on agreements providing for co-operation in the field of nuclear energy, and 206 concerning association agreements, furnish examples of such references to agreements which the founding fathers of Euratom considered particularly important.

With respect to the organ competent to commit the Community on the international plane, the constituent instrument of Euratom also contains clear provisions. Moreover, it should be stressed that once again it does not entrust this competence to a single organ. Under Article 101, paragraph 2, it is the Commission which in principle expresses consent to be bound on behalf of the Community[73].

It follows that the Council too plays an important part under this provision. The Commission is to take its directives[74] into account while conducting negotiations. Furthermore, the approval of the Council is required for the act which definitively commits Euratom.

However, the aforementioned principle suffers an exception in virtue of Article 101, paragraph 3, which under certain conditions confers an exclusive competence on the Commission[75].

It may be added that in practice the obligation merely to inform the Council results in this organ's wielding a considerable influence over the contents of agreements concluded under Article 101, paragraph 3[76].

Finally, there exists a category of agreements where the competence to engage Euratom rests with the Council and not with the Commission. Under Article 206, paragraph 2 (just as under Article 238 of the EEC-Treaty), association agreements with a third country, with a union of States or with an international organization are concluded by the Council, the Assembly having again the right to be consulted.

To sum up this brief analysis, one cannot but be struck by the extent to which provisions on the conclusion of agreements differ within these three closely related and interdependent Communities. It

---

[73] Fischer, L'accord de coopération entre les Etats Unis et l'Euratom, 4 AFDI (1958), p. 540—555 (p. 541); Loercher, op.cit., p. 195; Raux, op.cit., p. 1033—1037.

Article 101, paragraph 2 reads as follows:

"Such agreements or conventions shall be negotiated by the Commission in accordance with the Council's directives; they shall be concluded by the Commission with the approval of the Council given by qualified majority decision."

[74] These directives are not of an imperative character but rather a "simple general orientation," which must be ignored, however, by the Commission. Raux, op.cit., p. 1029—1030.

[75] Article 101, paragraph 3 reads as follows:

"Agreements or conventions whose implementation does not require the intervention of the Council and can be effected within the limits of the relevant budget shall, however, be negotiated and concluded by the Commission, provided that it keeps the Council informed."

"Such agreements or conventions shall be negotiated by the Commission in accordance with the Council's directives; they shall be concluded by the Commission, provided that it keeps the Council informed."

[76] Loercher, op.cit., p. 198—199.

is furthermore noteworthy that in none of the Communities any organ enjoys a monopoly in this field.

The observer is also puzzled, and justly so, by the technically imperfect solutions conceived for ECSC and EEC. As regards ECSC, doubts crop up even with regard to the organ entitled to engage the Community on the international plane, at least in certain cases. With respect to EEC, there is considerable uncertainty whether the Community is empowered to enter into agreements not expressly provided for in the Treaty of Rome, although at least the organs competent to engage it are specified in the constituent instrument. Hence it is to be deplored that the solution provided for Euratom was not developed earlier or at least also applied to EEC. It will be recalled that the constituent instrument of Euratom expressly confers treaty-making power on the Community in general terms. Moreover, it names the organs endowed with this power and sets forth the procedure to be followed for the conclusion of an agreement.

D) The Council of Europe

The particular traits of the Council of Europe may justify a few remarks on this international organization[77]. On the one hand, its competences cover a wide range of matters, economic and social as well as cultural, scientific, legal, and administrative, only questions of national defense being expressly excluded[78]. On the other hand, its powers are limited to discussing problems arising in these fields and making recommendations for common action. For the Council of Europe is not authorized to make decisions which are binding on the member States. As to its structure, its two main organs are the Committee of Ministers, where each member State is represented on a footing of equality, and the Consultative Assembly composed of representatives elected by the national Parliaments, their number varying according to the population of the countries they represent.

As regards the competence to enter into agreements, there is again no general provision conferring treaty-making power upon the Organization. However, Article 15 (a) of the Statute of the Council seems to imply the possibility of the Committee's concluding agreements, both on the recommendation of the Consultative Assembly and on its own initiative. Moreover, Article 40 (b) provides for a special agreement to be entered into with the Government of France

---

[77] Robertson, The Council of Europe (1961); Duclos, Le Conseil de l'Europe (1964); Reuter, Organisations Européennes, p. 106—131; Ganshof van der Meersch, op.cit., p. 197—402; Cartou, op.cit., p. 4—18.

[78] Article 1 (d) of the Statute of the Council.

in order to define the privileges and immunities which the Council shall enjoy at its seat.

The somewhat vague authorization laid down in Article 15 (a) was clarified by a statutory resolution adopted by the Committee of Ministers in 1951. It conferred upon the Committee the monopoly of concluding agreements with other intergovernmental organizations[79]. In the course of time, such agreements were in fact entered into.

Yet since from a technical point of view the Committee as a collegiate organ is hardly the appropriate body for engaging in the complex process leading to the conclusion of an agreement, the agreements to which the Council became a party were as a rule negotiated and often also concluded by the Secretary-General, sometimes with and sometimes without the subsequent approval of the Committee[80].

What ought to be kept in mind with respect to the topic under discussion is the fact that under the Statute as further defined by the statutory resolution of 1951, one single organ possesses the treaty-making competence of the Organization, even if the execution of the agreement falls into the sphere of competence of another organ. The wording of the resolution indicates in fact that even purely administrative arrangements between the Secretary-General and the chief administrative officer of another organization require some internal authorization.

3. The Opinions of Writers

It is not surprising that in view of the incoherent picture resulting even from the above brief analysis, whose aim has only been to show the lack of uniform provisions in the field, authors are not agreed on the organ invested with the treaty-making power of an international organization in the absence of express provisions in the constituent instruments. This applies to cases where the organization is entitled to conclude an agreement but the competent organ is not named. The problem also arises if the organization engages in treaty activities not expressly provided for in its constituent instrument, unless the latter confers general treaty-making competence in unambiguous terms on one organ. Hence the question to be answered is whether the law of international organizations has developed a presumption in favor of the capacity of certain organs to express consent to be bound similar

[79] The text of the resolution can be found in Golsong-Kiss, Les accords entre le Conseil de L'Europe et d'autres organisations intergouvernementales, 4 AFDI (1958), p. 477—492 (p. 483).

[80] Ibidem, p. 483—486.

to Article 7, paragraph 2 (a) of the Vienna Convention on the Law of Treaties.

Five different views have been expounded by writers[81].

A) The Treaty-Making Power of the Organization Is Vested in Its Chief Administrative Officer

The residual capacity of the Secretary-General of the UN in particular was affirmed by Fitzmaurice[82], mainly on the ground that there are situations where organs consisting of an "assemblage" of States may be unable to act although the organization is entitled or even bound to do so.

A similar position is taken by Kasme[83]. He refuses to base his thesis on any particular provision of the UN-Charter, though Article 97 refers to the Secretary-General as the chief administrative officer of the Organization and Chapter XV entrusts him with important political functions. He also rejects an analogy with the constitutional law of States, under which the Secretary-General would appear as a combination of Chief of State, Foreign Minister and Ambassador[84]. Kasme feels that the practice of the UN and the principle of effectiveness sufficiently support his view. Moreover, in his opinion two practical considerations should be taken into account. The Secretary-General's independent status in contrast to other organs, whose members are bound by instructions of their governments, as well as his continuous contacts with the other organs and the permanent missions of the member States qualify the chief administrative officer of the UN for the task of concluding agreements. Kasme further points out that the bulk of the agreements not provided for in the Charter were in practice entered into by the Secretary-General.

These arguments mainly based on considerations of effectiveness miss the point. A collegiate organ which is invested with treaty-making power is not obliged to exercise it itself[85]. For reasons of convenience and expediency the power may be delegated to another organ better suited for the task. Yet such delegation does not deprive the collegiate organ of its original treaty-making competence. The

---

[81] A summary of these views is given by Detter, The Organs of International Organizations Exercising their Treaty-making Power, 38 BYBIL (1962), p. 421 to 444 (p. 421—427).

[82] Fitzmaurice, The Law and Procedure of the International Court of Justice: International Organizations and Tribunals, 29 BYBIL (1952), p. 1—61 (p. 12—13).

[83] Kasme, op.cit., p. 187—194.

[84] The same point is made by Rosenne, op.cit., p. 408—409.

[85] Chiu, op.cit., p. 89.

same observation applies to treaties concluded by States, where originally competent organs frequently authorize other organs to enter into less important treaties.

The argument advanced by Fitzmaurice seems even less persuasive. If the authors of the constituent instrument of an international organization intended only a particular organ to exercise a specific function, even the most liberal interpretation must not lead to a different result. If in a specific case the competent organ is prevented from acting, because the majority required for a decision is lacking, the will of the sovereign States setting up the organization and posing certain conditions in the constituent treaty ought to be respected. If they insisted on a certain majority for the decisions of an organ or retained an individual right of veto, this means that they wanted to control the activities of the organization closely. Therefore no other organ should be permitted to act instead of the paralyzed organ, however desirable action by the organization may seem in a given situation. Even if one leans to the view that international organizations should be prohibited from invoking violations of their constitutions as a ground for invalidating agreements, the principles of effectiveness and the security of treaty relations should at least not cover manifest violations[86].

What is more, the above theory elaborated for the UN cannot be extended to all international organizations. The structure of the European Communities seems to exclude the application of this thesis[87] to these three organizations. It is not clear who could be considered their chief administrative officer. The suggested rule is also at variance with the statutory resolution adopted by the Committee of Ministers of the Council of Europe in 1951[88].

On the other hand, there is no denying that in practice chief administrative officers play an increasingly important part in the conclusion of agreements in simplified form[89]. However, at least some implicit and general authorization, be it previous or subsequent, by the organ endowed with treaty-making competence is required de lege lata even for these agreements, unless the chief administrative officer is directly empowered by the constituent instrument to enter into certain agreements on his own. Such provisions are, however, rather exceptional[90].

---

[86] See below, p. 254—268.

[87] See above, p. 208—215.

[88] See above, p. 216.

[89] See below, p. 233—238 and 243—246.

[90] Article XIII, paragraph 2 of the constituent instrument of FAO furnishes an example. See above, p. 206.

It is doubtful whether by virtue of their functions chief administrative officers are entitled to conclude purely administrative arrangements with their counterparts in other organizations. The very existence of even such a limited autonomous competence as well as the legal character of these agreements are far from established. This does not mean that a customary norm to this effect may not emerge one day from the practice of international organizations.

The security of treaty relations may make it desirable to include in a future Convention on the treaty law of international organizations a general presumption in favor of chief administrative officers. The suggested presumption could be justified as progressive development of the law. However, even then a line ought be drawn between the possession and the exercise of the treaty-making power. It is further suggested to distinguish between the internal and external spheres of international organizations in the Convention. This would mean a distinction between the possession of treaty-making power and its exercise. It may be convenient to use the terms "competence" for the internal and "capacity" for the external aspect of the treaty-making power of international organizations. The organs possessing competence need not be identical with the organs exercising capacity. The treaty partners of international organizations would not be required to bother about the competence of agents claiming to represent organizations unless the lack of competence was or ought to have been manifest to them. Hence chief administrative officers would only be entitled to exercise treaty-making capacity by virtue of a presumption laid down in the Convention. The fact that they have no competence may become relevant if it is manifest that they have not been authorized by the organ or organs possessing competence. For under the system developed in this paper, this defect may be invoked as a ground for invalidating the agreement. On the other hand, the organ endowed with competence would thereby be entitled to conclude any agreement within the limits of the constitution of the organization.

B) The Treaty-Making Power of the Organization Is Vested in Its "Executive" Organ

This theory was to apply to ECSC in particular. According to its authors, the High Authority as the Community's executive body was to enjoy the jus representationis omnimodae and exclusive treaty-making power[91].

[91] Ophuels-de Rossi-Reuter, Opinion on the Participation of Observers from the Council of Europe in the Common Assembly and on the Conclusion of an Agreement to this effect (1952); Reuter, La Communauté Européenne du Charbon et de l'Acier (1953), S. 124.

The following arguments were advanced in support of this thesis:

Article 8 of the Treaty of Paris charges the High Authority with the general task of ensuring the attainment of the objects of the Community, whereas the Assembly has only powers of control and the Council of Ministers is mainly to harmonize the action of the High Authority with that of the Governments of the member States.

Moreover, only the High Authority is entitled under specific provisions of the Treaty to act on the international plane.

Finally, an analogy is drawn between the structure of ECSC and that of States under whose constitution the executive branch is invested with treaty-making power[92]. According to this theory, the High Authority occupies a similar position within the framework of the Community.

We have already seen that upon analysis of the constituent instrument of ECSC much can be said against the first two arguments[93]. As regards the third one, the distribution of powers presently underlying the constitutions of most States is not so much the result of logical necessity but rather the product of a given historical evolution[94]. Other systems are conceivable and have prevailed in the course of history. At any rate, analogies between different branches of law have to be drawn with the greatest caution. This is particularly so in the present case, as the most frequent structure of international organizations, which as a rule are composed of two representative bodies and one administrative organ, does not resemble that of States at all[95].

The aforementioned theory is therefore of questionable value even if confined to ECSC. Applied generally, it would invest all chief administrative officers with treaty-making power. The reasons why this thesis ought not to be retained have already been adduced[96].

C) The Treaty-Making Power of the Organization Is Vested in Several Organs According to the Distribution of Competences within the Organization

This theory met with considerable support[97]. According to the principle of "parallelism[98]," "pluralism[99]" or "speciality[100]," each

[92] See above, p. 199—200.

[93] See above, p. 209—211.

[94] Hallier, op.cit., p. 432.

[95] Zemanek, op.cit., p. 31—42.

[96] See above, p. 217—219.

[97] Balladore-Pallieri, La formation des traités dans la pratique internationale contemporaine, 74 RCADI (1949), p. 465—545 (p. 490); Capotorti, op.cit., p. 197 to 198.

[98] Reuter, Cours d'Organisations Européennes (1960), p. 143.

[99] Dupuy, op.cit., p. 504.

[100] Kasme, op.cit., p. 181—182.

organ is competent to represent the organization within its material sphere of competence and hence also to enter into agreements within these limits.

Admittedly, this principle prevails to a certain extent within the European Communities. As already indicated, no organ enjoys an exclusive competence to conclude agreements in any of the Communities, however dominant its position may be in general[101].

The theory applies to the UN, at least in so far as the distribution of powers between the General Assembly and the Security Council is concerned. In virtue of Article 24 of the Charter, it is obviously the Security Council which is to commit the UN whenever the maintenance of international peace and security appears to call for the conclusion of an agreement, although there is no special authorization in the Charter for it[102].

Critics of this thesis[103] have remarked, however, that even within the framework of the UN, other organs have participated in the drawing up of certain agreements—the Trusteeship Council was for instance allowed to take part in the negotiation of agreements which were of direct interest to it[104]—but that these agreements were in fact concluded by the General Assembly alone. Furthermore, although the framers of the Charter seem to have regarded the Economic and Social Council as the principal organ for the co-ordination of the activities of the UN not only with the Specialized Agencies but with other international organizations too, agreements between the UN and the League of Nations and the Council of Europe were entered into by the General Assembly[105]. Moreover, the Relationship Agreements under Article 63 have been concluded by the Assembly, which expressed the Organization's consent to be bound by its approval of the Agreements, whereas the Economic and Social Council only negotiated them.

The above theory needs therefore further specification. It is submitted that it ought to apply only if the organs concerned are placed on a footing of equality, which means that they can act autonomously within their respective spheres of competence. This additional condition would explain why the principle is applicable to the "directive" organs of the European Communities and to the Security Council of the UN vis-à-vis the General Assembly, but not between the latter organ and the Economic and Social Council or the Trusteeship Council.

---

101 See above, p. 208—215.

102 Zemanek, op.cit., p. 37.

103 Dupuy, op.cit., p. 509—511; Kasme, op.cit., p. 181—183.

104 Kasme, op.cit., p. 181.

105 Dupuy, op.cit., p. 510.

Since these two organs are to discharge their functions under the authority of the Assembly[106], they need its authorization in some form, even for the conclusion of agreements on matters they are empowered to deal with under the Charter. The same is true of subsidiary organs like UNICEF, UNRWA, and the UN Special Fund, all of which have entered into numerous agreements[107]. The conclusion of all these agreements was authorized somehow by the General Assembly.

This further qualification reduces the number of organs empowered to conclude agreements on their own under the principle of decentralization. Hence the probability of chaos in the external relations of international organizations, due to the fact that practically every organ could conclude at least certain agreements, does not seem to be high. Moreover, subordinate organs are often under the obligation to report regularly on their activities to the main organs. These and other less formal contacts between the various organs of an international organization further reduce the danger of chaos against which Detter[108] and Chiu[109] caution so emphatically.

If on the other hand two or more organs enjoy parallel treaty-making competences, the rule "prior tempore, potior jure" should apply. In the case of joint competences, all the organs concerned have to agree to an agreement before it can be entered into.

D) The Treaty-Making Power of the Organization Is Vested in the Plenary Organ

This fourth theory has also met with considerable approval among writers[110].

In fact, both political and legal reasons seem to support the view that the organ on which all member States are represented shall be competent to engage the organization in cases of doubt, especially if

---

[106] Articles 60 and 87 of the UN Charter.

[107] Chiu, op.cit., p. 95—96 and 173—177.

[108] Detter, op.cit., p. 423.

[109] Chiu, op.cit., p. 86.

[110] Article 4, paragraphs 1 and 3 of Brierly's Draft Convention on the Law of Treaties. The two provisions read as follows:

"Article 4 (1) The capacity of a State or international organization to make treaties may be exercised by whatever organ or organs of that State or organization its constitution may provide.

. . .

(3) In the absence of provision in its constitution to the contrary, the capacity of an international organization to make treaties is deemed to reside in its plenary organ."

2 YILC, 1950, p. 223. Subject to certain qualifications, the same conclusion is reached by Dupuy, op.cit., p. 511.

the agreement in question is not expressly provided for in the constituent instrument but has not to be covered by the theory of implied powers. For more often than not, the obligations incurred by an international organization will impose new burdens on its members, last but not least as regards their financial contributions.

It is therefore suggested to include a presumption in favor of the plenary organs being invested with treaty-making competence in a future Convention on the treaty law of international organizations. A few further explanatory remarks seem to be appropriate in this context.

Objection has been raised to theory D) on the ground that it is at variance with the distribution of competences laid down in some constituent instruments. There are in fact instances where plenary organs possess only restricted competence, at least as regards the conclusion of agreements.

For example, under Article XI, paragraph 1 of the Charter of UNESCO the general treaty-making power appears to be vested in the restricted body and not in the plenary organ, although practice is somewhat ambiguous so far as agreements with States are concerned. It will be recalled that this type of agreement is not expressly covered by the constituent instrument of UNESCO[111].

It has also be maintained that in IMCO it is the Council and not the Assembly which occupies the central position, because the Assembly depends on the Council's recommendations which it cannot alter but only refer back to the Council with its comments[112].

Finally, this theory does obviously not hold in regard to ECSC and Euratom, where the organ endowed with general treaty-making competence is again not the Council composed of the representatives of States but the independent organ, although the Council is entitled to enter into certain types of agreements[113].

The obvious answer to this objection is that one will of course have to look first at the constituent instrument of an organization in order to determine the organ endowed with general treaty-making competence. Hence the proposed presumption is only to apply if no answer can be found in the constituent instrument. In consequence, all the cited examples would fall outside the scope of the presumption since the residuary competence of the restricted organs can be inferred from the constituent treaties.

Furthermore, presumptions are not limited to cases where all express regulations of an issue are identical and this identical solution

---

111 See above, p. 206—208.

112 Bowett, op.cit., p. 106—107.

113 See above, p. 208—211 and p. 213—215.

is merely extended to situations for which no explicit provision has been made. In the case at hand, it is therefore not necessary that constituent instruments confer general treaty-making competence on no other but the plenary organ.

The fact that plenary organs do possess this competence in the majority of international organizations and the practical considerations already referred to lend sufficient support to the suggested presumption. Furthermore, a comparison between the constitutions of States and those of international organizations yields a result which points in the same direction.

Most States have adopted the concept of separation of powers as the principle underlying their constitutions. Under this system, treaty-making power is vested in the executive branch. Yet the organ competent to conclude treaties is not of necessity competent to implement it. An act of the legislative is often required for the fulfilment of a treaty obligation. For instance a law may have to be passed to allocate the necessary funds.

As for international organizations, competence to conclude and competence to implement agreements appear to be linked. It is submitted that in the absence of express provisions each organ is entitled to enter into those agreements which it is in a position to perform. If this theory were retained, the principle of effectiveness would therefore furnish the decisive criterion.

This consideration endorses the thesis put forth under C). It can also be invoked in support of the presumption in favor of the residuary treaty-making capacity of plenary organs. For as a rule the competence to take the material steps necessary for the discharge of obligations incurred under an agreement is vested in the organ comprising representatives of all member States. This is particularly true of the power to provide for the necessary funds in the budget of the organization. As already indicated, agreements frequently impose new financial burdens on international organizations. Agreements not provided for in the constituent instrument are no exception to this rule. For practice shows that their scope is not limited to matters involving no additional obligations for the organization concerned.

Finally, brief mention should be made of the legal aspects of the suggested presumption. It would not mean that in each concrete case the plenary organ possesses a residuary treaty-making competence under the constituent instrument of the organization. The presumption would be confined to the external sphere of organizations. Its purpose would be the protection of good faith of the other contracting parties. These parties would not have to interpret ambiguous provisions in a constituent instrument. As a general rule, they could take the treaty-making competence of plenary organs for granted. Yet the presumption ought to be subject to one exception. Parties to an agreement should not be permitted to invoke it in case of a manifest lack of competence[114].

E) The Treaty-Making Power of the Organization Is Vested in the Most Powerful Organ

Detter tries to eliminate the objections she raises to the preceding theory by replacing the plenary by the "most powerful organ[115]." This version is designed to cover cases where, like under the constituent instrument of ICAO or ECSC, the "supreme" organ is not the body where all member States are represented but a restricted or independent organ.

It is submitted, however, that this thesis does not really solve the problem discussed by Detter, because the question which organ is most powerful within a given organization is often hard to answer.

What in fact is the criterion of power? Political science shows that the weight of the various elements of which power is composed is extremely hard to define[116]. Theories basing power on a single factor, like population number[117], economic strength[118] or geographical position[119], have to be rejected.

In respect of international organizations, is the number of competences conferred upon the various organs by the constituent instrument decisive? Is an organ with a more general competence of necessity more powerful than an organ with only specific powers? Which organ is for instance more powerful within the framework of the UN, the General Assembly or the Security Council? How is their respective power to be measured? Moreover, delegation or simple practice may result in a gradual shift in the distribution of power within an organization. Such a slow change is for example not to be excluded, at least theoretically, within EEC, once the Council has complied with its legislative task of filling the gaps left open by the general formulae of the "traité-cadre," provided the member States

---

[114] See below, p. 254—268.

[115] Detter, op.cit., p. 426—427.

[116] Padelford-Lincoln, International Politics (1954), in particular p. 194—195; Aron, Paix et guerre entre les nations (1962), in particular p. 63—68; Morgenthau, Politics among Nations (1967), p. 97—158.

[117] On the problem in general see Organski, Population and World Power (1961).

[118] Various aspects of this factor are discussed in Russett, Economic Theories of International Politics (1968).

[119] Mackinder, Democratic Ideals and Reality (1919).

permit the Commission to profit to the full from the possibilities contained in Treaty of Rome[120].

What is more, Detter's theory is disclaimed by the constitutions of UNESCO and Euratom, where the organ which appears to be most powerful is not invested with general treaty-making capacity[121].

Finally, it is submitted that the solution proposed under D) would also solve the problem raised by Detter. The examples quoted by her against the theory in favor of the plenary organ would be irrelevant since the first step would be to examine the constituent instrument of the organizations concerned. In the cases mentioned by Detter the general treaty-making competence of the "most powerful" organ can be inferred from these instruments.

4. Conclusions

The present writer feels that the elements of truth these theories contain might be combined. It is therefore submitted that whereas the theories B) and E) should be discarded, A), C) and D) ought to be retained subject to the qualifications developed above.

In the first place, one should of course always examine the constituent instrument of the international organization in question in order to find the organs invested with treaty-making competence. The practical application of the instrument and its possible development and modification resulting therefrom should also be taken into account. As we have seen, however, constituent instruments rarely provide for a satisfactory answer to our problem. It is also quite obvious that more often than not the evaluation of practice is bound to be difficult as this practice is often incoherent and because sources of information are not complete.

So the question arises whether international law confers general treaty-making competence on a given type of organ whenever the constituent instrument and the practice of an international organization are ambiguous. It may be argued that existing law furnishes no clear answer. This should not prevent, however, the draftsmen of a future Convention on the treaty law of international organizations from laying down uniform rules on the matter. Since codification

---

[120] Loercher, op.cit., p. 171, note 35.

[121] See above, p. 206—208 and p. 213—215.

As for Euratom, it may be added that it is somewhat doubtful which organ occupies the central position. The relationship between the Council and the Commission has indeed been referred to as one of "approximate equilibrium," Loercher, op.cit., p. 172.

also includes progressive development of the law[122], even norms at variance with lex lata can be included in such a convention. It is submitted that unless the constitution otherwise provides, the plenary organ should be considered as possessing the treaty-making power of the organization and ought to be competent to perform all acts relating to the conclusion of an agreement, in particular to express consent to be bound. However, the authors of the Convention should not content themselves with this provision, although it may be tempting to lay down a presumption in favor of a single organ. This would not only present the advantage of simplicity. Such a rule would also resemble the constitutional law of States where one organ is endowed with ultimate treaty-making power.

Attractive as this analogy may be, there should nevertheless be a lex specialis to this rule. If it can be established that another organ is placed on a footing of equality with the plenary organ, which means that it is endowed with an autonomous sphere of competence, the principle of decentralization ought to apply. Hence the organ in question should be regarded as possessing a limited treaty-making competence within that particular sphere, even if the constituent instrument does not provide for the conclusion of agreements on the matter in question.

Finally it is suggested to include in a future Convention on the treaty law of international organizations a presumption in favor of chief administrative officers. By virtue of this presumption, however, these officers could only be relied upon as lawfully exercising capacity but not as possessing competence to conclude agreements. This may indeed seem a nice distinction, yet it would have practical consequences too. For it is further submitted that the rules just set forth should operate subject to the exception of a manifest violation of the constituent instrument.

As for the presumption in favor of the capacity of chief administrative officers, it would mean that the validity of an agreement concluded by them could also be challenged in the case of a manifest lack of authorization by the organ endowed with treaty-making competence. With respect to plenary or autonomous restricted organs, only the lack of competence under the constituent instrument would be relevant since they need no further authorization once their competence is established.

[122] See Article 1, paragraph 1 of the Statute of the ILC: "The International Law Commission shall have for its object the promotion of the progressive development of international law and its codification." On the ILC in general, see Rosenne, The International Law Commission (1949—54), 36 BYBIL (1960), p. 104—173. On the problem of codification in general see Kaegi, Kodifikation, Wörterbuch des Völkerrechts II (1961), p. 228—237.

III. The Procedure of Concluding Agreements

If one compares treaties concluded by States with agreements entered into by international organizations from a procedural point of view, one discovers practically the same phases in the conclusion of both types of international agreements. As regards formal treaties, some of these phases are indeed indispensable or at least useful from a technical angle. This is for example true of authentication which marks the end of a negotiating stage by establishing a definitive text. The procedural device of authentication may of course not always be the same, yet in this respect too a far-reaching similarity can be observed in the practice of States and that of international organizations. Furthermore, both under the constitutions of States and those of international organizations, more than one organ usually participates in the treaty-making process, although it should be borne in mind that the structures of States and those of international organizations differ considerably. At least with regard to formal treaties, the organs negotiating the text are as a rule not identical with the organ invested with treaty-making power. Therefore, a separate act expressing the competent organ's consent to engage the State or the organization in question is necessary.

On the other hand, there is a marked trend in the treaty practice of both States and international organizations towards shortening the somewhat complicated procedure of concluding formal treaties as much as possible. In this connection it may be mentioned that treaties in simplified form are not confined to matters of secondary importance but frequently deal with important problems[123].

1. The Procedure of Concluding Inter-State Treaties
(Articles 9—17 and 24—25 of the Vienna Convention on the Law of Treaties)

A synthesis of the different steps in the conclusion of a treaty between States had been presented by the ILC in articles 7—14 and 21—22 of its final draft. Since the questions involved were mainly of a technical character, the provisions just mentioned were rather quickly disposed of at both Sessions of the Vienna Conference on the Law of Treaties which did not adopt any significant amendments[124]. This was consistent with the general tendency to modify as little as possible the ILC's draft articles, which the Communist and many

[123] Numerous examples are quoted by Weinstein, op.cit., p. 212—213, and Chayet, op.cit., p. 5.

[124] Neuhold, op.cit., p. 62—65.

young States regarded as the most acceptable compromise. This attitude may account for the fact that only one out of 75 articles proposed by the Commission was rejected as a whole[125]. The provisions on the procedure of treaty conclusion were included as Articles 9—17 and 24—25 in the Vienna Convention on the Law of Treaties.

The following phases had been distinguished by the ILC: at the end of the negotiating stage, there must be a point where the form and the contents of the proposed treaty are settled. This is brought about by adoption of the text which takes place either by consent of all the States participating in the drawing up of the treaty or by a two-thirds majority if the text is drafted at an international conference. In the Commission's opinion, recent practice has modified the unanimity rule in the latter case.

Then a procedure is needed which establishes the draft adopted by the parties as the text of the proposed treaty not susceptible of alteration, so that the competent organs know the definitive text they subscribe to. To this end, the text of the treaty is authenticated. Authentication is usually brought about by signature, signature ad referedum or initialling.

The next step in the treaty-making process consists of the competent organ's expressing consent to be bound by the treaty on behalf of its State. In regard to formal treaties, this decisive consent is expressed by ratification. Formerly ratification was only an act of confirmation by the sovereign to the effect that his representative had not exceeded the full powers issued to him. With the advent of modern democracies, it has gradually become an independent act whereby the organ invested with treaty-making power eventually engages the State on the international plane. If a State is not an original party to a treaty but allowed by the contracting parties to accede to it, its consent to be bound is expressed by accession.

Parallel expressions of consent do not suffice, however, for concluding a treaty. To use the term put forth by the ILC, consent to be bound must be established, which means that the legal nexus between the parties is created. To this end, they usually proceed either to the exchange of the relevant instruments or provide for their deposit with

---

[125] Article 38 of the ILC's draft. It provided for the modification of treaties by subsequent practice and was denounced, inter alia, as running counter to the principle pacta sunt servanda. Neuhold, op.cit., p. 77. For a general discussion of the issues involved see Cot, La conduite subséquente des parties à un traité, 70 RGDIP (1966), p. 632—666, and Casanovas La Rosa, La modificación de los acuerdos internacionales por la práctica posterior, 21 Revista Española de Derecho Internacional (1968), p. 328—345.

the appointed depositary or mere notification to the other contracting States or again to the depositary.

More often than not the establishment of consent also brings the treaty into force. Article 21 of the Commission's draft (which became Article 24 of the Vienna Convention), however, lays down only a subsidiary rule to this effect. In the first place, it is up to the negotiating States to agree upon the manner and date they deem most appropriate for the entry into force of their treaty. In fact, multilateral conventions often make the entry into force dependent on the establishment of the consent of a certain number of contracting States or stipulate a time-lag between the establishment of consent and the actual entry into force[126].

In view of this somewhat cumbersome and time-consuming process employed for concluding formal treaties, it is hardly surprising that recent practice has resulted in the emergence of more expedient procedures. Thus treaties in simplified form dispense with the production of full powers and ratification[127]. The crucial consent to be bound is expressed by signature or the mere exchange of instruments as in the case of notes verbales. Though unsigned and not even initialled, they nevertheless are covered by the definition of treaties contained in Article 2, paragraph 1 (a) of the Vienna Convention on the Law of Treaties. The ILC had confined itself to mentioning this more and more important category of treaties in its Commentary and did not refer to it in the draft articles. The issue was raised, however, at the 1968 Session of the Conference and discussed at some length. Various amendments[128] with a view to including special provisions on these treaties were eventually adopted and are embodied in Articles 11 and 13 of the Vienna Convention.

2. The Procedure with Respect to Agreements Concluded by International Organizations

A) Form of Agreements[129]

From the formal point of view the practice of international organizations is even more confusing than that of States. At least four types of agreements can in fact be distinguished.

[126] This is for instance true of the four 1958 Geneva Conventions on the Law of the Sea and the 1961 and 1963 Vienna Conventions on Diplomatic and Consular Relations (22 ratifications, time-lag of 30 days). As for the Vienna Convention on the Law of Treaties itself, 35 instruments of ratification or accession are required under Article 84, whereas the time-lag is once again 30 days.

[127] Chayet, op.cit., p. 4.

[128] A/CONF. 39/C. 1/L. 88 and Add. 1 (Poland and USA), A/CONF. 39/C. 1/L. 111 (Belgium), and A/CONF. 39/C. 1/L. 89 (Poland).

[129] See the article by Osakwe, this volume, p. 164—193.

a) The first category comprises formal treaties, whatever their particular designation. They strongly resemble formal treaties concluded by States in two respects: on the one hand, they usually are contained in a single instrument and consist of the same three parts, preamble, dispositive provisions, and final clauses[130]. On the other hand, the same procedural phases can be observed in their conclusion[131].

b) Exchanges of notes or letters form another group of agreements. They usually consist of an instrument proposing the text of the agreement and an instrument by which the other party accepts this text which is repeated in full. Sometimes, however, especially when the proposed agreement is lengthy, its text is not repeated in the instrument of acceptance but only referred to in general terms[132].

A simpler form of this type of agreement is the so-called letter agreement[133]. It consists of a letter in duplicate sent to the party with whom the agreement is to be concluded. The latter is requested to sign the copies and return one of them to the party making the offer.

Exchanges of notes or letters frequently deal with minor matters. They may for instance be used to bring another agreement into force[134]. Yet this kind of agreement is also employed for regulating important political problems. The establishment of UNEF is a case in point[135]. Similarly, the legal status of the Force in Egypt was determined in an exchange of letters between the Secretary-General of the UN and the Egyptian Foreign Minister[136].

---

130 No general conclusions on the contents and the importance of an agreement can be drawn from the form which the contracting parties chose for it. For instance, IAEA concluded two agreements dealing with the same subject matter, namely the making available of special fissionable materials, with the USSR and the United Kingdom on the same day, 11 May 1959. Whereas a formal agreement was made with the Soviet Union, an exchange af letters was preferred in the case of the United Kingdom. 339 UNTS, p. 341—357.

131 Dupuy, op.cit., p. 490; Kasme, op.cit., p. 139.

132 This remark applies to the exchanges of letters between the UN and various member States which set up UNEF. The lengthy text of the proposal of the UN was not repeated in the answering letter which contained only the express acceptance of the State in question. See for example the agreements with Canada (274 UNTS, p. 47—57), Denmark (ibidem, p. 81—91), Brazil (ibidem, p. 199—209), and India (ibidem, p. 233—243).

133 Schneider, op.cit., p. 45, who quotes a few examples.

134 Thus in the case of the 1947 Headquarters Agreement between the USA and the UN consent was established, under section 28 of the Agreement, by an exchange of notes. 11 UNTS, p. 38—40.

135 See above note 132. On the problem of UN peace-keeping forces in general see Weissberg, op.cit., p. 106—140; and Seyersted, United Nations Forces in the Law of Peace and War (1966).

136 260 UNTS, p. 61—88.

c) A third category of agreements is characterized by even less formality and usually by the different character of the offer and the acceptance constituting the agreement. The term "disjunctive exchanges of notes" has been used to describe them[137]. As regards agreements belonging to this type, the offer or proposal of one party contains no express reference to the conclusion of an agreement. The same is true of the more or less formal act by which the other party accepts the proposal. In fact, acceptance by conduct in conformity with the offer or proposal suffices in some cases.

Such an agreement "*lato sensu*" was for instance concluded between Switzerland and the UN in 1946[138]. It concerned a point which was not covered by the provisional agreement between the same two parties. On 22 October 1946, the Swiss Foreign Minister sent a letter to the Secretary-General of the UN, demanding that in case of a conflict between member States of the UN, or between the UN and a third State, Swiss territory should not be used for military actions. He asked that his letter be submitted to the General Assembly for approval. Approval of the letter was granted in Resolution 98 (I), in which the main agreement was also approved. Yet only the latter was published. Nevertheless, the letter of the Swiss Foreign Minister and the approval of the General Assembly may also be construed as a legally binding agreement, although it does not seem to have been referred to as such and despite the fact that is was not published. Consequently, if the UN did not comply with it, this violation would entail the responsibility of the Organization under international law.

We have already come across other examples of such agreements within the framework of the UN. If for example a non-member State accepts the conditions laid down in Article 32 of the Charter, the determination of the conditions of participation by the Security Council coupled with the acceptance by the non-member State can be said to form an agreement[139]. The problem of this kind of agreement was also discussed at considerable length by the PCIJ in the Mavrommatis Concession (Jurisdiction)[140] case and by the ICJ in the South West Africa cases[141] with respect to the legal nature of Mandates. They were held to be international agreements composed of a proposal made by the Council on behalf of the League of Nations

---

[137] Chiu, op.cit., p. 53—61, who borrows the term from Myers, The Names and Scope of Treaties, 51 AJIL (1957), p. 547—605 (p. 591).

[138] Kasme, op.cit., p. 156.

[139] See above, p. 203.

[140] P.C.I.J. Series A, No. 2, p. 6—37.

[141] I.C.J. Reports 1962, p. 319—347 (p. 330—332).

and its members and the acceptance of this proposal by the Mandatory[142].

d) Finally, even parallel resolutions adopted by the competent organs of international organizations have been construed as legally binding agreements. It ought to be stressed, however, that their legal nature is far from clear and must be determined on the merits of each concrete case.

Parallel resolutions were adopted in particular to effect the succession between international organizations. Thus various transfer matters between the League of Nations and the UN and between the International Meteorological Organization and WMO were dealt with by such resolutions in 1946 and 1951 respectively[143]. Here the intentions of the parties become relevant as regards the question of whether they meant to enter into legally binding agreements which may not be modified or denounced unilaterally. If identical resolutions are adopted after previous consultations between the organizations concerned, a strong case can probably be made for their contractual effect[144]. In this case, however, the oral understanding, even though arrived at informally, forms the legal basis of the agreement.

B) Negotiation and Adoption

The organ invested with treaty-making competence is usually too clumsy to conduct negotiations, both because of its collegiate structure and non-permanent character. Consequently, it usually delegates the authority to draw up the text of agreements to other organs better suited for the task. Since more than one organ often participates in the conclusion of agreements, the procedure is sometimes rather complex and time-consuming. International organizations encounter in this respect many of the problems one comes across in the treaty practice

---

[142] A similar situation arose under Annex XI of the 1947 Peace Treaty with Italy. The four Great Powers agreed that the UN General Assembly should be competent to pass a recommendation on the further fate of the former Italian colonies if they were unable to reach agreement on the matter among themselves within one year after the entry into force of the Treaty. Moreover, the pledged themselves to execute this recommendation. Since the Big Four in fact could not solve the issue unanimously, they submitted it to the General Assembly which recommended certain measures in Resolution 289 (IV A) adopted on 21 November 1949. The preamble of the resolution refers to the General Assembly's acting in accordance with Annex XI, paragraph 3 of the Peace Treaty with Italy. It seems to be safe to maintain that by taking the steps envisaged in the Treaty the General Assembly tacitly accepted the proposal of the Four Powers, the two acts forming again an agreement "*lato sensu.*" Kasme, op.cit., p. 159; Chiu, op.cit., p. 54—55.

[143] Rosenne, op.cit., p. 394—396; Chiu, op.cit., p. 62.

[144] Dupuy, op.cit., p. 523—524.

of States[145]. It stands to reason that more often than not the organ charged with negotiations is the chief administrative officer of the organization. Given the permanent nature of his functions, he is in close contact with many other organizations and the member States of the organization.

The possibility of sub-delegation is also sometimes resorted to. Thus the plenary organ endowed with treaty-making power may entrust the exercise of its power to a restricted organ, which in turn may authorize the chief administrative officer either to negotiate or even to conclude the agreement in question. Chief administrative officers sometimes delegate this task to one of their deputies or regional representatives.

It is worth noting that authorization to negotiate is but rarely given for a specific agreement. It is frequently couched in rather general language and covers a series of agreements[146]. On the other hand, if the chief administrative officer is empowered to conclude agreements of course no special authorization to negotiate is necessary.

There are instances, however, where it is impossible to ascertain even an implied authorization to negotiate. The organ in question, for instance a chief administrative officer, seems to have acted on its own. Hence the question arises whether a future Convention on the treaty law of international organizations should contain a rule similar to the presumption laid down in Article 7, paragraph 2 (b) and (c) of the Vienna Convention on the Law of Treaties. Under this rule, the chief administrative officer would be considered as representing his organization for the purpose of drawing up and adopting the text of agreements simply by virtue of his functions and without having to produce any evidence of his authority to do so.

It is doubtful whether the practice of international organizations has already resulted in the emergence of a norm of customary law to this effect. For one thing, the existence of customary law is always difficult to prove. Even if the material element, "the constant and uniform usage[147]" can be established beyond doubt, the proof of the

---

[145] Thus all the four organs of EEC may possibly take part in the conclusion of an agreement by this Community. In addition to the two "directive organs," the Council and the Commission, the Assembly plays a certain role in the entering into of association agreements, as it has to be consulted before definitive consent to the bound is expressed (Article 238). Finally, the Council, the Commission or a Member State may request a decision of the Court of Justice on the compatibility of a contemplated agreement with the Treaty of Rome (Article 228). See above, p. 211—213.

[146] Detter, op.cit., p. 427—437.

[147] Columbian-Peruvian Asylum Case, I.J.C. Reports 1950, p. 266—289 (p. 276—277).

psychological component, the "opinio juris," gives rise to further difficulties. What is more, the practice of negotiating agreements is not uniform, although in most cases chief administrative officers do act as negotiators for their organizations. There are in fact instances where, even in organizations whose chief administrative officer seems at first sight to be invested with the jus representationis omnimodae, the organs endowed with treaty-making competence charged other bodies or persons with the task of negotiation.

As indicated above[148], the Economic and Social Council is to negotiate the Relationship Agreements with the future Specialized Agencies under Article 63 of the Charter. Though the Council decided not to discharge this function itself, it did not delegate its power to the Secretary-General. Instead it established a Special Committee on Negotiations which was given partly mandatory and partly discretionary instructions[149]. Similarly, the Relationship Agreement between the UN and IAEA[150] was drawn up by a collegiate body, the Advisory Committee on the Peaceful Uses of Atomic Energy, which had been authorized to this end by the General Assembly in Resolution 1115 (XI)[151]. Likewise inter-agency agreements were drafted by negotiating committees set up for this purpose by the organizations concerned[152].

Other agreements were drawn up by chief administrative officers, who were assisted, however, by a commission appointed by the organ invested with treaty-making competence. Thus the Headquarters Agreement between the UN and the USA was, on behalf of the UN, originally drafted by the Secretary-General with the assistance of a Negotiating Committee[153]. He was expressly authorized to negotiate (and only to negotiate) by General Assembly Resolution 22 B (I) of 13 February 1946. Even signature for authenticating purposes was subject to the approval of the General Assembly, which was then to proceed to another act of approval before the Agreement was to enter into force. It may be added that Resolution 99 (I) which authorized the Secretary-General to conduct further negotiations after New York had been determined as the site of the Headquarters did not require the approval of the General Assembly before the signing of the Agreement.

---

[148] See above, p. 202.

[149] Rosenne, op.cit., p. 397—398; Weissberg, op.cit., p. 42; Detter, op.cit., p. 427—428; Chiu, op.cit., p. 129—130.

[150] Balekjian, op.cit., p. 88—93.

[151] Chiu, op.cit., p. 130.

[152] Ibidem, p. 131.

[153] Rosenne, op.cit., p. 402—405.

Moreover, even subsidiary organs are often empowered to negotiate agreements or "act in consultation" with governments. The ad-hoc Committee of UNRRA under General Assembly Resolution 6 (I) or the UN Commissioners in Lybia or for Eritrea by virtue of Resolution 289 A (IV) may be quoted as examples[154].

Even this quick glance shows that practice is far from uniform, so that at best a presumption under which chief administrative officers would be regarded as negotiators of their organizations might be in the making within the framework of certain organizations. To lay down such a presumption as a general norm could on the other hand be defended as progressive development of the law if the law governing agreements concluded by international organizations were to be laid down in a Convention. The decision will depend on the value the international community attaches to the bulk of practice and several mainly practical arguments.

Such a presumption would above all add to the security of treaty relations. Indeed, one of the main shortcomings of the treaty-making process of international organizations is due to the fact that the effects of a delegation of power to the organ conducting negotiations are confined to the internal sphere of the organization, whatever form the delegation may take. No documents comparable to full powers in State practice are issued by the organ endowed with treaty-making power[155].

It would be rather unrealistic to expect international organizations to change a well established practice by requesting them to provide their representatives with full powers. They may point to the practical difficulties involved. It is not clear by whom and how full powers to act on behalf of international organizations would have to be issued. Furthermore, organizations might argue that full powers are the product of a historical evolution in State practice and are dispensed with even there in an ever increasing number of cases.

On the other hand, it cannot be denied that parties which want to enter into agreements with international organizations are in a rather awkward position. They have to rely on the statement of the agent purporting to represent the organization that he is competent. If the agreement is to be concluded with a member State, the difficulty is more easily surmounted: a member of the organization can be expected to be familiar with the constituent instrument and the practice of the organization. Consequently, it ought to know whether

---

[154] Kasme, op.cit., p. 58; Detter, op.cit., p. 428.

[155] Schneider urges that more attention should be paid to the introduction of such documents. Op.cit., p. 64.

the organ in question is competent under the constitution or not. If in view of the subordinate position of the organ a particular act of authorization by the organ endowed with treaty-making power is required, a member should have no trouble to find out whether such authorization has in fact been granted.

Yet non-member States and other organizations may face a real dilemma. If they do not confine themselves to simply accepting the claim of the agent of the organization to be competent or duly authorized, they will have to interpret the constitution of the organization. Such an attempt will not only meet with practical difficulties, since the practice of the organization will also have to be taken into account. It is further almost bound to be objected to by the organs of the organization which may insist, and rightly so, that it is for them to interpret their constitution. Moreover, they might regard the attempt at interpretation as an unfriendly act and break off of the negotiations before they really get under way. On the other hand, it is equally hard to imagine that in practice a negotiating organ asks its counterpart representing an international organization, especially a high official, to prove his authority for drawing up the text of an agreement. The official may consider such a demand rather insulting. The result will certainly not be beneficial to the intensification of treaty relations with the organization concerned.

All these difficulties could be met if, by virtue of the suggested presumption, negotiators could rely on the chief administrative officer's authority to negotiate under international law. The issue of confining the presumption to the negotiating stage or extending it to the expression of consent will be discussed below[156].

It is further submitted that the presumption should be of a sub sidiary character. Hence it would only apply if no other organs, like negotiating committees etc., were authorized in a specific case. These organs should on the other hand be requested to produce some proof of their authority so that their priority could be established. Reference to a resolution of the superior organ may suffice. If as suggested below the lack of internal authorization does not affect the validity of an agreement unless it was or ought to have been manifest to the other party[157], even an informal evidence of authorization will prove to be workable. For in cases of doubt the organs purporting to represent an organization will consult with the competent organs before performing acts relating to the conclusion of a treaty for fear of internal sanctions. In contrast, chief administrative officers would not have

---

[156] See below, p. 243—246.

[157] See below, p. 254—268.

to prove their authorization, although they may of course refer to it informally. Because of the stricter control the competent organs can be expected to exercise, if the theory of manifest violation were adopted, and in view of the disciplinary measures which are bound to be taken against them, chief administrative officers will probably refrain from acting ultra vires, if they are not competent to represent their organization because of some internal restriction.

The adoption of the text of an agreement does not give rise to any particular problem in the sphere of international organizations. As already mentioned, there is a tendency in inter-State relations to depart from the unanimity rule, which seems less and less practicable in view of the increasing number of States participating in multilateral treaties. The Vienna Convention on the Law of Treaties accordingly requires only a two-thirds majority of the States present and voting for the adoption of the text of a treaty at an international conference, unless by the same majority they decide to apply a different rule[158]. Since as a rule agreements by international organizations are bilateral or limited only to a few parties[159], there seems to be no doubt that the unanimity rule ought to prevail with respect to this category of treaties. If on the other hand international organizations were to participate in the adoption of multilateral conventions, there seems to be no reason why the rule laid down in the Vienna Convention should not apply. This does not mean that international organizations have to submit to majority decisions against their will; for they accept the rule in advance and can furthermore make reservations or refuse to approve the treaty in question.

C) Authentication

Authentication does not raise any particular problems in respect of agreements concluded by international organizations. It may be recalled that there has to be a point where the text of the agreement adopted by the negotiators is established as definitive. In principle, further changes in the contents of a treaty can only be effected by making reservations. In the case of bilateral agreements such demands for modification are not reservations but constitute an offer to reopen negotiations and conclude a different treaty. Moreover, in the practice of some States[160], authentication does not necessarily amount to the

---

[158] Article 9, paragraph 2 of the Vienna Convention on the Law of Treaties.

[159] The Standard Technical Assistance Agreements raise a particular problem in this respect because they combine bilateral and multilateral elements. Rosenne, op.cit., p. 302; Chiu, op.cit., p. 171.

[160] Information obtained from Mr. Nettel, Legal Adviser at the Austrian Ministry for Foreign Affairs.

establishment of a definitive text but only marks the end of one negotiating phase, the possibility of further negotiations not being excluded.

The methods developed in the practice of States have been adopted by international organizations too, so that Article 10 of the Vienna Convention on the Law of Treaties could be applied *mutatis mutandis*[161].

If an agreement is signed but a further act of the organ endowed with treaty-making power is necessary to commit the organization, signature serves only the authenticating purpose just referred to[162].

The procedure of signature ad referendum also has its place in the practice of international organizations. Such a signature is affixed provisionally and subject to confirmation by the organ invested with treaty-making competence. When confirmed, it constitutes a full signature and renders the party a signatory as of the original date of signature.

Thus the President of the ICAO-Council was authorized to sign ad referendum on behalf of the Council new agreements approved by the Conference of Geneva on 6 September 1956, to review existing Danish and Icelandic arrangements.

When approving the new provisional agreement with the Technical Assistance Administration, the Administrative Council of ITU requested the Secretary-General to submit any new arrangement to the Council for approval. Yet in cases of emergency he was allowed to sign *ad referendum*[163].

Finally, international organizations also use the procedure of initialling for authenticating the text of an agreement. The Relation-

---

[161] It is worth noting that initialling is regulary resorted to within the framework of EEC. This is due to the distribution of functions under Article 228 of the Treaty of Rome (see footnote 63) and to political considerations. At the end of the negotiating stage, the text agreed upon by the parties is initialled by a representative of the Commission which is entrusted with the task of negotiation. Yet even in cases where signature by the Council does not express consent to be bound, because the Assembly has to be consulted before an agreement may be concluded on behalf of EEC (Article 238 concerning association agreements), the Council proceeds to signature. Although legally this type of signature has merely an authenticating effect, it usually has far-reaching political consequences. In fact, it is hard to imagine that the Council will eventually refuse definitely to commit EEC to an agreement which its representative has signed at a solemn ceremony receiving a certain amount of publicity. This is all the more so as the view of the Assembly on the agreement concerned is not binding on the Council. Melchior, op.cit., p. 195—198.

[162] Examples of this procedure are legion. See for instance the Headquarters Agreement between the UN and the USA. 11 UNTS, p. 11—34.

[163] These two examples are quoted by Schneider, op.cit., p. 52—53.

ship Agreements between the UN on the one hand and FAO[164] and UPU[165] on the other hand may be quoted as examples.

It ought to be added that not all agreements concluded by international organizations are authenticated. There are in fact cases where signature in particular is affixed after approval so that one cannot speak of authentication proper.

D) Expression of Consent to Be Bound

After the negotiating stage has come to a close, the parties in question are not yet bound, at least not in the case of formal agreements. The final decision lies with the organ competent to engage the organization on the international plane by expressing its consent to be bound. In the case of formal treaties, this is done by approval. For some agreements signature by another organ suffices, which must have been authorized to this effect in the internal sphere.

It may mentioned already at this point that as a rule agreements concluded by international organizations set forth express provisions on how consent to be bound is to be expressed. Hence the problem of a residuary rule in favor either of approval or signature, whenever an agreement remains silent on the matter, is of little practical significance. For the same reason, the ILC had decided not to include a provision on this mainly doctrinal issue in its final draft on the law of treaties between States instead of giving preference either to ratification or signature. However, the problem was raised at the First Session of the Vienna Conference. Yet the amendments calling for a residuary norm were defeated so that the solution adopted by the Commission prevailed once again[166].

a) Approval

Approval by the organ possessing treaty-making power corresponds to a large extent to ratification in the practice of States. Possibly because of the structural differences between States and international organizations, the term "ratification" is but rarely used by the latter[167].

Approval usually takes place after the text of the treaty has been authenticated by signature or another method referred to above.

As a rule, agreements are approved by a collegiate organ. In this connection, the question may arise whether the decision to commit the organization concerned has to be made unanimously or whether a simple or qualified majority suffices. This clearly is a problem to be

---

[164] 1 UNTS, p. 210.

[165] 19 UNTS, p. 232.

[166] Neuhold, op.cit., p. 63—64.

[167] A few cases were the term was used are quoted by Schneider, op.cit., p. 55.

solved by the constituent instrument, the internal regulations or the practice of each international organization.

It is worth noting in this connection, however, that some agreements are signed after approval and their entry into force. This procedure was for example followed in the conclusion of the Relationship Agreement between ECSC and ILO[168] which came into force on 16 July 1953 after exchange of approvals, but was signed on 12 August of the same year. Similarly, the Co-operation Agreement between IAEA and UNESCO was signed by the two Directors-General on 27 November and 5 December 1958, after the Agreement had been approved by the Executive Board of UNESCO on 26 September and by the General Conference of the IAEA on 1 October 1958[169]. Under Article XII, the Agreement entered into force on the date of the latest approval, hence on 1 October 1958. In these cases, signature seems to fulfil a recording function, confirming that all the required formalities have been accomplished[170].

From a technical angle, several variants of approval can be found in practice[171].

(1) The normal procedure appears to require that all parties approve or, if States are concerned, ratify the agreement.

(2) Yet there are instances of ratifications by States alone, whereas signature sufficed to bind the organization. The Consultation Agreements between ECSC and Switzerland can be cited as example[172]. As regards ECSC, a particularly interesting category of agreements seems worth mentioning. Because of the overlapping of competences, they are signed not only by the Commission (formerly the High Authority), but also separately by the six member States. Whereas mere signature engages the Community, compliance with constitutional requirements is again stipulated on the part of the member States and the non-member State with which the agreement is entered into. This solution is to be found, for example, in the agreement between ECSC and Switzerland signed in Luxemburg on 28 July 1956[173].

---

168 Ibidem, p. 53.

169 339 UNTS, p. 373—384. (See note 1 on p. 374.)

170 The writer cannot concur in the view held by Schneider, according to whom signature after approval and entry into force "is resorted to for formal purposes, i.e., for initialling or authenticating a text or for effectuating a ne varietur of it." Schneider, op.cit., p. 54. This theory would mean a contrario that the text of a treaty already in force could still be altered before the ultimate signature provided for by the parties is affixed!

171 Detter, op.cit., p. 439—443.

172 Loercher, op.cit., p. 103—105.

173 Amtsblatt der Europäischen Gemeinschaften, 29 May 1957.

(3) Conversely, other agreements call for approval by the competent organ of the organization without requiring ratification by the contracting State. Thus section 34 of the agreement between France and WHO on privileges and immunities signed in Paris and Geneva on 23 July and 1 August 1952 reads as follows:

"The present Agreement shall enter into force as soon as it has been signed by the Government (of France) and adopted by the World Health Assembly[174]."

(4) Likewise, agreements among international organizations do at times not require the approval of all parties. The agreement between WHO and the Pan-American Sanitary Organization of 24 May 1949 only provided for the approval of the World Health Assembly, the Director of the Pan-American Sanitary Bureau being authorized to commit his Organization by signature[175].

(5) Furthermore, agreements between international organizations are not invariably approved by the plenary organs on both sides because of the different constitutional provisions on treaty-making competence. Accordingly, agreements concluded between UNESCO and other international organizations were approved by the Executive Board of UNESCO, whereas the plenary organ expressed the consent of the other party[176].

On the other hand, it ought to be pointed out that certain procedures similar to approval should clearly be distinguished from it. The organ possessing treaty-making power is sometimes informed of the conclusion of an agreement by an organ it has previously authorized to this end. Schneider mentions the following example: the Secretary-General of UNESCO had been empowered to enter into an agreement with the United Nations Korean Reconstruction Agency. Having concluded the agreement he subsequently submitted its text to the Executive Board[177].

In such a case, it should be borne in mind that the definitive consent to be bound is expressed by the organ previously authorized to do so. Therefore, the submission of the text of the agreement only informs the organ endowed with the original treaty-making power that the subordinate organ has profited from the authorization or complied with an order to enter into an agreement. However, such a report does not affect the agreement on the external plane, especially

---

[174] 209 UNTS, p. 231—253 (p. 253).

[175] 32 UNTS, p. 387—392 (p. 392).

[176] See for example the Agreement between FAO and UNESCO, 43 UNTS, p. 315—324, and UNESCO and WHO, ibidem 44, p. 323—332.

[177] Schneider, op.cit., p. 48—49.

not its entry into force[178]. It is only designed to facilitate co-operation between the organs within the organization.

b) Signature

Since the organs endowed with treaty-making competence do usually not exercise their functions permanently but only meet at regular intervals, agreements requiring approval may take a long time to come into force. Hence an increasing number of less formal agreements are concluded by signature which is usually affixed by the chief administrative officer or his representative.

As these officials do in principle not possess treaty-making competence, they need some authorization to express the consent of their organization granted to them by the competent organ.

There are a few exceptions to this rule. In the first place, the constituent instrument of international organizations may confer on the chief administrative officer a treaty-making competence of his own within a limited sphere where he therefore can enter into agreements without any further authorization[179]. In the second place, the practice of a given organization may have resulted in the chief administrative officer's assuming treaty-making power in respect of certain agreements for which originally the consent of another organ was required. Finally one could perhaps argue that, by virtue of their functions, administrative officers are in general entitled to conclude agreements on co-operation in purely administrative matters with one another. However, whether it is possible to prove such a limited independent competence as a general customary rule is open to question, just as the legal character of such administrative understandings.

Yet as a rule, chief administrative officers do need some kind of internal authorization when purporting to engage their organization by their simple signature. True enough, such an authorization is rarely granted for the conclusion of just one agreement but usually covers a series of agreements[180]. Authorization to conclude is usually granted by a resolution of the organ endowed with treaty-making competence. Furthermore, it may be contained in some previous agreement[181]. The authorization may also be couched in rather broad

---

[178] Ibidem, p. 48; Dupuy, op.cit., p. 514; Detter, op.cit., p. 444; Chiu, op.cit., p. 105.

[179] Article XIII, paragraph 2 of the constituent instrument of FAO is a case in point. See above, p. 206.

[180] See above, p. 233—234.

[181] Thus there is a standard clause in the Relationship Agreements between the UN and the Specialized Agencies empowering the respective chief administrative officers to enter into such supplementary arrangements for the implemen-

terms in resolutions on the general policy of an organization, without express reference to the conclusion of agreements at all. This holds true whenever chief administrative officers are requested to take the measures they deem necessary for attaining certain goals. For instance, UNEF was established on the basis of such a general resolution.

Acts of authorization are at any rate confined to the internal sphere of the organization. No documents comparable to full powers are issued in the treaty practice of international organizations. So the other parties again face the unpleasant situation already described with regard to the negotiating stage. They have in fact to rely on the contention of the official who claims to be empowered to express the consent of his organization by signature.

Admittedly, in many cases the agent in question will not simply allege to be competent to commit his organization but refer to some resolution of the plenary organ or indicate another act of authorization. Moreover, if the other party is a member of the organization and has misgivings about the capacity of the latter's agent, it may make inquiries without too much difficulty.

There will still be cases, however, where the authority of the official is far from clear and where the other parties could dispel their doubts only by asking the official to produce some conclusive evidence of his authority or by trying to interpret the constitution of the organization. It ought to be stressed once more that they should refrain from either course of action. Otherwise they run the risk that the proposed agreement will not be concluded at all, as the organization may regard such action as an unfriendly act.

On the other hand, it must be emphasized that the consequences of an unauthorized signature are much more serious than those of the lack of authority to conduct negotiations. The other party, which believes that it has definitely concluded an agreement, would be confronted with the claim that the illegal signature has not expressed consent to be bound on the part of the organization and that no agreement has not come into being. In many cases parties which intend to enter into agreements with international organizations cannot be absolutely certain that the organization will not assert the lack of capacity of the organ which had purported to express its consent by signature.

As this state of affairs is highly unsatisfactory at least from the legal point of view[182], attempts should be made to remedy it in a

---

tation of the Relationship Agreement as may be found desirable in the light of the operating experience of the two organizations concerned. Jenks, op.cit., p. 233.

[182] The present writer does not know of any case where this issue gave rise to a dispute in the actual treaty practice of international organizations.

future Convention codifying the treaty law of international organizations. The question arises whether the presumption in favor of chief administrative officers which has been developed with respect to the negotiating stage should be extended to expression of consent. An affirmative answer is proposed, because the arguments advanced in regard to negotiations apply with equal force to this later phase. The presumption would once again enhance the security of treaty relations and protect the good faith of the contracting parties. It is again urged that a solution should be chosen which takes account of the practical considerations just put forth and existing treaty practice as much as possible. Therefore the codification should not impose on international organizations the obligation to issue full powers. Although their introduction into the sphere of international organizations would protect the other contracting parties, it would involve considerable practical difficulties which have already been pointed out[183].

Hence the parties to the codification treaty should not shrink from venturing into the field of progressive development of the law. The proposed presumption would again imply a distinction between the internal sphere of international organizations and the external plane. In conformity with existing practice, an act of authorization would be relevant only internally. In the external relations of organizations, contracting parties could rely on the administrative officer's (and possibly his representatives', whose competence is apparent by virtue of their functions) signature as valid expression of consent to be bound on behalf of his organization. Restrictions on his power could only be invoked by the organization if they had been previously brought to the knowledge of the other parties or if the organization could prove that they were otherwise manifest to them.

Otherwise the agreement would be valid and the organization bound, even if the executive officer signed without sufficient authorization.

The issue of the effects of unconstitutional acts on the validity of agreements will be discussed at some length later on[184]. May it therefore suffice to stress at this point that the risk which the sovereign member States of international organizations run under this presumption of being committed without their consent or against their will is rather slight in practice. For they are bound to instruct their representatives in collegiate organs to see to it that a stricter control be exercised over and measures taken against a chief adminis-

---

[183] See above, p. 236.

[184] See below, p. 254—268.

trative officer who is suspected of being unreliable or who has indeed acted ultra vires. Since conflicts with member States will hardly further their careers, chief administrative officers will consult with the other organs and obtain their consent if their capacity is doubtful. It may be pointed out again that this solution does not amount to conferring upon chief administrative officers possession of the treaty-making power of their organization. They would only be regarded as having capacity to exercise it on the external plane. The consequence of the difference between possession and exercise would be that the organ possessing treaty-making power could restrict or exclude the authority of the chief administrative officer to express consent by signature and invoke such restrictions against the other parties if they were informed or ought to have been aware of the restrictions. Moreover, a certain degree of diligence and watchfulness can be expected from parties dealing with chief administrative officers, as in certain cases the lack of authority on his part will be regarded as manifest to them.

The following example shall illustrate the point. A party has concluded several agreements on the same matter, all of which required approval by the plenary organ of the organization. A further agreement of the same kind is to be entered into. All of a sudden the chief administrative officer claims that approval is not necessary any more and that his signature suffices to bind his organization. In this case the other party should not content itself with the officer's contention but ask for further evidence. On the other hand, contracting parties can take the competence of the organ endowed with treaty-making power to conclude agreements for granted.

E) Reservations

An issue which is one of the principal apples of discord in the treaty-relations of States[185] should at least be briefly mentioned in this context. Does the problem of the admissibility and the effects of reservations arise with respect to agreements concluded by international organizations? The question seems to raise no particular difficulties since most of these agreements are bilateral. As mentioned above, reservations are confined to multilateral treaties. If an alteration of the text is demanded by a party to a bilateral treaty, this amounts to a proposal to resume negotiations and conclude a

---

[185] Holloway, Les réserves dans les traités internationaux (1958); Anand, Reservations to Multilateral Conventions, 1 The Indian Journal of International Law (1960), p. 84—91; Rao, Reservations to Multilateral Conventions, ibidem, p. 92—99; Bishop, Reservations to Treaties, 103 RCADI (1961), p. 249—341; Neuhold, op.cit., p. 66—71.

new one. But even such demands seem to be rather exceptional in the treaty relations of international organizations. Rarely if ever are negotiations resumed.

At the most, conditions are sometimes posed by organs invested with treaty-making power on approving the agreement. The other party usually accepts or just tacitly complies with the condition.

A well known example of a plenary organ's making its approval dependent on the fulfillment of a condition is furnished by the Relationship Agreement between the UN and ICAO[186]. In Resolution 50 (I) of 14 December 1946, the General Assembly made its approval conditional on the ICAO's complying "with any decision of the General Assembly regarding Franco Spain." It will be recalled that at that time most members of the UN objected to the policies of the Franco regime. Consequently, General Assembly Resolution 39 (I) of 12 December 1946 recommended that the Franco Government be debarred from membership in international agencies established by or brought into relationship with the UN and from participation in conferences or other activities arranged by the UN or these agencies. On 23 May 1947, the ICAO-Assembly accepted the condition put forward in Resolution 50 (I) and the Relationship Agreement accordingly entered into force. It may be noted that in reality ICAO ignored the condition posed by the UN, although it amended its constituent instrument in accordance with the Resolution. Yet in fact Spain, an original signatory of the ICAO-Charter, remained a member of the Organization[187].

Conditions such as this one should not be confused, however, with reservations, because they only affect the entry into force of the agreement. Once they are complied with, the agreement comes into force as a whole and without modifications. On the other hand, when making a reservation, a party aims at excluding or modifying certain provisions of the agreement[188].

Nor does an interpretative declaration, which merely clarifies a party's position without purporting to exclude or vary any provision of the agreement, constitute a reservation proper. Some of the

---

[186] 8 UNTS, p. 315—320.

[187] Rosenne, op.cit., p. 372.

[188] The following "reservation" was made by the representative of the EEC-Council upon signature of certain association agreements:

"Sous réserve que la Communauté ne sera définitivement engagée qu'après notification à l'autre partie contractante de l'accomplissement des procédures requises par le traité instituant la Communauté économique européenne et notamment la consultation de l'Assemblée parlementaire européenne." Melchior, op.cit., p. 209. This of course is not a reservation as defined by the Vienna Convention on the Law of Treaties.

examples listed by Schneider as reservations fall into this category. For instance, on approving the agreement between the Interim Commission of WHO and Switzerland, WHO claimed the right to conclude a General Convention on Privileges and Immunities later on[189]. This claim can hardly be called a reservation, since it does not affect the contents of the agreement in question.

The problem of reservations in the field of international organizations did arise in 1953, when the USA refused to grant visas for transit to the UN Headquarters to representatives of two non-governmental organizations in consultative relations with the Economic and Social Council[190]. The USA attempted to justify this refusal on the ground that it had made a reservation to this effect when concluding the Headquarters Agreement. The UN maintained that it had not been informed of the alleged reservation contained in the approbatory Joint Resolution of the US Congress. The issue was eventually not treated as one concerning a reservation. Attempts were made to solve it by negotiations between the Secretary-General and the respective US authorities.

However, it must be recalled that the possibility of international organizations becoming parties to multilateral conventions is not to be ruled out. In this case, genuine reservations may indeed become relevant. Yet there appears to be no reason why the norms on reservations set forth in the Vienna Convention on the Law of Treaties (Articles 19—23), which mark the end of the former unanimity system and are characterized by great flexibility, should not apply to international organizations as well.

F) *Establishment of Consent and Entry into Force*

Even after consent has been expressed individually by the parties, the process of treaty conclusion is not completed. For one thing, the expression of consent of only one party is of course not sufficient. But even if more than one party has subscribed to the agreement, the legal nexus between these manifestations of will must still be established. This procedure usually also brings the agreement into force, as time-lags between establishment of consent and entry into force do not often occur in the practice of international organizations. So the two phases which the Vienna Convention on the Law of Treaties regulates separately in Articles 16 and 24 can be treated together in this context.

Parties are of course free to choose the way of establishing consent and the moment of entry into force which they deem most appro-

[189] Schneider, op.cit., p. 57.

[190] Rosenne, op.cit., p. 356—358.

priate. Like States, international organizations may and do in practice pose conditions or agree upon the provisional entry into force or retroactive effect of agreements to which they are parties[191]. In this connection, three main devices have been developed in the treaty relations of international organizations.

a) Establishment of Consent and Entry into Force on Approval

Agreements subject to the approval of the organs endowed with treaty-making power frequently provide for entry into force on approval by the organs concerned. For instance, the Relationship Agreements between the UN and the Specialized Agencies contain a standard clause stipulating that they shall come into force on their approval by the General Assembly of the UN and the plenary organ of the respective Agency. The same applies *mutatis mutandis* to certain inter-agency agreements[192]. Hardly if ever are these approvals granted at the same time, given the sporadic and not simultaneous sessions of the plenary organs of the various organizations. In the dates of approval differ, it is the latest one which is decisive in as much as it establishes consent and brings the agreement into force.

It is worth noting that entry into force takes place automatically on the date of the latest approval. From a legal point of view, no further act is required, as is indicated by the laconic wording of the agreements just mentioned. This will of course give rise to difficulties. For how are the other parties to know of the latest approval and realize that the agreement has come into force, especially in view of the fact that the headquarters of the organizations concerned may be located in different cities? In practice, the problem is usually solved by notifications between the secretariats. Yet there still may be time-lags before the information reaches its destination. During this period the agreement will be in force without the other parties being aware of it.

---

[191] A series of agreements between the UN and six States (Canada, Denmark, Finland, New Zealand, Sweden, and the United Kingdom) which had placed national contingents at the disposal of the United Nations Forces in Cyprus established in 1964 furnishes examples of agreements having retroactive effects. On 21 February 1966, exchanges of letters concerning the service with the UN-Peace Keeping Force of these contingents were concluded. In his letters to the respective Permanent Representatives, Secretary-General U Thant suggested that the agreements "shall be deemed to have taken effect from the date that the national contingent provided by your Government departed from its home country to assure duties with the Force." This solution was accepted by the six States concerned. UNTS 555, p. 119—180.

[192] See for instance the agreement between IAEA and WHO, 339 UNTS, p. 388—398.

In practice, the problems resulting from this legally unsatisfactory situation do not bother international organizations particularly[193].

The entry into force is also sometimes recorded in protocols. This additional formality was resorted to in the case of the Relationship Agreements between the UN and the Specialized Agencies.

However, both notifications of approval and protocols on entry into force have only an evidentiary value in these cases[194], the agreements coming into force independently of them.

b) Establishment of Consent and Entry into Force on Signature

The less formal agreements like exchanges of notes or letters in their various forms usually enter into force on signature, which also establishes the consent of the parties, or on exchange. Whole categories of agreements like the Technical Assistance Agreements[195] or those concluded by UNICEF[196] as a rule contain provisions to this effect.

No particular problems arise if the instruments in question are signed simultaneously. The text of complex agreements is sometimes unofficially communicated to the other party in order to give the latter sufficient time to study it before the official exchange of instruments takes place. Thus the parties can sign at the same time without accepting obligations prematurely.

But signatures are often affixed not only at different places; the dates of signature also differ quite frequently. It would again seem logical to attribute to the latest signature the decisive effect of establishing consent and bringing the agreement into force, unless the parties express a different intention. Here too the parties should be informed as rapidly as possible of any signature and, in particular, the entry into force of their agreement resulting from the latest expression of consent. However, any such act of notification has only an evidentiary function and does not affect the entry into force of the agreement, which comes into being automatically, regardless of whether the other party or parties are aware of it or not.

It may be mentioned in this connection that signature, which is usually performed by the chief administrative officer or his representative to whom he delegates his power, is a rather complex phenomenon in the law of international organizations.

---

[193] This writer at least does not know of any disputes where the issue of this time-lag was raised.

[194] Rosenne, op.cit., p. 413.

[195] Chiu, op.cit., p. 171. For a general discussion of the Technical Assistance Agreements see Feuer, Les aspects juridiques de l'assistance technique dans le cadre de l'ONU et les Institutions Spécialisées (1957), and the contribution by Miss van Wouw, this volume, p. 105—126.

[196] Chiu, op.cit., p. 174.

Firstly, if the agreement is subject to approval, signature authenticates the text if affixed before the approval. This is not too say that signature subject to approval by the organ possessing treaty-making competence is without effect on the freedom of action of the organization concerned. In fact, there seems to be no reason why Article 18 lit. (a) of the Vienna Convention on the Law of Treaties, under which States are to refrain from acts which would defeat the object and purpose of a treaty after they have signed it, should not apply to agreements concluded by international organizations. For this obligation derives from the principle of good faith which also governs the treaty relations of international organizations[197].

Secondly, if signature takes place after the approval, it usually serves only a recording purpose.

Thirdly, signature may express consent to be bound, if the agreement is not of a formal character. Furthermore, if linked to other similar expressions of consent to be bound, it may bring about the entry into force of an agreement.

c) Establishment of Consent and Entry into Force by Exchange of Notes or Notification

In rather exceptional cases, agreements do not come into force on the latest expression of consent, but a further act is required, apart from compliance with material conditions laid down upon expressing consent. Such an act is then not a mere formality, since the agreement would not come into being if this act were not performed. This holds true only if it is provided for by the parties to the agreement.

These additional formalities include for instance exchanges of notes. Such an exchange of notes was stipulated in section 28 of the Headquarters Agreement between the UN and the USA[198]. It was to be concluded by the Secretary-General, duly authorized pursuant to a resolution of the General Assembly of the United Nations, and the appropriate executive officer of the United States, duly authorized pursuant to appropriate action of the Congress. The notes in question were signed by Secretary-General Trygve Lie and Warren R. Austin, the Permanent Representative of the USA at the Seat of

[197] The ILC's proposal to extend the obligation in Article 18 to the negotiating stage did not meet with approval at the 1968 Session of the Vienna Conference. This was one of the extremely few substantive provisions of the draft which was not retained by the Conference. For the reasons of the negative attitude of the majority see Neuhold, op.cit., p. 65. For a criticism of article 15 of the ILC's draft see Morvay, The Obligation of a State not to Frustrate the Object of a Treaty Prior to its Entry into Force, Comments on Art. 15 of the ILC's Draft Articles on the Law of Treaties, 27 ZaöRV (1967), p. 451—462.

[198] 11 UNTS, p. 11—34.

the UN, on 21 November 1947, whereupon the Agreement entered into force[199].

A less formal way of establishing consent and making sure that all parties are aware of the agreement coming into force is to provide for reciprocal notification. Thus an additional agreement on co-operation between Euratom and the USA signed on 11 June 1960 was to come into force "on the first day on which each party shall have received notification that it has complied with all the statutory and constitutional requirements for the entry into force of the agreement[200].

In conclusion, it is submitted that a future codification of the treaty law of international organizations should in the first place stress that it is up to the parties to agree upon the mode of establishment of consent and entry into force. They may of course stipulate a certain date, pose conditions, provide for provisional entry into force in urgent cases or opt for the retroactive application of an agreement. A Convention should also suggest the desirability of the parties including some express provision on the two matters in the agreement, which international organizations as a rule do anyway in their treaty practice. Finally, a residuary rule could be added that in cases where the agreement simply provides for signature or approval or just refers to entry into force on signature or approval, the agreement is to come into force on the latest signature or approval. The Convention should also urge the parties to inform one another as quickly as possible of any expression of consent to which they proceed. The present writer again feels that a Convention should not impose on international organizations new obligations at variance with their established practice by requesting them to proceed to some formal act of exchange, deposit or notification in order to bring an agreement into force. If on the other hand international organizations become parties to multilateral conventions, they should comply with the rules developed in the treaty law of States.

IV. The Consequence of Unconstitutional Agreements

Finally, another delicate issue, which fortunately will give rise only exceptionally to disputes in practice, must be discussed in this connection. For the presumptions suggested above would not be com-

[199] Liang, Notes on Legal Questions concerning the United Nations, 42 AJIL (1948), p. 435—447; Gross, Operation of the Legal Adviser's Office, ibidem 43 (1949), p. 122—127; Brandon, The Legal Status of the Premises of the United Nations, 28 BYBIL (1951), p. 90—113; Rosenne, op.cit., p. 405.

[200] Amtsblatt der Europäischen Gemeinschaften 1961, p. 668—674 (p. 673).

plete without a provision dealing with violations of constitutional provisions governing the conclusion of agreements by international organizations. The matter is at best superficially dealt with by the relatively few writers on the treaty law of international organizations[201].

1. The International Law of States (Articles 46 and 47 of the Vienna Convention on the Law of Treaties)

Here the ILC had to take a stand on a question on which opinion was sharply divided and in regard of which the decisions of international tribunals offered but little guidance[202]. One school of thought (which incidentally prevailed within the Commission in 1951)[203] maintains that, since international law leaves the determination of the organs competent to conclude treaties and the procedure to be observed in their conclusion to the domestic law of each State, this reference of international law to constitutional law makes the latter part of the former. Consequently, an agent purporting to bind his State in breach of a constitutional limitation imposed on him is incompetent to commit his State under international law. It follows that the treaty in question has to be considered void or at least voidable. In practice, this theory is bound to give rise to considerable difficulties. For other parties could not even rely on the apparent authority of Heads of Government, Foreign Ministers etc., but would have to check their constitutional powers in each case if they wanted to be sure of entering into a valid treaty. It has already been shown[204] that such an investigation into the constitutional sphere of another party is hardly compatible with the obligation not to interfere with the internal affairs of other States. According to the opposite view, international law is only concerned with the external manifestations of the will of a State, which may express its will as it deems fit. Consequently, international law only regulates the external procedures for concluding a treaty and the conditions under which certain types of State organs are to participate in this process. If these conditions are met, the agent regarded as representing his State by international law engages his State on the international plane, regardless of whether

---

[201] Schneider op.cit., p. 62—63; Kasme, op.cit., p. 65—103; Chiu, op.cit., p. 81—84 and 97—100.

[202] See for instance the Cleveland Award, Moore, 2 International Arbitrations (1898), p. 1945—1968. For a general discussion of the issues mentioned below see Geck, Die völkerrechtlichen Wirkungen verfassungswidriger Verträge (1963).

[203] 2 YILC, 1951, p. 73.

[204] See above, p. 199.

he has complied with internal formalities or not. Although in the latter case the treaty may be invalid as domestic law, its validity under international law is thereby not affected.

The ILC eventually tried to strike a balance between these diametrically opposed views. It opted for an approach which enhanced the security of treaty relations and protected the good faith of contracting parties.

Under article 43 of the Commission's draft, States were precluded from invoking unconstitutional expression of consent unless the violation of internal law regarding competence to enter into treaties was manifest. The ILC further provided for the situation where, in regard of a particular treaty, a representative failed to observe specific restrictions of his authority to bind his State. In virtue of the same principle, such limitations were to be invoked only if brought to the knowledge of the other negotiating States prior to the expression of consent (article 44 of the ILC's draft).

The position adopted by the ILC prevailed once more at the Vienna Conference[205]. Thus an amendment calling for the absolute irrelevance of violations of constitutional law[206], thereby suggesting a return to the second theory just mentioned, was rejected by a large majority at the 1968 Session. On the other hand, a proposal to limit the scope of the exception to the principle to violations of norms of fundamental importance was adopted[207]. A British amendment which specified that the criterion of a "manifest" violation was of an objective character[208] also met with approval. However, it only inserted in the Convention the ILC's standpoint as explained in its commentary to article 43 of the draft. The two articles in question became in turn Articles 46 and 47 of the Vienna Convention on the Law of Treaties.

2. The Law of International Organizations

As regards agreements by international organizations, two kinds of constitutional restrictions have to be distinguished in this context. In the first place, the agent performing an act relating to the conclusion of an agreement may be incompetent. As shown above, this problem also exists with respect to treaties concluded by States.

---

[205] Neuhold, op.cit., p. 78—79. A solution similar to article 43 of the ILC's draft is advocated by Dahm, Völkerrecht III (1961), p. 21—30.

[206] A/CONF. 39/C. 1/L. 184 and Add. 1 (Japan and Pakistan).

[207] A/CONF. 39/C. 1/L. 228 and Add. 1 (Peru and Ukrainian Soviet Socialist Republic).

[208] A/CONF. 39/C. 1/L. 274.

The second type of restrictions is limited to international organizations. Whereas States, by virtue of their sovereignty, may in principle enter into treaties on any subject matter, international organizations have to observe more or less far-reaching restrictions in this respect, because it is submitted that their powers are not unlimited[209]. This second type of unconstitutionality will be discussed first, in being understood that the same solution is proposed to both kinds of constitutional violations.

A) Unconstitutional Agreements in View of Their Contents

Even if the constituent instruments of international organizations contained as a rule and not only exceptionally a general provision on the treaty-making power of the organization, the question of whether such an authorization entitled the organization to conclude agreements on any matters whatever would still have to be answered. As already pointed out, however, more often than not constituent instruments at best confer express authorization to enter into specific agreements. Hence the question arises whether such enumerations are to be regarded as exhaustive or whether the organization concerned may conclude other agreements as well. The second reply which is borne out by practice appears to be correct. It may be recalled that in the first place cases where the authors of the constituent instruments more or less clearly envisage the conclusion of agreements without using the term have to be included. Examples of this type of authorization have already been given. In the second place, some agreements can be justified along the lines of the implied power theory: the fulfillment of the functions entrusted to the organization seems to require the entering into of an agreement, although not even a vague provision to this effect can be detected in the constituent instrument[210]. Whether a given agreement is still covered by the implied powers of the organization concerned or whether it is beyond or even contrary to the will of its founding fathers will often be a delicate problem of interpretation.

---

[209] A different position is taken by Seyersted, op.cit.

[210] Rosenne, for example, sums up this theory as follows:

"... it is clear that the implied treaty-making power of the United Nations (and indeed of any international Organization enjoying an objective international personality) is not unlimited, but is one derived from the necessity of ensuring to the Organization the ability to perform the functions for which it was created, if this needs capacity to conclude treaties and that capacity can be said to arise by necessary intendment out of the Charter." Rosenne, op.cit., p. 296. Dupuy for his part refers to the notion of functional competence based on the interplay of the principles of speciality and effectivity, Dupuy, op.cit., p. 536.

However, there may be agreements which are clearly illegal and cannot be brought under the terms of the constitution even by the most liberal interpretation. This will for instance be true if an international organization which is expressly prohibited from dealing with military matters entered into a military agreement[211].

It is with such obviously unconstitutional agreements that we are concerned here. Weighty arguments can indeed be adduced for the invalidity of an agreement not covered by the constitution of the organization concerned.

a) If such an agreement were valid, the organs of the organization would be at liberty to extend the powers of the organization and hence their own competences at will. The could in fact enter into agreements on matters expressly excluded by the States which set up the organization. This would be tantamount to a revision of the constituent instrument. Many of these instruments contain provisions on their modification and require certain formalities in order to enable the member States to control the evolution of the organization[212]. These safeguards would be thwarted if the organs were allowed to conclude agreements beyond the competences of the organization, even if they are convinced that they are serving the interests of their organization.

b) A second argument also seems to endorse the conclusion that unconstitutional agreements ought to be held invalid. Otherwise the unlimited treaty-making power resulting from the irrelevance of violations of the constituent instruments would, in the final analysis, be a step towards the sovereignty of international organizations, at least in their treaty relations. Sovereign member States would be bound without their consent or even against their will by the act of an organ in which they may even not be represented. A restricted body or even a single agent could impose new obligations, especially financial burdens, on them. True enough, dissenting member States may be bound by majority decisions of certain collegiate organs of international organizations. But this is only so if they have consented to comply with such an act on becoming a party to the constituent instrument. Hence they have pledged themselves in advance to accept the will of the majority, but only in the cases provided for by the constituent instruments. Moreover, they can attempt to convince the other members that their point of view should prevail and plead their case at least in the plenary organ, provided this organ is competent to make the decision in question. Yet no consent to unconstitutional

---

[211] The Council of Europe is a case in point. See above, p. 215.

[212] See for example Article 109 of the UN-Charter.

treaty obligations can be presumed whenever majority decisions are accepted by States which become parties to the constituent instrument of an international organization.

c) Furthermore, it is maintained that a decisive argument advanced in favor of the validity of treaties concluded by incompetent organs of States cannot be extended to agreements to which international organizations are parties. With respect to inter-State treaties, it is sometimes pointed out that international law and internal law are of a different character, because international law overrules domestic law whose requirements and restrictions are irrelevant on the international plane. It is stressed that no such line can be drawn in regard of agreements entered into by international organizations. For the constituent instruments of international organizations are multilateral treaties, this argument runs, and therefore fall within the sphere of international law.

All these considerations appear to support the conclusion that a materially unconstitutional agreement must of necessity be regarded as invalid. This view is also held by the few authors who have dealt with the issue[213].

However convincing this point of view may be from a purely theoretical angle, its application may prove to be difficult. It is therefore urged that the discussion be again not confined to the abstract level but that the feasibility of the solution based on theory should be examined from a practical viewpoint. Furthermore, even on the theoretical plane, the above arguments are not as irrefutable as they might appear at first sight.

If the principle of invalidity were to apply, the other contracting parties would frequently not be sure whether in cases not expressly covered by the constituent instrument an agreement with an international organization is covered by its implied powers or on the contrary unconstitutional and hence invalid. Even if the other parties could be expected to be familiar with the constitution of their treaty partners—a controversial requirement even in inter-State relations—this knowledge would have to be confined to the unambiguous provisions of the constituent instrument, leaving aside cases where the competence to conclude agreements can be ascertained only by way of interpretation. It must be emphasized once again that it is for the organs of the organization concerned and not for other parties to interpret the statutes of international organizations. Moreover, it is hard to imagine that in practice a contracting party will request a

---

[213] Schneider, op.cit., p. 62—63; Kasme, op.cit., p. 65—67; Chiu, op.cit., p. 81—84.

restricted or individual organ concluding an agreement to produce some evidence of authentic interpretation by the plenary organ to the effect that the agreement falls within the terms of the constitution. On the contrary, the other party will in principle rely on the organs of the organization correctly interpreting their powers.

If it does so in good faith, it may be submitted that a solution along the lines of Article 46, paragraph 1 of the Vienna Convention on the Law of Treaties is more practicable and would contribute to the security of treaty relations, an advantage not to be ignored nor underestimated. The principle of good faith, one of the cornerstones of international law, also suggests such a solution.

Thus the member States or another organ of the organization should not be allowed to invoke the infringement of the competences of the organization by the organ concluding the agreement as invalidating the agreement unless the transgression was manifest. According to this theory, other contracting parties are precluded from invoking the violation of the constituent instrument of the organization. If they were aware of it at the moment of the conclusion of the agreement, good faith would require that they lose the right to claim invalidity by nevertheless entering into the agreement. If a contracting party discovers the infringement later on, the agreement may be terminated if the organization agrees. But this really would be a case of termination by mutual consent, which does not give rise to any particular problem. On the other hand, if the organization refuses to terminate the agreement, it is highly doubtful whether the other party or parties should be free to denounce or withdraw from it unilaterally. For one thing, this situation may lead to a dispute concerning the interpretation of the constituent instrument of the organization, for which the organs of the latter are competent. The organization may also argue that it has remedied the constitutional defect at least tacitly by applying the agreement without any objection. However, in most instances where the issue of unconstitutionality will be raised in practice, it will be the organization concerned which will invoke it in order to get rid of burdensome obligations under the agreement.

As to the determination of the manifest character of a transgression of the constitution, subjective criteria should be admitted as well, in contrast to Article 46, paragraph 2 of the Vienna Convention on the Law of Treaties.

A line will for instance have to be drawn between member States of the organization on the one hand and non-member States and other international organizations on the other.

a) A much higher degree of knowledge of the constitution of the organization can be expected from member States. The fact that the constituent instrument has been transformed, in some way or the other, into domestic law of the State concerned like any other international treaty, may even justify the presumption that the infringement must have been manifest to it, unless it can prove the contrary. As international organizations, especially those of universal character, conclude far more agreements with their members than with non-member States[214], the theory just put forth will more often than not authorize organizations to invoke violations of their constituent instruments as invalidating agreements with States. For they will be in a position to prove that the infringement was or ought to have been manifest to the other party. It stands to reason that in the second case ignorance due to the lack of diligence should not protect member States but ought to have the same effect as action in bad faith. Consequently, the practical result of the suggested solution will frequently be identical with that under the theory regarding any unconstitutional agreement as invalid, at least so far as agreements with States are concerned.

b) In regard of non-member States, the answer will have to vary according as a State has frequent contacts with the organization in question or not.

c) As to agreements concluded between international organizations, one may distinguish between agreements concluded by organizations composed to a large extent of the same members (universal organizations like the UN and its Specialized Agencies are cases in point) and those between organizations of totally different membership (agreements between regional organizations representing different parts of the globe could be cited as example). A higher degree of knowledge may be assumed in the first case, especially if the representatives of a State to both organizations receive instructions from and are controlled by the same governmental department. The frequency of contacts between the organizations concerned will also have to be taken into account.

Apart from these considerations which are almost completely ignored by the writers who advocate the automatic invalidity of materially unconstitutional agreements, the reasons they adduce in support of their theory are not wholly persuasive upon closer analysis.

a) As regards the argument that an agreement transgressing the sphere of competence of an international organization amounts to a revision to the constituent instrument, this may indeed be so. If one

---

[214] Concrete figures can be found in the article by Hartmann, this volume, p. 147.

examines this contention more closely, trying to imagine the possible reactions to such a transgression, three situations must probably be kept separate.

(1) Firstly, the other organs and the member States may take no action whatever, although it is evident that the agreement is unconstitutional. They may simply not object to such an agreement entering into force upon signature. What is more, all the member States may even approve the agreement in the plenary organ later on. Their silence can be construed as consent to an informal revision of the constitution, although the constituent instrument might provide for some special procedure to this end.

However, it is generally admitted that what counts, even from the viewpoint of international law, is not the written instrument but the constitution as effectively applied in practice[215]. This rule developed in inter-State law should also govern the constituent instruments of international organizations. Moreover, there seems to be no special reason why clauses concerning revision should be excluded from the scope of this rule.

(2) Secondly, only some member States may object to the agreement which they denounce as unconstitutional, whereas the majority regards it as covered by the implied powers of the organization. These contradictory contentions will give rise to a dispute within the organization on the correct interpretation of its constituent instrument. It is worth noting that the problem is not confined to the particular hypothesis of unconstitutional agreements, but will arise whenever the minority opposes decisions made by the majority on the ground that they are unconstitutional. The controversial decision need of course not always envisage the conclusion of an agreement. To return to the above example, let us suppose that the organs of the organization not allowed to deal with questions of defense may make majority decisions under its constituent instrument. Accordingly, a majority of the members may conceivably request all member States to furnish arms and ammunitions to an international police force. A minority might denounce the decision as unconstitutional, whereas the majority interprets the constitutional limitation relating to matters of defense restrictively, claiming that the force in question has nothing to do with defense and that at any rate only the furnishing of troops is prohibited. However unfortunate such a situation may be, the minority will eventually have to submit to the will of the majority or refuse to accept new obligations and withdraw from the organization.

---

[215] Verdross, op.cit., p. 159.

(3) Thirdly, another organ, all or the majority of the member States (the latter probably within the plenary organ if the agreement concerned was entered into by a restricted or individual organ) may assert the unconstitutionality of the agreement. Under the above principle, the agreement ought to be valid even in this case, provided the other contracting party or parties concluded the agreement in good faith. The burden of proof that this was not so in view of the manifest character of the violation would rest with the organization. This third situation of an organization being bound by an unconstitutional agreement against the will of all or the majority of its member States will occur very rarely indeed. For as already indicated, it will often be possible to prove that the infringement was manifest, especially if the other contracting party is a member of the organization[216]. It ought to be added that in the few remaining eases the conclusion of an unconstitutional yet internationally valid agreement will not of necessity result in a revision of the constituent instrument. Such an agreement will not constitute a precedent for a tacit extension of the competences of the organization in view of the express disapproval of the member States. It is further to be expected that the other organs, especially the plenary organs as well as the member States individually see to it that no agreement of the same kind be entered into again. As the chief administrative officer is most likely to be the organ concluding an unconstitutional agreement under this third hypothesis, internal measures will certainly be taken against him. A tight control will be exercised over his activities. Moreover, his further career will be jeopardized, especially if he wants to be re-elected. It is therefore in his own interest to consult with the other organs and member States before entering into an agreement of doubtful constitutionality in order not to be disavowed by them later on.

If these considerations are correct, the manifest violation theory may have as a by-product a beneficial effect on the cohesion between the organs of international organizations without necessarily resulting in a greater reluctance to enter into agreements.

b) To the argument that the validity of an agreement transgressing the competence of an international organization would be incompatible with the principle of sovereignty, one may object in the first place that this does not apply to all unconstitutional agreements but only to those which impose new obligations on the member States of the organizations. It could further be pointed out that this is a risk—a very slight one indeed—a State should be willing to run when

---

[216] See above, p. 258—259.

joining an international organization. Furthermore, it may protect its sovereign rights by refusing to execute the agreement and ceasing to be a member if its view is not shared by the majority. It ought to be stressed again that situations where the risk materializes are bound to occur but rarely. The encroachment on sovereignty resulting from the validity of a materially unconstitutional agreement can of course not be argued away completely. In this respect, the parties to a future Convention on the treaty law of international organizations will have to take a stand, just as the ILC did in regard of unconstitutional treaties between States. They will have to choose between the security of treaty relations and the protection of good faith on the one and sovereignty on the other hand. In his connection, it should be borne in mind that the very existence of international organizations proves that sovereignty in its original rigid form had to be adapted to the needs of international co-operation.

c) Thirdly, adherents of the invalidity theory point out that international law cannot overrule "domestic" law in the case of international organizations. There is of course no doubt that the constituent instruments of international organizations form part of international law. It is submitted, however, that the distinction should not be made between a higher and a lower legal order. It has been the main thesis of this paper that the constituent instruments of international organizations ought rather to be considered as the "internal" law of the organization which is placed on a footing of equality with general international law. Yet non-member States as well as other international organizations should not be concerned with this internal law. It should be enough for them to rely on the apparent capacity of the organ which purports to bind the organization on the external plane.

B) Agreements which Are Unconstitutional because they Have Been Concluded by an Incompetent Organ

The second category of unconstitutional agreements suffers from a defect which comes into play in the treaty relations of Staates too. The agreements concerned fall within the material competence of the organization but are entered into by an organ lacking either direct constitutional competence or authorization by the competent organ. The most frequent case will be that of an administrative official, be it the chief administrative officer or one of his deputies or regional representatives, purporting to express consent to be bound on behalf of his organization without the authorization of the organ endowed with treaty-making power. The question of whether such an agreement should be valid is again answered in the negative by most writers[217]. The reasons adduced to support this conclusion carry once more considerable weight. However, since the arguments are in part identical with those advanced in respect of materially unconstitutional agreements, only the additional points made with regard to agreements concluded by incompetent organs will be developed in this context.

a) Some writers again stress the necessity of protecting the sovereignty of the member States. They maintain that the division of competences among the various organs of an international organization is certainly not a matter of purely internal concern. If the member States insisted on approval by the plenary or some other collegiate organ, they obviously wanted to control the activities of the organization with regard to the conclusion of agreements. Hence especially an individual agent like an administrative officer should not be allowed to ignore the will of sovereign member States and to impose on them treaty obligations without their consent or even against their will. In view of these far-reaching consequences, the argument runs, it cannot be argued that any organ is entitled to act

---

[217] Kasme, op.cit., p. 99—103, who points out that within the UN the issue of the "extrinsic" constitutionality came to the fore when the Soviet Union criticized the Trusteeship Agreements as contrary to Article 79 of the Charter. Under this provision, these Agreements are to be agreed upon by the States directly concerned prior to their approval by the General Assembly. The meaning of the term "States directly concerned" has never been established. See Vedovato, Les accords de tutelle, 76 RCADI (1950), p. 613—699; Leroy, La nature juridique des accords de tutelle, 69 RGDIP (1965), p. 977—1018. Kasme's conclusion concerning the invalidity of agreements concluded by incompetent organs is endorsed by Chiu, op.cit., p. 97—100. Another of the very few examples of an agreement being denounced as unconstitutional because the organ concluding it allegedly lacked the required authorization by the competent organ occurred in 1965. By an exchange of letters with Belgium dated 20 February 1965, Secretary-General U Thant agreed on behalf of the UN to pay $ 1,500.00 for damages caused to Belgian citizens by members of O.N.U.C. during military operations (text in 1 Revue belge de droit international (1965), p. 559—560). In a letter of 2 August 1965, Mr. Morozov, Permanent Representative par interim of the USSR, claimed that this agreement ran counter to international law, because it was for Belgium as the aggressor to assume responsibility for the consequences of its aggression. Moreover, Mr. Morozov drew the attention of the Secretariat to the fact that is was not entitled to conclude the aforementioned agreement without authorization by the Security Council. In his reply of 6 August 1965, the Secretary-General justified, inter alia, the conclusion of the agreement in the following terms:

"En concluant ces arrangements, le Secrétaire général a agi en sa qualité de chef des services administratifs de l'Organisation, conformément à la pratique établie [sic!] de l'Organisation des Nations Unies qui veut que les réclamations adressées à l'Organisation par des particuliers soient examinées et réglées sous la responsabilité du Secrétaire général." Security Council Documents, S/6589 of 3 August and S/6597 of 6 August 1965. Ibidem, 2 (1966), p. 314—316.

on behalf of the organization as long as the action remains within the material competences laid down in the constituent instrument.

Even if the conclusion of an agreement appears highly desirable in a given situation in order to enable the organization to fulfil the functions entrusted to it, an incompetent organ should not be permitted to act on its own. In particular, it ought to be barred from committing the organization if the organ invested with treaty-making competence opposes an agreement because the necessary majority is lacking. This holds true even if only one member of a collegiate organ exercises a right of veto which it enjoys under the constituent instrument.

For example, if a permanent member of the UN Security Council objected to an agreement under Article 43 of the Charter, because it thinks that the member State concerned should furnish more assistance than it offers under the proposed agreement, the Secretary-General of the UN should not be allowed to argue that after all some assistance is better for the attainment of the goals of the Organization that none at all and conclude the agreement on his own.

b) Another argument in favor of the invalidity theory has already been mentioned in regard of the first type of unconstitutional agreements. It points to the danger of drawing an analogy from the treaty law of States, where it can be asserted that international law overrules the restrictions of domestic law, which is of a different, even inferior character. No such distinction can be made in respect of international organizations whose constituent instruments are multilateral treaties and form part of international law.

Although these arguments carry considerable weight, they do not of necessity entail the invalidity theory as the only acceptable solution to the problem at hand.

a) As for the protection of the sovereign rights of member States, it is again suggested that States should be willing to accept in advance the very slight risk of being bound by unconstitutional acts when joining international organizations.

If as suggested the manifest violation theory were adopted, it would afford a certain protection to the organization and thereby to its sovereign members too. The agreement will fall to the ground if it can be established that the violation of the constitution was or should have been manifest to the other party. This will be possible in many cases, especially with regard to member States, but at times even in respect of agreements with non-member States and other international organizations.

b) As for the second argument in support of the invalidity theory, it may be repeated that from the point of view of non-member States or other international organizations, the constituent instrument of an international organization ought to be considered the latter's "internal" law with which they should not interfere. Above all, they ought to refrain from interpreting the constituent instrument of an international organization with which they intend to conclude an agreement. This does not mean that constituent instruments are not part of international law and inferior to it.

Other considerations strongly support a solution based on the principle underlying Articles 46 and 47 of the Vienna Convention on the Law of Treaties so far as this second type of unconstitutional agreement is concerned too.

Since international organizations ignore the safeguard of full powers[218], their treaty partners can rarely be quite sure whether the organ purporting to bind the organization is duly authorized, especially if this organ is the chief administrative officer or his representative. Yet in practice the other parties are frequently confronted with this situation. They should again refrain, however, from interpreting the constituent instrument of the organization.

One solution would be to ask the organ for evidence of its authorization. This would mean requesting international organizations to adopt a new practice by issuing documents comparable to full powers. However, it is once more submitted that even progressive development within the framework of a codification should not lay down the rules totally at variance with existing practice.

Moreover, if the other party acts in good faith and without undue negligence, so that the lack of competence of its counterpart is not manifest to it, good faith would again be protected and the security of treaty relations greatly increased if such an agreement were considered valid.

Considerations similar to those put forward in regard of material unconstitutionality should come into play in this context too[219].

Thus a line may be drawn between member States, non-member States and other international organizations when the manifest character of a constitutional violation is to be determined.

a) A member State can be presumed to be familiar with the particular restrictions of the competences of the various organs. Accordingly, as a rule the violation of the constitution will be or should have been manifest to it.

b) As to non-member States, the answer will in part depend on the intensity of its relations with the organization in question. Less

---

218 See above, p. 236.

219 See above, p. 255—262.

knowledge is to be expected if it enters into an agreement with the organization for the first time. On the other hand, a strong case could probably be made for the manifest character of the constitutional violation, if for example a non-member State has concluded several agreements on the same matter which were all subject to the approval by the plenary organ. To repeat the above example[220], in case the chief administrative officer of the organization, who up to then has only conducted the negotiations, all of a sudden declares that no such approval is necessary for a similar new agreement, but that his signature suffices to express consent, the non-member State should not simply accept this contention but ask for further explanations.

c) As regards agreements between international organizations, the considerations already discussed apply to the second type of unconstitutionality as well.

With respect to the reactions of the member States and the other organs of the organization, the three situations mentioned above can also be distinguished in regard to agreements concluded by incompetent organs[221].

a) If the matter is not raised at all, one may speak of tacit approval. Such tacit approvals may furthermore set a precedent and eventually confer new competences on the organ which has been originally incompetent under the constituent instrument. Consequently, the international organization concerned may finally be precluded from invoking the lack of competence of the organ in question, because practice will have brought about a modification of the constituent instrument. The very principle of good faith entitles other parties to rely on such practice.

b) If the competent organ makes majority decisions and only a minority of its members objects, the backing of the originally unconstitutional expression of consent by the majority will also constitute approval. Dissenting members will have to accept this decision or quit the organization.

c) A real problem arises only if unanimity is required, for in this case the objection of just one member prevents approval. Similarly, in cases of majority decisions within the competent organ, the refusal of all or of the required majority of members to subscribe to the unconstitutional act will have same effect. Nevertheless, the agreement would be valid under the proposed rule if the lack of competence of the organ concluding it were not manifest. However, this situation will arise but rarely. Moreover, the organization will most probably take

---

[220] See above, p. 246.

[221] See above, p. 260—261.

the necessary measures to prevent the guilty organ from acting again in breach of the constitution. For fear of these measures, the organ intending to commit the organization will contact the competent organ in cases of doubt before proceeding to the conclusion of an agreement.

Moreover, support for the suggested principle can be found in the advisory opinion of the International Court of Justice in the Certain Expenses case[222].

3. Conclusion

It has been the thesis of this paper that a rigid approach to the codification of the treaty law of international organizations should be avoided. On the one hand, rules developed in inter-State relations ought not to be applied ipso facto to agreements concluded by international organizations, a point which is stressed by many authors[223]. But one should not fall into the other extreme of excluding them in principle. For the underlying political, sociological, and legal needs they respond to may be the same in both cases. These should be carefully examined with respect to each rule. Furthermore, progressive development of the law and the practical aspects of the eventual application of a norm should also be taken into account. The adoption of a given norm will often mean the rejection of other solutions for which arguments of considerable weight can be advanced. The present writer hopes to have developed such an alternative as regards the organs competent to conclude agreements on behalf of international organizations and the effects of unconstitutional agreements[224].

On the basis of the foregoing considerations, it is therefore suggested that the provisions of the Vienna Convention on the Law of Treaties dealing with problems discussed in this paper apply mutatis mutandis and subject to slight additions taking into account the particular procedural practices of international organizations to agreements concluded by international organizations. As regards the

[222] I.C.J. Reports 1962, p. 151—180. The following passage is particularly relevant: "If the action was taken by the wrong organ, it was irregular as a matter of that internal structure, but this would not necessarily mean that the expense incurred was not an expense of the Organization. Both national and international law contemplate cases in which the body corporate or politic may be bound, as to third parties, by an ultra vires act of an agent." (Ibidem, p. 168.)

[223] "L'application par analogie des règles du droit international à ce phénomène ne peut se faire qu'en tenant compte des particularités de la nature juridique des accords, à savoir notamment de la qualité juridique spéciale des contractants." Golsong-Kiss, op.cit., p. 477.

[224] Similar conclusions are reached by McRae, this volume, p. 1—55.

main issue, viz. the organs competent to conclude agreements, Article 7 of the Vienna Convention should be replaced by the following provisions which resulted from an attempt at codification made at the end the end of the 1969 Research Seminar of the Hague Academy and to which the writer fully subscribes:

"*Article 7*

1) The constituent instrument of every international organization shall determine the organ or organs competent to conclude agreements.

2) In the absence of express provisions in the constituent instrument of an international organization, the following organs shall be considered as representing an international organization for all acts relating to the conclusion of an agreement:

a) the plenary organ or other organs when the agreement comes within the framework of autonomous functions conferred upon them by the constitution of the international organization (in particular the 'chief administrative officer') or

b) any other administrative official whose competence is apparent by virtue of his functions.

Article 7 bis

If an organ possessing competence in respect of all acts relating to the conclusion of an agreement delegates its competence to another organ of the international organization or to a negotiating committee, the latter organ or committee must be able, where necessary, to prove such delegation of competence."

Druck: R. Spies & Co., 1050 Wien